Ghost Dance

Also by David Humphreys Miller

CUSTER'S FALL
The Indian Side of the Story

Ghost Dance

DAVID HUMPHREYS MILLER

University of Nebraska Press
Lincoln and London

First Bison Book printing: 1985
Most recent printing indicated by the first digit below:
2   3   4   5   6   7   8   9   10

Library of Congress Cataloging in Publication Data
Miller, David Humphreys.
   Ghost dance.
   "Bison books."
   Reprint. Originally published: New York: Duell,
Sloan and Pearce, 1959.
   1. Ghost dance. 2. Dakota Indians—Wars, 1890–1891.
3. Dakota Indians—Religion and mythology. 4. Indians
of North America—Great Plains—Religion and mythology.
I. Title.
E99.D1M6 1985   299'.74   85-5876
ISBN 0-8032-3099-0
ISBN 0-8032-8130-7 (pbk.)

Reprinted by arrangement with E. P. Dutton, Inc.

This book is for Jan—

Wica-cante-yuha-winyan—

CAPTURES-EVERYBODY'S-HEART-WOMAN

A Word to the Reader

THIS book is about a dance—a strange dance practiced by Indian men and women less than seventy years ago in the vain belief that it would restore them and their deceased ancestors to a fast-disappearing way of life. Because the weird ritual involved supplication to the spirits of Indian dead, it was known to white men as "the ghost dance." Whites also came to know it as the Dance of Death for it inspired Indians to die fighting for their hopeless dream of a better life in a world of spirits.

Thus this book is also the story of a war, a clash in which the Indian dreamers were as earmarked for doom as characters in a classic Greek tragedy. In many ways the last major American Indian uprising, known as the Sioux Ghost Dance War of 1890-91, was one of the most dramatic conflicts since the Crusades. Although it involved comparatively few combatants by standards of modern warfare, it marked the final desperate attempt of Indian tribes in the United States to throw off the yoke of the white man's domination. Moreover, it put an end forever to the frontier of the old West.

The significance of the ghost-dance uprising has long been obscured under coats of official whitewash diligently applied by the practical white men who finally overpowered the Indian dreamers. The outcome was perhaps an inevitable step in the juggernaut advance of our so-called civilization.

And yet it must not be misconstrued that the Indians who dreamed so blindly and struggled so futilely against insurmountable odds were mere childish savages. While trapped in the moiling death-throes of their old free way of life, the Sioux were a uniquely cultured people, instinctively nomadic and inured to violence, yet far from primitive. One of the ironies of history is that the ghost dance and the ensuing conflict which consigned it to oblivion were actually sparked by grave misinterpretations of the teachings of the greatest peacemaker of all time, Jesus Christ; for the messianic conception had no place in native Indian religions but was taught to the red men by white missionaries.

The story of the ghost dance rightfully belongs to the Indians, however, and only they can properly tell it. Nearly all accounts written by the ghost dancers' white contemporaries were obviously slanted for the unknowing or bigoted white readers of their time. Consequently, I have gotten this story direct from Indians who were themselves ghost dancers, or were otherwise involved in the flare of religious excitement which swept through the tribes nearly three-quarters of a century ago. This book is largely a compilation of data gleaned from my own personal interviews with some one hundred thirty-five Indian men and women of twenty different tribes.

Although the ghost dance seems remote in time, a number of my informants are still alive at this writing, including an even dozen Indian survivors of the Wounded Knee massacre. I have known these brave people, as well as many who later took the spirit trail, since I began research on the ghost dance in 1935. When the late Black Elk, famed Ogalala Sioux medicine man and battle-scarred warrior, adopted me as his son in 1939, I promised him that someday I would tell white men the true story of the Indian ghost dance—just as Black Elk and other members of his race had told it to me. The purpose of this book is to tell that story.

Several other individuals who figure prominently in the ghost-dance story have also been almost as close to me as members of my own family. The late Iron Hail (or Dewey Beard), who lost his entire family during the Wounded Knee holocaust and was, incidentally, the last Indian survivor of the 1876 Battle of the Little Big Horn, adopted me as his son after old Black Elk passed away.

I am proud to say that many other Indian men and women still regard me as a near kinsman. Among them are such marvelous old characters as Frank Kicking Bear, whose boyhood recollections of his dynamic father helped greatly in a reconstruction of the Sioux ghost-dance movement, and Simon Helper (or Wallace Hump), who told me many things about the ghost dance never before known to any white man and who, on several occasions, showed me over the ghost-dance Stronghold and the so-called Battlefield at Wounded Knee where he, as a young man, narrowly escaped death.

Any author is indebted to his friends—for their patience and encouragement as well as their assistance. In addition to the above-mentioned persons, I am particularly grateful to the following Indians: Chief Ben American Horse, Howard Bad Bear, Zona Bad Bear, Peter Two Bulls, Charlie Fire Thunder, Henry Weasel, Ben Black Elk, Margaret One Bull Tremmel, Thomas Short Bull, Norman Short Bull, Gus Knox, and Frank White Buffalo Man—all Sioux.

Certain white people have also been of much help, including John Boland, Sr., Gus Haaser, Raleigh Barker, Mrs. Gus Craven, Mrs. George Philips, Ed Rentz, Mrs. Mamie Duhamel, John Peters, George C. Robb, Mrs. Cushman Clark, Bernard Tabakin, and Reginald Laubin.

I am also glad to express my gratitude to my mother, my late father, and my uncle, Eugene Chauncey Humphreys, for glowing recollections of life in the eighties and nineties, and to my friend Paul I. Wellman, whose writings have ever been inspirational to me.

One person, however, has performed an indispensable task in making it possible for me to write this book—my wife, Jan. Besides maintaining a tranquil household in which I could work, she has lent her most welcome critical analysis of these pages. In a very real sense, this book is an experience which we have shared together.

DAVID HUMPHREYS MILLER

Contents

The People in Ghost Dance

At CHEYENNE RIVER RESERVATION (located in central South Dakota)

Agents: F. W. McChesney
P. P. Palmer (later)

Indians: Kicking Bear—High priest of the Sioux ghost dance (Ogalala and Brûlé by blood, but an acting band chief of his wife's people, the Minneconjous); Woodpecker Woman —his wife; his son (now known as Frank Kicking Bear)
Big Foot—a Minneconjou band chief; his wife
Pipe-on-Head (later known as James Pipe-on-Head)
Iron Hail—a Minneconjou warrior (also known as Dewey Beard)
Hump
Touch-the-Cloud } Minneconjou Scalp Shirt Men
White Bull
Helper (later known as Wallace Hump or Simon Helper)
Yellow Bird—a medicine man and ghost-dance fanatic

At STANDING ROCK RESERVATION (located in north central South Dakota and south central North Dakota)

Agent: James McLaughlin

Indians: Sitting Bull—Chief of the Hunkpapas; Seen-by-Her-Nation—his wife; Four Times—another of Sitting Bull's wives; Deaf-mute adopted son (later known as John Sitting Bull); Crow Foot—Sitting Bull's son; One Bull—Sitting Bull's nephew and adopted son; Scarlet Whirlwind—his young wife

Gray Eagle—Sitting Bull's brother-in-law
Little Assiniboin
Catch the Bear } Followers of Sitting Bull
Henry Bullhead—Lieutenant of Indian Police
Charles Shave Head—First sergeant of Indian Police
Marcellus Red Tomahawk—Sergeant of Indian Police
Little Soldier
White Bird
He-Alone-Is-Man } Indian Policemen
Cross Bear
Mary McLaughlin—James McLaughlin's mixed-blood wife

Whites: Mrs. Catherine Weldon—field representative of the National Indian Defense Association
Reverend T. L. Riggs—a missionary
Mary Collins—a missionary
Father Bernard—a missionary

At PINE RIDGE RESERVATION (located in southwest South Dakota)

Agent: D. H. Gallagher
D. F. Royer (later)

Indians: Red Cloud—Head chief of the Ogalalas; Jack Red Cloud—his son
American Horse—an Ogalala chief; Tom American Horse—his son; Ben American Horse—another son
Black Elk—a medicine man and ghost-dance priest
Good Thunder—a ghost-dance priest
Yellow Breast
Flat Iron
Cloud Horse } Delegates to visit the Wanekia in Nevada
Sells-a-Pistol Butt (Little Gun)
Broken Arm
Eagle Elk—a ghost dancer
Young-Man-Afraid-of-His-Horses—an Ogalala chief

Little Wound—an Ogalala chief
No Flesh—a sub-chief
George Sword—captain of Indian Police
Black Horn—a visitor at Wounded Knee
No Water—a sub-chief
Standing Bear—an Ogalala chief
Few Tails—an old man; his wife
One Feather—a young man; his wife
Ten Fingers ⎱
Little   ⎰ Ghost-dance fanatics
Hugh Top Bear—a schoolboy
Catching Spirit Elk—a traveler
Dr. Charles Alexander Eastman—an educated Santee
    physician
Reverend Charles Smith Cook—an educated Yankton minister
Philip F. Wells—a mixed-blood interpreter (later Army scout)
Big Road—an Ogalala chief
William Selwyn—mixed-blood postmaster of Pine Ridge
Louis Shangraux—mixed-blood scout
Big Bat Pourier—mixed-blood rancher
Little Bat Garnier—mixed-blood scout
Stands First—an Ogalala scout
Highbackbone—an Ogalala scout
Woman's Dress—an Ogalala scout
Yankton Charlie—a Yankton scout
Lucy Lone Eagle—a disillusioned young girl
Pete Richards—Red Cloud's son-in-law, a half-breed
Feather-on-Head—an Ogalala scout

Whites: Elaine Goodale—supervisor of Indian schools in the
    Dakotas and Nebraska
Mrs. Charles Smith Cook
Father Craft ⎱
Father Jutz   ⎰ Missionaries
James H. Cook—a rancher
Isaac Miller—a rancher

William D. McGaa—a rancher

Gus Haaser—a cowboy

General Nelson A. Miles—Commander of Department of the Missouri

General John R. Brooke—Field Commander of the Sioux Campaign

Colonel James A. Forsyth—Commander of the Seventh Cavalry

Major S. M. Whiteside—Seventh Cavalry

Captain Myles Moylan—Seventh Cavalry

Private Francischetti—Seventh Cavalry

Corporal Paul Weinert—Second Artillery

Lieutenant E. W. Casey—Chief of Casey's Cheyenne Scouts

Colonel W. F. Cody—"Buffalo Bill," famous scout turned showman

Valentine T. McGillycuddy—former agent at Pine Ridge Agency

Pete Culbertson—leader of an outlaw gang

At ROSEBUD RESERVATION (located in south central South Dakota)

Agent: James G. Wright
   E. B. Reynolds (later acting agent)

Indians: Short Bull—a ghost-dance priest
   Mash-the-Kettle—a ghost-dance priest
   Two Strike—a Brûlé chief
   Turning Bear—a Brûlé sub-chief
   Crow Dog—a Brûlé sub-chief (Spotted Tail's murderer)
   Luther Standing Bear—a schoolteacher and storekeeper
   Hollow Horn Bear—a Brûlé chief
   Plenty Horses—an educated ghost dancer
   Hard Heart—a Brûlé leader
   Black Horn—a Brûlé sub-chief

elsewhere—

At TONGUE RIVER RESERVATION (located in southeast Montana)

Agent: James A. Cooper

Indians: Porcupine—a healer
Head Swift ⎫
Young Mule ⎭ Ghost-dance fanatics and murderers

At WIND RIVER RESERVATION (located in west central Wyoming)

Indians: Sherman Sage—a medicine man and ghost-dance priest
Sharp Nose—a Northern Arapaho chief
Yellow Calf—a Northern Arapaho chief
Black Coal—a Northern Arapaho chief
Spoonhunter—a Sioux by blood but Arapaho by marriage;
Two Crows—his half-Arapaho, half-Ogalala son
Sitting Bull—a medicine man (later at Darlington, Indian Territory)

At KIOWA RESERVATION (located in west central Oklahoma)

Indians: Wooden Lance—a man with a quest
Bianki—a dreamer

At WALKER RIVER RESERVATION (located in western Nevada)

Indian: Wovoka—whose vision started it all

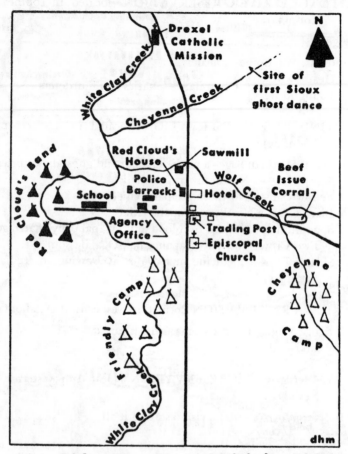

Map labels:
- Drexel Catholic Mission
- White Clay Creek
- Cheyenne Creek
- Site of first Sioux ghost dance
- N
- Red Cloud's House
- Sawmill
- Wolf Creek
- Beef Issue Corral
- Police Barracks
- Hotel
- Red Cloud's Band
- School
- Agency Office
- Trading Post
- Episcopal Church
- Friendly Camp
- Cheyenne Camp
- White Clay Creek
- dhm

Pine Ridge Agency and Vicinity, 1890

Sioux Country 1890–91

North Dakota

SCALE
0 20 40 Miles

Cannonball River

Standing Rock Agency
STANDING ROCK
Fort Yates

RESERVATION

Grand River
Sitting Bull's Camp

Indian trail

Missouri River

South

Dakota

Moreau River

CHEYENNE RIVER

RESERVATION

Kicking Bear's Camp
Cheyenne Agency

Hump's Camp
River
Fort Bennett
Cheyenne City
Fort Sully

Cheyenne

Fort Meade
Deadwood
Few Tails ambushed
Big Foot's Camp

Pierre

Rapid City
Indian trail
Bad River

LOWER BRULE RESN.

Black Hills

Big Foot Pass
badland wall
Bad Lands
White River

Hermosa
Bad Lands

Strong hold
Cuny Table
PINE RIDGE
RESERVATION
ROSEBUD
RESERVATION

Buffalo Gap

Pass Creek

Rosebud Agency

Mission
Wounded Knee massacre

Pine Ridge Agency

Fort Robinson
Chadron
Nebraska
Fort Niobrara

Rushville
DHM

The Time the Sun Died

THE noonday sun was blotted out, and darkness spread like a mantle of night across the snow-swept prairie. Past the frozen banks of Cherry Creek, as far as the eye could see, the bleak Dakota plain undulated, dark and forbidding. In every direction the old, familiar look of the land was gone.

For some minutes on this first day of the new winter the close-knit band of Kicking Bear had watched the coming of the strange shadow, which drooped across the sun like a monstrous black eyelid. Several of the younger warriors had impulsively fired their Winchesters high in the air, thinking to frighten away the terrible specter that hovered between them and the sun, shutting off all light and warmth. But now, with gun smoke still riding on the chill air, even the bravest among them submitted to this strange power, seemingly greater than the sun itself. With the total eclipse at its zenith, the people fell prostrate to the ground and wept.

Awe-stricken like the others, Kicking Bear, band chief of the Minneconjou Sioux, lay motionless while his mind groped for some explanation of this horrendous thing that now blotted out the sun. As a medicine man and healer, as well as a leader, he was the one person to whom the people would look for an answer—if the sun appeared again and the world survived. He wondered if life could go on indefinitely in total darkness. Far better, he thought, if the end to everything came suddenly than to drag on without the warmth and power of the sun.

While the ominous shadow was spreading across the sun, the people had searched Kicking Bear's blank stare with terrified

3

eyes. Until the white men's government had made them stop,[1] the Sioux annually performed a dance to the sun in supplication to the mysterious powers of Wakantanka, "The Great Spirit." Through the brazen eye of the sun, Wakantanka had peered down with satisfaction at his Indian children. Then white men had tried to turn the Sioux away from their God, whose very eye was now closed against them.

Kicking Bear had taken care to keep his inward fear from showing. His fighting heart somehow provided courage for this perilous moment. Yet, one by one, the people had turned hopelessly away, enmeshed in the toils of a nameless horror. Soon, if the darkness passed, they might seek his eyes again. And he would have to be ready. He must think. Somewhere he must find the knowledge. Almost audibly his thoughts cried out for a vision of understanding. Yet there had been no warning in the foregoing days in which to prepare oneself for a *hanblecheyapi*—the lonely vigil of vision-seeking.

Kicking Bear had barely had time to purify himself with sagebrush and mumble a few select incantations before the darkness was upon his village. On sacred occasions he normally would paint his lean face with the old elaborate war markings—sun circles and lightning streaks and protective hail spots. In his present haste, however, the symbols had been reduced to a few spit-wetted smears across his high cheekbones. He had managed to tie a small bundle of hawk feathers and a dirty eagle plume into his loose-flowing hair.

Stirring slightly, he felt behind his ear for the tiny rawhide medicine bundle, tied inconspicuously under the fall of hair and seldom seen by another human. Few, in fact, knew it was there; and only two or three people knew of its contents. Through the little hide pouch Kicking Bear fingered the smooth round brown stone and a relieving sense of its great protective power coursed through him.

It was no ordinary stone. Far from it, for, although it was ap-

---

[1] The Sun Dance of the Plains Indians was banned by federal statute in 1886, largely because of the missionaries' misunderstanding of the self-torture features. With certain modifications, the ceremony was again legalized in 1934.

parently only an ordinary small sphere of polished sandstone, wrapped in eagle down and sweetgrass, it reputedly had certain supernatural properties that protected its wearer in battle. As long as he engaged in warfare, he would be safe from all enemies—seen or unseen. The stone's history was remarkable. Many winters ago it had belonged to the greatest fighting leader the Sioux ever had—the daring, invincible Crazy Horse.

In spite of his renewed courage, Kicking Bear lay prone through the terrible moments of darkness, his fingers clawing at the earth, frozen flint tough by the icy northern gusts that swept the prairies. Combing through crackling clumps of buffalo grass, his hands caressed the brittle stalks. It would be evil, he knew, to break off the grass, for that would be cutting off the sacred hair of the Earth Mother of all living creatures—a sacrilege he dared not commit.

The white men, of course, believed differently. They had no understanding of the Earth Mother when they dug up the ground and plowed under the rich grasses. Worse yet, white agents and missionaries were doing everything possible to get the Indians themselves to engage in agricultural pursuits. Farming was fit, perhaps, for the womanish Arikaras and soft-living Gros Ventres, but hardly suited for the warrior Sioux. Kicking Bear's lean belly churned in an old torment of hatred against the whites. Deep within him an unplumbed well of bitterness roiled that time could never drain.

Dark thoughts of the present led to black memories of the past. Nearly twelve winters had passed now since that fatal day in the Moon of Scarlet Plums (September 5, 1877) when white soldiers had tricked Crazy Horse into coming to Nebraska's Fort Robinson for a council. Once lured into a little prison with barred windows, Crazy Horse had fought desperately to escape. As the Indian struggled, a soldier had stabbed him with a bayonet.

Kicking Bear had not been at Fort Robinson to see Crazy Horse's life blood ooze from him, but other Sioux had seen it happen. Black Elk, his kinsman, had told Kicking Bear many times how, when federal troops released Crazy Horse's body to the Indians, soldiers had crammed the corpse into a small coffin.

Both legs of the dead war chief had been broken off to make the body fit the cramped coffin. The box was turned over to Crazy Horse's parents, who carried it away on a pony drag toward the Dakota Badlands. Nobody followed the old people as they rode off across the lonely hills with all that remained of their murdered son bumping along behind them. Few persons—even Indian relatives—knew Crazy Horse's final resting place.

It mattered little now where Crazy Horse lay, a bleached pile of broken bones on a rotting scaffold grave. The important thing, Kicking Bear decided, was that Crazy Horse's "medicine"—the *tunka,* or sacred round stone that had given him power in battle—had been preserved. One day, months after the murder, Crazy Horse's mother, a sister of Kicking Bear's mother, had given the tiny rawhide bundle to her nephew.

Since then Crazy Horse's medicine had served Kicking Bear well. His possession of it not only afforded him "strong protection," but also spurred him into deeds of great daring. He had led the warrior Sioux against the enemy Piegan and Flathead and hated Crow. Many small, fierce battles were won through his courageous leadership.

But, as white men swarmed into the northern plains, the intertribal wars soon waned. Old contests between Sioux and Crow dwindled off to a few annual horse-stealing raids. While Kicking Bear was eminently successful in leading these forays,[2] the white men again interfered. Soldiers who garrisoned the forts scattered across Dakota and Montana turned back Sioux raiders time and again.

Overnight, the tribes were forced to follow an unfamiliar trail —the white man's road. Truly, thought Kicking Bear, the old days of glory were gone. Thinking of the past was like swallowing stones.

Only one spark flickered in the shadowy past, the recollection of a slim, sloe-eyed girl who walked beside him under a courting blanket. He had been proud that she responded to his attentions,

[2] On one notable raid north of Dakota's Bear Butte in the seventies, Kicking Bear and twenty-three Ogalalas and Minneconjous captured one hundred and thirty-nine Crow ponies.

he remembered, for she was the niece of Big Foot, a chief of the Minneconjous. And when, instead of words of love, he had poured out his warrior dreams to her, she had listened and seemed to understand his restless striving for honor and glory. He bought her from her uncle in the old Sioux way with many fine ponies captured from the Crows.

His marriage to Woodpecker Woman had long been a fine match, he reflected, happy in every way save that it marked the curtailment of his career as a fighting leader. He could hardly blame his young bride for that, however, since being wedded to her made him a chief among her people. He was only a band chief, of course, but a chief nevertheless.

Still prone on the frozen ground, Kicking Bear felt the sun's warmth on his outstretched hand. Hardly daring to look directly at the sky, he glanced about him with hooded eyes slitted against the growing light on the sun. The other Indians cowered, fear-quivering under their tattered blankets, no face yet upturned.

It was then that he heard the sharp rising wail of the wind, sounding full and clear like a wolf howling at close quarters. Above it all, in a piercing falsetto, a voice was shrieking out words.

"An omen!" the voice screamed. "An omen!"

Looking overhead, Kicking Bear saw a sun shaped like a half-moon, its brilliance steadily increasing. Against it he saw wings flapping. A young spotted eagle had come soaring up out of the cedar brakes downstream. Kicking Bear had heard the eagle's voice riding on the wind. Glancing about, he saw the trembling people stir under the sun's growing warmth. He was certain none of them had heard the voice. To himself alone the eagle had spoken, as in a vision. For long moments he waited in silence, until all the mysterious darkness was gone from the sun. At last no trace of the earlier blackness lingered in the sky. One by one the Minneconjous stood and gathered around Kicking Bear.

"Father, what does it mean?" the people asked, surprised to have survived the dreadful darkness.

Standing lean and tall and gaunted by famine, Kicking Bear

took his time answering. Although still in his early forties, he had long since adopted the mien of an elder chieftain. His vulpine features were grim and humorless in these trying days. Every mood and act showed the blood line of true chieftains, for he was the son of Black Fox, chief of the Oyukpe band of the Ogalala Sioux. Many Minneconjous accepted him as chief and addressed him with fitting respect in spite of his lack of great age. Most of them would follow him blindly.

As usual, Kicking Bear was tempted to utter hot words of anger against the white men. But this matter of blotting out the sun was hard to explain simply by blaming the whites. Furthermore, it would seem to give them undue powers in the eyes of his people, and Kicking Bear himself suspected that some far greater agency was behind the mysterious darkness that had so frightfully come and gone. At last he forced himself to speak, letting his voice sound distant and a little off pitch, as though coming from another person.

"A voice I heard, a sacred eagle's voice," he intoned. "The sun died, but a new sun has taken its place. The sacred voice of a young spotted eagle told me this was a portent—an omen of great things yet to come."

After that he said no more, but turned on his moccasined heel and moved in long, easy strides toward his lodge.

Along the timbered banks of Cherry Creek the conical lodges of the Minneconjous squatted like huddled tatterdemalions, their ragged smoke flaps turned in against the howl of the weather. Few cook fires burned these days, for all along the creek game was scarce. Above the smoke-blackened tepee cones rose bare-limbed cottonwoods, gaunt and ominous against the cheerless sky. Throughout the camp cowskin lodges were less common than ever, for more than five winters had passed since the last prime buffalo cowhides were taken by the Sioux. Nowadays tepees had to be made from half-rotten government-issue canvas —at best a poor substitute for tight, warm cowskins.

Kicking Bear threaded his way among the lodges, passing willow-stick meat racks that were falling apart from disuse. It had been a long time now since they had been festooned with fresh, tasty intestines and bladders or lined with strips of jerked meat to cure in the sun. Even the handful of skulking dogs that pawed around the burned-out cook fires were no longer worth eating; they were hardly better than prowling skeletons covered with mangy hide.

As befitted the dwelling of a chief, Kicking Bear's lodge was somewhat set apart from the others. His wife gone across country to Deep Creek to visit her uncle Big Foot for a few days, the Ogalala knew the tepee would offer him seclusion for a while. Stooping to enter the lodge, he let the blanket fall away from his shoulders. Out of the wintry gusts he felt the dank interior tolerable if not warm. Clad in his greasy buckskins, he was not uncomfortable. Settling himself on an old buffalo robe opposite the entrance, he reached for the long, beaded bag that contained his medicine pipe and *kinnikinic*—willow-bark tobacco—and the flint chips he used instead of white men's matches to start a fire.

The Sioux call it the Winter That Red Shirt's Sister Killed Herself [3] and have no way of pinpointing days. As white men figure dates it was January 1, 1889, when the sun "died." For several days following the eclipse Kicking Bear shut himself away from the people and sat alone in his womanless lodge, mulling over the strange shadow across the sun and the screaming eagle's voice.

The tepee was bare of food. What little had been on hand he had given to Woodpecker Woman and the children for their journey. Lacking food, he smoked many pipes of fragrant *kinnikinic*. Although smoking traditionally had a ritual purpose as part of a religious ceremony, it also served as an adjunct of profound thought and soul searching. Sometimes men used it as a prelude to lengthy or important conversation. But now, more often than not, it merely served to allay hunger. Kicking Bear's solitary meditation soon turned to dark brooding.

For all American Indians this was a time of trial and tragedy, but roving warrior tribes of the plains—Sioux, Cheyenne, Arap-

[3] Some Sioux bands also refer to that year as the Winter That "Gray Fox" Came to Buy Land. "Gray Fox" or "Three Stars" was the Sioux name for General George Crook, chairman of the 1889 Sioux Land Commission.

aho, Kiowa—suffered most. Short years earlier, their very existence dependent on the vast buffalo herds that roamed the prairies, they had lived free and wild on the virgin grasslands.

In a handful of years everything changed abruptly. With the coming of white men to the plains, the game herds fell victim to lustful killing. Ruthlessly butchered by white hide hunters and Sunday sportsmen, the buffalo all but vanished in less than a decade. And the white invaders threatened the Indian tribes with destruction as thorough as their wasteful slaughter of some sixty million bison. With the near extermination of the buffalo, the Indians and their way of life were doomed. The last Sioux buffalo hunt had taken place in the fall of 1883. Since then the heart and the hope of the tribes had withered away.

Ruefully, Kicking Bear recalled the treaties with the whites to which honorable Sioux leaders had "touched the pen" in all good faith, giving up the sacred land in exchange for promises of beef allotments to replace the vanished buffalo.

For a while after the establishment of the reservations longhorn cattle had been provided in sufficient quantity to keep the Sioux pacified. But within the last year or so the allotments had been steadily decreased. As soon as the Indians were settled down at their agencies, the whites built a Thieves' Road across Sioux lands to the Black Hills of Dakota. Thousands of white settlers as well as gold seekers flooded into the newly opened country. Steel rails were laid across the prairie and soon great iron horses came panting and churning to frighten away what little game was left. Settlements mushroomed into big white men's towns such as Pierre and Rapid City and Hot Springs and Crawford. Even the whites who had made the treaties no longer cared what happened to the Indians. With beef issues cut, the tribes were desperately hungry; many Indians were starving. It mattered little. The swarming whites encroached everywhere on Indian lands, illegally grazing their own cattle on Sioux grass, or hunting out the few remaining deer or antelope. The land of the Sioux seemed lost to the white men.

In angry despair, Kicking Bear's thoughts turned back to the dying of the sun and the screaming eagle's voice. Like the high, soaring flight of the young bird, the meaning of the sun's death eluded him. For a brief time some great momentous understanding seemed almost within his grasp. Then suddenly, like the eagle's flight, it was beyond his perception.

A sudden flapping broke the chilled silence outside the lodge. Kicking Bear looked up sharply. It seemed as though a great bird, far bigger than an eagle, was beating its wings against the thin tepee wall. Kicking Bear grunted his disgust at this intrusion on his reverie, for it was a person with a blanket draped from the arms who waited outside.

Cramped from long sitting, Kicking Bear got up with deliberation and moved toward the hide-covered entrance of the lodge. Thrusting aside the heavy flap, he peered out into cold sunshine, beady eyes squinted to slits against the day's brightness.

Woodpecker Woman stood there, her natural thinness padded by the bulk of her shawl and blanket. She smiled shyly up at him, but he kept his face sober and scowling. Beyond the woman, their four children [4] waited—three small boys and a girl. Although they had all been visiting with their mother's uncle and had been away from the camp for some days, their father barely glanced at them.

"Why would you not enter as any wife should?" he asked the woman, his annoyance ill concealed.

"One has come to stay a while with us," she answered.

Kicking Bear looked past her shoulder to the blanketed figure sitting motionless on his horse a few paces away. It was Big Foot, his wife's uncle, waiting respectfully for the show of hospitality that was customary between in-laws. For some time since his journey to Washington with his brother, Touch-the-Cloud, Big Foot [5] had been a chief of considerable importance among the Minneconjous. Though only a band chief (while Touch-the-Cloud was a "scalp-shirt chief"), Big Foot had proved so cooperative to the whites that he had received much attention from high officials. Upon his return from seeing the Grandfather

[4] Only one of the children is alive at this writing: Frank Kicking Bear of Manderson, South Dakota.

[5] Big Foot was also known to intimates as Spotted Elk.

(President), he had urged his people to do the white man's bidding. He even tried to set the Minneconjous an example by becoming one of the first Sioux on Cheyenne River to cultivate corn according to Indian Department Instructions.

But following the wishes of the whites had cost Big Foot much respect among certain elements of the tribe, particularly Kicking Bear and his following. Added now to the formality of the in-law relationship was the cool restraint between men of opposing beliefs.

"I wished to make certain my uncle would be well received," said Woodpecker Woman, explaining her hesitancy in entering the family dwelling.

"There is nothing to eat," said Kicking Bear. "There is no food for us—let alone enough for extra mouths."

Smiling faintly under his hawk nose, Big Foot reached beneath his blanket and brought out several strips of jerked beef—dry as leather and far from fresh killed, but meat nevertheless.

"A humble offering of food, my niece," said Big Foot, pointedly addressing Kicking Bear's wife.

"Tell your uncle to get down and enter," Kicking Bear said without enthusiasm, turning back into the lodge.

Later in the day Kicking Bear's wife prepared the meat and the two men ate in strained silence while the woman and her children sat apart and waited. Only after the men and boys had finished would she and the little girl eat. There might be enough beef left over for a taste, at least, but it was only proper that her husband eat his fill. Casting side-glances at him from time to time, she noticed the extreme gauntness of his cheeks and the lack of flesh on his arms which made his wrists and hands look larger than ever.

In many ways, she knew, these times were unbearably difficult for her husband. Born and bred a warrior, he now seemed more like a caged, starved wild animal than a man. A quiet sorrow grew inside her as she saw the widening breach within her family.

As the situation demanded, Kicking Bear at last took down his pipe bag, removed the pipe and packed it and lighted it—going through the preparations with obvious reluctance. After three ceremonial puffs he passed the pipe to Big Foot. The older man smoked a moment before handing it back.

"I have talked at length with our father, the agent." Big Foot's tone carried a wary note as he studied Kicking Bear's firelighted features.

"Our *father!*" Kicking Bear snorted contemptuously.

Among the Sioux, chiefs as well as elders were politely called *"Ate"* (father). Such a term of respect, however, was also applied by many Indians to the agent of the white man's government.

"There are many things he and the Grandfather in Washington will do for us—if we give him the cooperation he seeks," Big Foot said defensively. For some time he had attempted to ameliorate the harsh attitude of the wilder Minneconjous. Years of strain and concern had already left their mark on his old wrinkled face.

"The best any white man can do for us is to leave us alone with our old tribal ways," growled Kicking Bear.

"But the whites offer many things, nephew." Big Foot's voice was soothing, almost caressing. "All that the white men themselves know—this can be ours also. This they will teach to our young people."

Kicking Bear grunted.

"Knowledge for which we have no use."

"But the days of hunting *pte*—our sacred buffalo—are forever gone. Making war is no longer allowed. We must do as the white men say and follow their teachings. Perhaps then we can learn the way of the white man's road."

"The 'Thieves' Road'!" Kicking Bear spat out the words. "Can we eat what the white men teach us? Will their empty promises fill our hollow bellies? Can we turn deaf ears when our starving children cry for food? Are we to cut the sacred hair of our Mother, the Earth, so we may plant corn like Arikaras—or women?"

This last was a deliberate insult aimed at Big Foot. Yet the older man let it pass without comment. As a chief of prominence, he must hold himself aloof from personal offense at anything said or done to him. Presently he spoke.

"For many winters I have urged the agent and his government to give us schools for our Minneconjous. Now, at last, it is promised. There will soon be a mission school on Cheyenne River!"

Big Foot had spoken with heartfelt pride; his deep emotion had been ill concealed. But he was hardly prepared for Kicking Bear's sudden outburst.

"School! A white man's school—on our river? I'll die before I see it happen!" Kicking Bear suddenly sprang to his feet. "Old man, I'll tell you something: a world lies between you and me— our Indian world that Wakantanka has given his red children. Believe in what the white liars tell you! Before you are through, the white men will kill you! But I care not what happens to you!"

With his angry words echoing in the hushed chill of the lodge, Kicking Bear strode to the entrance, grabbed up his blanket, and stepped outside into the cold winter afternoon.

Not until after sundown, when Big Foot finally rode off alone toward Cheyenne River, did Kicking Bear return. Through all the lonely night hours his wife nursed her heartache at this new trouble between her husband and her mother's brother. Silent and sullen, Kicking Bear brooded at his side of the lodge and never came near her.

After her week's absence, Woodpecker Woman longed for his touch and his firm tenderness. Had propriety permitted, she would have crossed to his part of the lodge. Yet something more than custom held her back. Now she held her husband in a strange sort of awe and to her it seemed almost as though he belonged to another tribe, another race, another world. As people around camp had already warned her, Kicking Bear had not been himself since the time the sun died.

Backdrop

IT WAS the gingerbread age. The realities of life were muffled by heavy drapes and obscured by rococo trappings and neo-classic false fronts. Once considered a period of innocent charm and effervescent romanticism, the era can be seen in perspective as a time of artificial standards and spurious morality.

Britain's aging Queen Victoria, having given her name to an age of respectability, rocked her empire by retreating into a life of overindulgence. Emperor Francis Joseph of Austria-Hungary was more furious than sad when his only son, the neurotic Crown Prince Rudolf, defied tradition and the crown by taking the life of his paramour, the Baroness Vetsera, as well as his own after an illicit rendezvous at Mayerling.

American Indians, unlike European royalty, were fast breaking under stresses and pressures they had never before imagined. An entire way of life had almost disappeared among such fighting tribes as the Sioux and Cheyennes in the short thirteen-year span since their high-water mark at Little Big Horn in 1876. The buffalo had been virtually exterminated, to be replaced by the spotted long-horned cattle of the white men. The tribes were corraled on great barren areas known as reservations, ruled like small empires by white agents and missionaries. Old tribal authority was grudgingly giving way to the alien law of the whites. Missionaries had succeeded in stamping out many of the ancient customs. Where rare crime within the tribes had once been settled calmly by giving ponies or other gifts to the aggrieved parties, agents now dealt harshly with the most trivial offenders.

In America, as well as in Europe, white men lived in a universe of inherited ideals that had fast become hollow notions.

Free thought was restricted to such diverse intellectuals as ex-
patriates Henry James and Lafcadio Hearn. American mores
were still largely dictated by repressive doctrine. Conformity
was the rule, and only a daring few stepped over the traces.

*The Hunkpapa and Blackfeet and Yanktonnai Sioux quar-
tered at Dakota's Standing Rock Agency were hopelessly divided
in their waning allegiance to proud, aging Sitting Bull and in
their increasing obeisance to the "squaw man" agent they called
"White Hair"—Major James McLaughlin. At Pine Ridge Agency,
some two hundred miles south, the Ogalalas looked in vain to
feeble old Red Cloud for the firm leadership he had once given
them. At neighboring Rosebud Agency the arch-conservative
Chief Two Strike was vigorously opposed by a minority of regu-
lation-abiding progressives among the Brûlés. Only on Cheyenne
River, in the rugged heart of Sioux country, were the tough Minneconjous and Sansarcs following Kicking Bear's lead and holding out against white encroachments and tribal deterioration.
And even here Big Foot was already showing signs of knuckling
under to the juggernaut of civilization.*

In the civilized world the forward look was a rarity. Enthu-
siastically supported by young Frank Lloyd Wright, architect
Louis Sullivan was decrying the fact that Victorian buildings
were merely boxes over which ornament was appliquéd. Although Chicago already boasted the first true skyscraper (the
Home Insurance Company Building), New Yorkers were so wary
of their first tall building, the eleven-story Tower Building on
lower Broadway, that for want of tenants designer Bradford L.
Gilbert was forced to occupy the topmost floors and offices. J. P.
Morgan's lavish Manhattan mansion became the first residence
in America to be completely lighted by electricity, but the public
was far more fascinated by accounts of the first electrocution of
a criminal (a murderer) at Sing Sing Prison.

Technological advances, however, were few and far between.
At West Orange, New Jersey, Thomas Alva Edison was tinkering
with a gadget he called the "kinetoscope," with which he demonstrated the first motion-picture film. After twenty-five years of
experimentation, a man named Doty had perfected a washing

machine. George Washington Ferris labored on his unique con-
traption, the Ferris wheel, slated to dominate the Midway at
the World's Columbian Exposition three years hence at Chicago.
Another inventor neared concepts of power far in advance of
his age when he devised a rocket cluster for travel in outer space.

People dutifully took notice of such wonders, yet found trivial
matters more to their liking. Everybody sniffed again at the old
Tabor scandal when wealthy convention-flouting H. A. W. Tabor of Leadville, Colorado, and his second wife, the beauteous
Baby Doe, christened their infant daughter "Silver Dollar." Dime
novels flourished, perpetuating such innocuous heroes as "Bottle
Nose Ben, the Indian Hater."

*Agency employees at Standing Rock laughed contemptuously
at the devoted letters written to Sitting Bull by Catherine Weldon of Brooklyn, New York, field representative of the National
Indian Defense Association. Opened by the agent's son, young
Harry McLaughlin, and other self-appointed messengers, the
letters contained ardent passages in which the widowed artistic
Mrs. Weldon laid bare her heartfelt admiration for the Hunkpapa chief and proclaimed over and over her desire to pay him
an early visit. Deliberately misconstrued as words of naked passion, Mrs. Weldon's messages were read aloud with many a guf-
faw on the part of agency personnel long before they reached
Sitting Bull. After all, the employees laughingly decided, old
"Bull" had already had nine wives and two of them were still
with him. What did a man his age want with another squaw—
and a white squaw at that?*

The public steadfastly refused to look at the realities of life—
even in the theater. Audiences preferred a dream world, and
few true-to-life dramas were produced. Gilbert and Sullivan were
far more popular. The maudlin sentimentality of an earlier era
was kept alive in small towns and rural areas with special effects
such as could be provided by traveling stock companies. One road
show spruced up *Uncle Tom's Cabin* with a climactic sparring
bout between the Uncle Tom and the Simon Legree. John L.
Sullivan, "The Strong Boy of Boston," was a popular hero. After
winning twenty thousand dollars and a diamond-studded belt

(donated by the *Police Gazette*) by battling challenger Jake Kil-
rain for seventy-five rounds in New Orleans, John L. even talked
hopefully of running for Congress. Florenz Ziegfeld achieved a
higher degree of respectability and created an overnight sensa-
tion in exploiting strongman Eugene Sandow—"Mighty Hulk
of Muscle and Sinew Whose Torso Haunts Female Dreams"—by
persuading Mrs. Potter Palmer, revered dowager of the age, to
feel—publicly, of course—Sandow's muscles.

*Confined on their dreary reservations, the Indians knew few
pleasures. Most native dances had been banned by the authorities, for missionaries had convinced the government that all
vestiges of aboriginal religion or culture must be abolished. Even
the harmless public humiliation of the Sioux heyoka or Cheyenne
massuum—men who voluntarily exposed themselves to the ridi-
cule of the tribe as a manifestation of the presence of thunderbirds in their dreams—even the semi-comic actions of these
"contraries" or "fools" was prohibited by the stern agents of the
Indian Department. Although never a friend of the Indian,
Civil War hero General William Tecumseh Sherman allowed
that "an Indian reservation is a worthless parcel of land set aside
for Indians and completely surrounded by white thieves." Virtually sealed off from the white man's world, the life of an
Indian was a dull succession of days made bitter and wearisome
by his endless longing to return to the dead past.*

It was the age—long before income taxes—of ten-thousand-
dollar dinner parties at Delmonico's in New York and fabulous
soirees at the fashionable Hoffman House Bar. Earmarked indefinitely as "The 400" by a chance remark of social arbiter
Ward McAllister ("Society As I Have Found It"), the smart set
became more exclusive than ever as society's inner circle. Ruled
by etiquette books and snobbery, America unashamedly allowed
wealth and family to become the criteria of leadership.

*Since the passing of the buffalo, the Sioux were subsisting on
rations doled out by a patronizing government. Bolstered by the
cheapest grade of green coffee beans, coarse brown sugar, and
wormy "Indian flour" of a quality no white family would use,
the staple of diet was low-grade beef delivered on the hoof to*

the various agencies. After the old manner of running buffalo, the half-wild longhorns were turned loose and hunted on horseback by shouting young bucks armed with rifles. One bony steer was expected to feed as many as thirty people over a two-week period. Now the Sioux were threatened with the loss of fresh meat by angry Captain Richard Henry Pratt, mentor of Pennsylvania's Carlisle Indian School and head of the unsuccessful Sioux Land Commission of 1888. Seeking to even the score with the stubborn Sioux who resisted his attempt to force the public sale of Indian lands, Pratt was recommending that the Indian Department discontinue "the cruel butchering method of the Sioux" and substitute bacon for fresh beef. It mattered little to Pratt or his fellow commissioners that the ill effects of a salt-pork diet on Indians was widely known; or that, in the words of former Sioux agent Valentine T. McGillycuddy, "the government had better issue arsenic instead of bacon and get the poisoning process finished with decent expedition."

A few socially minded citizens were looking upon 1889 with some satisfaction. Strides were being taken—even in the realm of reform. Jacob Riis completed a photographic report (using only the newly developed portable "detective" camera) on the growth of poverty in American cities. Such agencies as the Salvation Army began to offer help for "down and outers." And in Chicago Miss Jane Addams established Hull House, the first American settlement for the advancement of the underprivileged.

While the federal government now had a Department of Labor, many trouble areas remained untouched. Growing numbers of children were employed in factories and the bulk of city sweatshops were located in tenements beyond the reach of laws regulating factory labor.

Far more acute, however, was the increasingly desperate plight of the Indians—largely owing to the fact that it presented problems few politicians felt worth tackling. After twenty-five years of bloody campaigning, the American Indian was considered by most administrators, as well as the public at large, to be well along the white man's road and no longer an obstacle to the spread of civilization. The average citizen did not know that red men were starving and were being ravaged by epidemics of grippe, smallpox, and scarlet fever.

Like most Americans, cautious Benjamin Harrison, twenty-third President of the United States, was hardly aware that any Indian problem existed. An honest middle-of-the-roader, a grandson of Indian-fighting President William Henry Harrison, the chief executive could vaguely trace his ancestry back to Pocahontas—and that was about the extent of his interest in the red man. Concerned primarily with keeping his administration free of scandal, Harrison was content to turn over such routine matters as dealings with Indians to his Commissioner of Indian Affairs, General Thomas J. Morgan.

Business, like government, was extremely conservative. Insurance policies, for instance, were invalidated if a person went up in a balloon. Only with special permission from the underwriter could a policyholder cross the ocean or even the Mississippi River.

Indians the country over were trying to make the jump from the Stone Age to modern times. What had taken the white man centuries to accomplish was to be done overnight by the Indian. The Sioux had always lived communally and shared land ownership, as they shared the wild buffalo and all the rest of Nature's bounty. Now the whites expected them to appreciate the value of individual land tenure and free enterprise. Never an agricultural people, the Sioux were forced by government policy to undertake dry farming in flinty badlands soil under conditions no white farmer would have tolerated.

More shattering to Indian morale than the white man's bewildering economics was the endless confusion of the white man's religion. In rapid succession missionaries representing the Black Robes (Roman Catholics), White Robes (Episcopalians), Long Coats (Presbyterians), and many other denominations and sects had attempted to convert the Sioux. With typical Indian logic, the Sioux decided that the missionaries were either lying or mistaken, or that none of them knew more about worshiping God than the Indians themselves.

While holding to abstract ideals of justice and reform, the average citizen paid lip service to a frightening array of petty prohibitions. The Victorian cult of decency is now best described as having been "nasty nice." Philadelphia's Academy of Art even arranged for ladies' days in order to permit the fair sex to "gaze upon plaster casts of the human body without being embarrassed by the presence of men who might be indelicate enough to notice what they were observing. . . ." [1]

Morals, generally, were reduced to terms of "Thou shalt not!" Instead of preaching Christian tolerance or classic moderation, reformists such as Miss Frances Willard were issuing stern warnings: "Touch not! Taste not! Handle not!" Blue bows were distributed among school children in a crusade against the evils of drink, a wineglass was likened to a Cup of Death. Old demon rum, the saying went, "biteth like a Serpent, and stingeth like an Adder."

Once eagerly hopeful that the wonderful world of the white man would soon be open to their people, Indian leaders now looked back ruefully at the old treaties—mere scraps of paper dirtied with white men's lies. Ironically enough, the one provision the whites thought worthy of honoring was a stipulation prohibiting the sale or use of alcoholic liquor among Indians. Originally intended as a safeguard to insure control of the fiery young warriors by their chieftains, the liquor ban was now only part of the enforced morality code on the reservations. Few Indian Department officials cared a whit whether or not the young men looked up to the chiefs. Here, in this living hell where leaders were needed more sorely than ever before, the chiefs and elders sat around in bitter apathy, waiting only for a surcease to their earthy misery and frustration.

Prostitution was banned in most communities, but enforcement was lax and commercialized vice was on the upswing. "Brides of the multitude" did business in every conceivable setting, from palatial bagnios to sleazy opium dens—their favors priced accordingly. Compromising with the tenor of the age, Allen's Dance

[1] Quotation from *As We Were,* by Bellamy Partridge and Otto Bettmann.

House in Manhattan, operated by a former theological student, featured a Bible in every upstairs room.

One by one the old tribal conventions which made up the moral fiber of a people were breaking down. At army camps near the Indian agencies comely Sioux and Cheyenne maidens were trading their affections for scraps of food to keep themselves and their families alive. Many were forced to lie with soldiers against whom their fathers and brothers had futilely battled to hold the land. In order to eat, the young men of the tribes were enlisting as scouts for the Army or as Indian police—never sure when they might be pitted against their own people.

Card playing was frowned on as immoral, and most citizens entertained guests only within the confines of the front parlor, suitably maintained as a formal showplace with groupings of Rogers' statuary or a well-varnished Chickering piano.

The showplace of the Sioux country was Red Cloud's house at Pine Ridge Agency. Built for him years ago when the agency had been established, it was an ugly two-storied frame structure from which jutted a tall flagpole, a fine barometer of the old chief's mood. When Red Cloud felt friendly to the whites, the Stars and Stripes bravely fluttered from the top of the pole. Visible for miles around, the American flag was a sign that all was well at the agency. Vaguely aware that a lowered flag meant some sort of trouble, the old chief allowed his banner to droop at half-mast whenever he plotted mischief.

Much to their annoyance, small American boys were often attired in the fashions set by Frances Hodgson Burnett's "Little Lord Fauntleroy." As dictated by Paris designers, well-dressed ladies decked themselves out in leg-of-mutton sleeves and gored skirts. Hourglass figures were in vogue in spite of one prominent physician's warning: "Woman, by her injurious style of dress, is doing as much to destroy the human race as is man by his alcoholism!" Although high-heeled shoes and cinched-in waists were considered unhealthful by many, the steel-reinforced corset was holding its own—causing well-padded Frances Willard to sniff: "Niggardly waists and niggardly brains go together." Even sophisticated New Yorkers were taken aback when Mrs. Jack Gardner commissioned a society portraitist to paint her in a daringly décolleté gown to emphasize her "modern sensuality."

By this time a large majority of the Sioux already wore the mark of degradation—"citizen's dress"—shabby, cast-off white men's clothing provided largely by the missionaries. Many younger men as well as a few elders were cutting their long hair, in spite of the prevalent old-time belief that spiritual power often came through unshorn locks. Only in scattered camps did the Sioux adhere to former customs. Long after other Indians had given up old ways, Kicking Bear and Big Foot and their bands on Cheyenne River were still living in old-fashioned clustered villages and wearing gee strings, breechclouts, and buckskins. Elsewhere, agents had long bribed chiefs and their bands with sewing machines, oil lamps, and even iron bedsteads to give up their tepees and build cabins and wear white men's clothes instead of blankets. At government insistence many chiefs were donning stiff-bosomed white shirts, black "undertaker" suits, and shiny silk hat for all official occasions.

Along with the cultivation of chin whiskers American males were taking up cigar smoking. While cigarettes were looked down upon as "coffin nails," the presentation of a stogie to one's friend had become a ritual. Smoking of any sort was tabu for ladies, but a gentleman was often judged by his choice of cigars.

Most religious denominations forbade dancing. Believing the devil dwelt in musical instruments, many rural churches banned fiddle playing, permitted dancing only to vocal accompaniment. Some city-bred women were gaining a degree of emancipation, however, in the "two-step" dance craze, an outgrowth of John Philip Sousa's stirring new "Washington Post March." As American women began to emerge from their Victorian shell, the old reels, quadrilles, lancers, gallops, and waltzes went out of style overnight. Even the once-daring "Portland fancy" gave way to the two-step.

Far from the gaslighted streets and teeming music halls of American cities another dance craze was sweeping the remote Paiute Indian country in Nevada's Mason Valley. Here, in a beautiful vale surrounded by tule-grass meadows and purple mountains, bronze-skinned people were holding hands and chanting in unison as they moved in stately shuffling circles. Even in Nevada few white men were aware of the weird new dance. The handful of whites who knew of the strange ceremony spoke of it with derision edged with idle curiosity. From the beginning the "ghost dance" was the most misunderstood religious movement in history. And the misconceptions of intolerant whites were to lead inevitably to tragedy.

For all its apparent novelty—even among Indians—the ghost dance was not new. Some eighteen years earlier, around 1870, the dance had its origin among the Northern Paiute of Nevada. Its author, a Paiute shaman named Tavibo ("White Man"), prophesied the end of the world and the sure destruction of the hated white aggressors who were already profitably ensconced in Virginia City and other nearby mining settlements. The earth would be reborn, Tavibo promised. The dead would return from beyond the grave to help living Indians populate a terrestrial paradise.

In the early seventies the ghost dance swept through many tribes in northern California and Nevada. Farther north, in the lava beds of southern Oregon, the dance helped fan the desperate Modoc tribe into an abortive outbreak in 1872. Scarcely known to whites, the early ghost dance flared briefly, then died out among the disillusioned Indians.

After Tavibo's death, the Paiute looked at his young son, Wovoka ("The Cutter"), and hopefully recalled those times of promise when the old shaman had walked among them, preaching of an Indian paradise on earth. Many wishfully thought the son might follow in the footsteps of his father. But early in life Wovoka turned away from his tribe and went to live with white people. With no one to perpetuate the ritual, even the Paiute forgot it.

From boyhood into early middle age Wovoka cut timber and performed various farm chores for David and Mary Wilson, gentle Christian Mason Valley settlers. Their humble God-fearing background had a profound effect on the strapping young Paiute. Almost daily they spoke of the wonders of Jehovah and the glory of

Christ. Each evening they read aloud from a heavy book that told of a wonderful age in which unbelievable miracles were an everyday occurrence.

The mightiest medicine man of all time, Wovoka learned, was Jesus, the son of God, who went around teaching everybody to be good. He could turn ordinary water into firewater. He could feed a whole tribe with two tiny fishes. He could make the sick well just by touching them. The blind could see again after He waved His hand across their eyes. He could raise the dead. In spite of all these attainments, unbelievers cropped up among His own tribesmen and killed Him by nailing Him to a tree. He went to heaven for three days and talked to God. Then he came back to life. Walking among His people, He proved to them that He had come back to life by showing them where the nails had pierced His hands and feet.

When ranch life grew tame, Wovoka joined a group of migratory Paiute field hands who worked the hop farms and garden patches of Oregon and Washington. He met members of other tribes, including apostles of several strange new religions which had recently sprung up in the Northwest.

Among these were the "Shakers," the followers of a Skokomish prophet named John Slocum who advocated complete abstinence from swearing, whoring, drinking, gambling, and other evils acquired from the white men. Borrowing the sign of the cross, candles and bells from Christianity, Slocum's converts swayed themselves into religious ecstasy to the rhythmic tinkling of bells and feverish demonstrations of quaking and trembling.

The first of Slocum's converts, Louis Yowaluch, led an offshoot sect called "Blowers." Instead of greeting a stranger by shaking hands, they waved and blew at him to chase away his badness.

The Yakimas and Klickitats of Washington had long been numbered among the adherents of a Wanapum chief named Smohalla, who taught that it was evil to uproot the soil and practice any sort of agriculture. Known as "Dreamers," Smohalla and his cult believed that men learned lasting wisdom only from reflection. Backbreaking labor was for fools—and white men. "Each person must learn for himself the highest knowledge," preached Smohalla. "It cannot be taught."

Wovoka returned to Nevada determined to become a shaman like his father. Shakers, Blowers, and Dreamers contributed much to his own growing ideology. Combined with his hand-me-down mastery of the shaman's art, his preaching soon brought him minor prominence among his tribesmen. But Wovoka sought even greater power such as Smohalla or John Slocum enjoyed. Casting about for a device to extend his influence, he quietly revived Tavibo's old ghost dance.

For all its promise, the revival of the old ceremony at first caused scarcely a ripple of excitement among the Paiute. Started up again around 1886, the ghost dance was long confined to Mason Valley.

Wovoka patiently kept the dance going. Unlike most Indian rituals in which the sexes danced separately, men and women together joined hands to form the great circles. They chanted sacred songs taught them by Wovoka himself, as he remembered them from early boyhood or made them up impromptu. No drum was used. The circle of dancers moved in simple, stately steps from left to right, the ring slowly revolving in time to the unison singing.

When interest began to flag, Wovoka decided to "die." For hours he lay in a deathlike trance. Coming out of it at last and "returning to life," he told the Paiute believers that he had gone to heaven where God had given him a holy message to bring back to his people. According to Wovoka, God had promised that a new world was coming—one in which the Indian would no longer be the slave and beaten dog of the white man. The Indian dead would return to life to people the new earth. In order to insure its coming, however, the believers would have to keep dancing the ghost dance.

For a while the dance was practiced by most Paiute in Mason Valley. Wovoka occasionally taught the people new songs or improvised some new feature to keep them dancing. Sometimes, after a strenuous five-night performance of the ghost dance, he led the dancers in a plunge into Walker River—"to wash away your sins," as the shaman explained.

Gradually, however, the fervor of the Paiute diminished. By the end of 1888 Wovoka's following had dwindled away to a bare handful of enthusiasts. Suddenly, when all else seemed to have failed, there was the startling death and rebirth of the sun.

In many ways the eclipse was a propitious event. Along with many another Paiute, Wovoka had been stricken that winter with one of the white men's most dreaded diseases, scarlet fever. Although the tribe expected him to die, he felt himself recovering as the old year waned. His youth among the whites had taught him the usefulness of an almanac. Quick to take advantage of this treasure-trove of facts and predictions, he cleverly timed a second "dying" to coincide with that of the sun. Again Wovoka lay stretched out like a corpse with the pallor of death upon him.

This time it was surely no accident, the superstitious Paiute decided, that life had left their medicine man at the same hour— indeed at the same moment—that all light was gone from the sun. Presently, like the rebirth of the sun, Wovoka once more miraculously came to life and told wondrous tales of his second visit to heaven.

Wovoka's second passing into immortality opened the eyes of the Paiute people. With his name on every lip in Mason Valley, he was quickly accepted by the entire Paiute tribe as the holiest of men. A stolid, heavy-set man in his middle thirties, he was well prepared for a life of adulation and ease. Soon after his second "resurrection from death" in January, 1889, Wovoka gathered his tribesmen around him.

"I have talked with God," he told them. "Soon now the earth shall die. But Indians need not be afraid. It is the white men, not Indians, who should be afraid, for they will be wiped from the face of the earth by a mighty flood of mud and water. When the flood comes, the Indians will be saved. The earth will shake like a dancer's rattle. There will be thunder and smoke and great lightning, for the earth is old and must die. Still, the Indians must not be afraid.

"Then, when the flood has passed, the earth will come alive again—just as the sun died and was reborn. The land will be new and green with young grass. Elk and deer and antelope and even the vanished buffalo will return in vast numbers as they were before the white men came. And all Indians will be young again and free of the white man's sicknesses—even those of our people who have gone to the grave. It will be a paradise on earth!"

Believing wholeheartedly in Wovoka's words, the Paiute turned with renewed zeal to the ghost dance. With sharp new impetus the dance spread like wildfire across Nevada, wherever the scattered Paiute bands dwelt. From far-flung branches of the tribe in Oregon came eager delegates one day to learn the ritual.

Eastern Paiute in Utah, long evangelized by Mormons, heard of the ghost-dance revival and were electrified into a belief that Wovoka's revelations in heaven heralded the Second Coming of Christ as promised by the angel Moroni to prophet Joseph Smith. Many Mormon Indian converts suddenly began to see another messianic prophet in Wovoka. The graven gold plates of Moroni which became the Book of Mormon had promised years ago that the American Indian would be lifted out of barbarism and would become "white and delightsome" people in a reclaimed world. And so almost within the shadows of Mormon chapels the circles of the ghost dance formed.

Paiute disciples fanned out across the land. The ritual was picked up by Uintah and Uncompahgre Utes in eastern Utah and western Colorado. Pit River and Digger visitors in Mason Valley carried the dance across the High Sierras to California. The Washoes of western Nevada, as well as the Walapai, Mohave, and Chemehuevi of northwestern Arizona began dancing. The Gosiute, Bannock, and Shoshoni of southern Idaho soon started the ceremony.

All through the West Indians began to stir with renascent vigor after decades of spiritual lethargy. Tribe by tribe, the new faith kindled hopes long dormant. In all history no religion ever spread with greater speed—or with more dramatic impact. Spiritually aflame, Indians carried Wovoka's word through one reservation after another. Inured to the pall of defeat and degradation, yet chafing under the white man's dominance, red men everywhere in the plateau and mountain states came alive with buoyant new hope.

Early in 1889 a Bannock from Idaho's Fort Hall traveled east across the Rockies to visit his kinsmen, the Wind River Shoshoni, who shared a Wyoming reservation with the Northern Arapahoes. He carried to the plains tribes their first knowledge of an Indian messiah.

By the time the ponies grew fat in June, 1889, five Shoshoni, headed by Täbinshi, journeyed west across the Shining Mountains to seek the new messiah. With them traveled an Arapaho medicine man, Sage (*Nakash*) or "The Well-Knowing One," once a prominent warrior who had helped his friends the Sioux and Cheyennes wipe out Long Hair Custer and his men.

In Nevada they attended a ghost dance at Mason Valley and met Wovoka. He told them they would be meeting all their dead relatives from the ghost world two years from the next turning of the leaves.[2]

"Dance often, my brothers," said Wovoka, "for only thus can the dead be brought back."

Returning to Wyoming, the delegates started ghost dances among both Shoshoni and Arapahoes. Although Wovoka's doctrine was completely new, the Shoshoni found that dancing in a circle with clasped hands was much like an old ceremony they had practiced more than fifty years earlier.

Many Arapahoes accepted the new religion without hesitation. While the Paiute had performed the ghost dance at night around a blazing fire, the Arapahoes and Shoshoni planted a cedar tree in the center of the dance circle, an important innovation on the plains, and usually performed the ceremony in broad daylight. Green and never-dying, the cedar symbolized enduring strength and lasting life. For countless generations the plains tribes had used straight cedar or pine saplings for tepee poles and lance shafts. It was now fitting that the tree should serve a formal religious purpose.

Full of fervid excitement, Sage as hero of the hour composed and sang a holy song at the first Arapaho ghost dance. Lifting his

[2] That is, in the fall of 1891.

voice above the din of the crowd which soon joined in the singing, he chanted:

> "My children—e'e'ye!
> My children—e'e'ye!
> Here it is, I hand it to you.
> The earth I give you—e'e'ye!"

In spite of his key role in bringing the ghost dance to the tribe and to the plains, Sage was gradually eased into the background by more avid leaders, including Yellow Calf, who became chief of the ghost-dance encampment. So intense was the fervor of the long-oppressed Arapahoes that each day saw dozens of eager supplicants swell the throng camped at a place called Ethete ("Good"), a few miles east of the agency at Fort Washakie.

Among participants and spectators at Ethete was Spoonhunter, an Ogalala Sioux married to the sister of Arapaho Sub-chief Sharp Nose. As excitement grew among the animated Arapahoes, Spoonhunter sent for his half-Arapaho son, Two Crows, who was learning to put talk into writing at the nearby mission school. Together father and son labored painstakingly over a short, fateful letter, the old Sioux dictating a message while Two Crows translated it into scrawling English words.[3]

The letter was an urgent request for a Sioux leader back in Dakota Territory to come at once to Ethete on a matter of greatest importance to the Indian race. It was addressed to Spoonhunter's nephew at Cheyenne River Indian Reservation, the band chief named Kicking Bear.

---

[3] In 1889 few Sioux or Arapahoes could read and write their own language and had to send messages to other Indians in English. Since then members of both tribes have become literate in their own tongues.

Journey into Sunset

KICKING BEAR often visited the Northern Arapahoes. His lonely horseback journey across eastern Wyoming was through country he had known a long time. Much of the land had once been Sioux hunting grounds. Short years earlier great buffalo herds had roamed here in an unending sea of grass.

Now, Kicking Bear noticed, the land was almost empty of game. Everywhere there were fence lines, cutting up the land into the ranches of the white men. Here and there ugly white men's towns sprawled like piles of dirty boxes. Furtive in his movements, Kicking Bear gave these settlements a wide berth, often circling miles out of his way to avoid meeting a white man. He sensed that the urgent matter at Ethete pertained only to Indians. His present caution as well as his standing hatred for the whites kept him restlessly on the move.

Day or night, he seldom stopped, kicking his buckskin pony into motion whenever the animal lagged. In spite of blustry winter winds he kept going. Some mornings after a hard night's riding he found his pony's dark mane and his own flowing hair rimed with hoarfrost. Yet the bitter weather only spurred him on.

He felt he had good reason to move as fast and inconspicuously as possible. This was a time in which Indian agents demanded that Indians secure official permission before leaving the reservation where they were enrolled, a hated technicality that made the Sioux and other freedom-loving tribes subject to their agents' merest whims and virtual prisoners in their own camps. Following his usual practice, Kicking Bear had not bothered to secure a pass which would give him official permission to be off the Cheyenne River Reservation. If Indian police or a roving cavalry patrol should intercept him, it might go hard with him back at the

agency. Agent McChesney, who was then in charge at Cheyenne
Agency, might jail him and cut off his rations. Even worse punish-
ment was sometimes meted out to frequent offenders such as
Kicking Bear.

So far as he knew, the only white man who might guess his
destination was storekeeper-postmaster at Howes Store who had
read Spoonhunter's letter to him. Although Kicking Bear had displayed no interest in his uncle's message, there was always a chance
that the little storekeeper might report the matter to McChesney.
Then Kicking Bear's absence might be discovered.

Kicking Bear's hooded eyes constantly scanned the horizon for
danger signs. From time to time he looked over his shoulder at
his back trail to see if anyone followed. As he rode on no horsemen were anywhere in sight.

His beaded pipe bag hung thonged to his greasy buckskin shirt.
Without letting the pony relax his gait, Kicking Bear reached
into the bag and felt the wadded paper of Spoonhunter's letter,
the first anyone had ever sent him. Soon he would learn what
great matter of importance lay behind the writing of this talking
paper.

During his long ride he thought often of the unasked question
in his wife's eyes as he had made ready to leave the Minneconjou
camp on Cherry Creek. He frequently rode off alone on some
private errand, telling no one his destination. Neither Woodpecker Woman nor his children had ever asked where he was going. This recent parting was like all the other times. Yet he had
sensed her awareness of a difference in his own attitude, some
sixth sense that told her this was no ordinary mission.

He felt a quiet surge of pride and tenderness for her as he recalled her wordless acceptance of his present errand. For days
after his dispute with her uncle, Big Foot, he had attempted in
his own strange, reserved way to bridge the gap that had fallen
between his wife and himself. They had known days and nights
of silent estrangement, each of them too proud to come to the
other.

Then on the day of his leave-taking he looked deep into her
eyes a long moment. Turning away abruptly, as was his habit, he

was assured for the present that no real gap lay between them, after all. She understood his going and knew the importance of it.

After crossing the Big Horn Mountains through lonely ice-clogged passes and wind-swept snowdrifts, Kicking Bear stopped briefly under a sheltered cut bank to make himself ready to meet his Arapaho relatives, for he was now a half-day's ride from Ethete. He first combed out his hair with handfuls of dry, spiky buffalo grass. This occasion of arrival was almost equal to a ceremony and he wanted to look his finest. To his braided scalp lock he tied a clean eagle plume, carefully saved for the purpose. Behind his ear, as usual, was the tiny medicine bundle containing the treasured smooth stone of Crazy Horse. Shaking out his old faded blue trade blanket, he wrapped it around his waist again so as to cover as much as possible of his travel-stained buckskins. Finally he daubed a finger of spit-wet red paint across his cheekbones and eyelids. To the Arapaho as well as the Sioux red was the color of life and happiness. Ready at last, he mounted the jaded little buckskin and rode on toward the Arapaho camp at Ethete.

Kicking Bear looked on in silent wonder at the shuffling circle of dancers. His eyes were wide in amazement as the Arapahoes reeled and spun and fell into rigid trances. During rare lags in the ceremony he listened attentively while Spoonhunter translated the magic words of Sage who could speak of nothing but the new messiah.

One day Täbinshi, the Shoshoni, paid a visit to the Arapaho ghost dance. Although the tribes seldom mingled and were traditional enemies, here was a Shoshoni meeting Arapaho and Sioux on common ground. Matters relating to the messiah were, after all, far above the petty tribal rivalries of the past. Now one Indian looked upon another as his brother, regardless of tribe or tradition. Kicking Bear absorbed it all, listening transfixed at everything he heard, a glowing flame leaping inside his breast like a living thing.

This great new faith must be made known to the Sioux, he decided, for here was a wonderful new power that might well mend the broken hoop—the sacred circle of the universe that mythically bound the Sioux and their old allies and friends together. Too long had the ancient symbol of a glorious past been reduced to mere remembering. Now it could be restored.

If only the Sioux could see this ghost dance! Kicking Bear knew few would fail to grasp its meaning. Even Big Foot would surely forget his stupid hankering for a white man's school on Cheyenne River.

In this new ceremony lay the answer to Kicking Bear's long soul-searching and brooding. Here, at last, even the meaning of his vision of the screaming spotted eagle became clear. And he knew it was no accident that the Indian messiah in the west had died, then returned to life at the same moment the eagle had spoken. The vision of the eagle, like the new ghost dance, meant a sure revival of Indian power all across the land. No longer would any red man be trodden under the white man's boot. As the wailing Arapaho voices rent the air, Kicking Bear watched the ghost dance with piercing eyes, his face agleam with the sweat of intense excitement and whetted for more knowledge of this great boon for all Indians.

News among the Sioux travels with uncanny swiftness. By the time Kicking Bear reached Pine Ridge Agency on his homeward route, a secret whisper was already running from person to person among the Ogalalas. The Wanekia—a "makes live savior"—had suddenly come alive in the minds of the Sioux and everyone was eager for word of him. Kicking Bear solemnly substantiated the rumors.

"Yes, a holy man lives far to the west in the land of those who wear rabbit-skin blankets and live in grass houses. He died and came to life again many days later—long after speaking with Wakantanka (God). While in the spirit world he learned a sacred dance, a dance he brought back to give to all Indians. The day will come, they say, when all our dead will come to life again with a whirlwind at their head. All of heaven and earth will be reborn.

But first the white men will be destroyed. We have only to learn this dance to be saved when the world ends."

The Sioux listened, some already convinced through their dark despair and yearning for a better world. Others were undecided, a few skeptical. Kicking Bear had always been a man of honor as well as courage, and few doubted his word; but this was strong talk. The whites had shoved the Sioux into barren badlands and had long been powerful lords of much of the old Sioux territory. Not since Little Big Horn and the great victory over Long Hair Custer had the tribes bested the pony soldiers of the white man's army; and that had been nearly thirteen years ago. Now they wondered about this man as Kicking Bear described him through the eyes of Arapahoes and Shoshoni—if, indeed, he were but a man.

"Let us see this man with our own eyes," said the Sioux elders, wise to the world's ways. "Let us hear him with our own ears, this man who dies and talks to Wakantanka and returns to life, so that we, too, may know how these things are done."

A chorus of approving "hau's" greeted the proposal. Still no definite plan was formulated whereby the Sioux might see the Wanekia for themselves. His patience spent, Kicking Bear headed north to his camp on Cherry Creek.

Wovoka himself may have written the letters. Or the scribe may have been one of his half-educated tribesmen. They were signed "Jack Wilson," the name Wovoka took when he lived with the white rancher and his family. Scribbled in English, the messages were sent to the leaders of every major Indian tribe in the country, who were asked to select brave and broad-minded men to come to Mason Valley to meet the messiah. These delegates were then to return to their people and help Wovoka found a new religious faith exclusively for Indians. Educated red men were expected to help out by reading the messiah's letters to tribal chieftains.

Across the land, wherever Indians lived and gathered, the new religion stirred the tribes into decision. While white citizens kept busy battling disastrous floods in Johnstown, Pennsylvania, and importing thousands of Australian beetles to combat a white scale which threatened citrus crops in California, Wovoka's message was carried far and wide through the spring and summer of eighty-nine. Far from the white men's towns and railways and ranches, Indian leaders sat in secret council, charting the destiny of their race.

Sparked by the letters from Nevada, rumors of the messiah trickled into the southern plains. Like chain lightning the word jumped from tribe to tribe in Indian Territory and the new Territory of Oklahoma. The Southern Arapahoes heard it from their northern cousins. The Cheyennes learned of it from the Arapahoes. The Kiowas, Caddoes, and Wichitas picked it up from the Cheyennes. Osages, Otoes, Cherokees, and many others got it from the Caddoes.

For all their wretched despair some tribes rejected outright the idea of an Indian messiah. Red men in the Pacific Northwest were firmly entrenched in the doctrines of Smohalla and John Slocum. Woodland tribes in the Midwest, such as the Ojibwa (Chippewa), Winnebago, Omaha, Sauk, and Fox, would have little to do with the new religion. Long under "civilizing influences," the Santee Sioux of eastern Dakota and Nebraska completely ignored it.

The Blackfeet, Bloods, Sarsis, and Plains Cree of Montana and Alberta displayed no interest in the letters, so fresh in their minds was the ill-fated Riel Rebellion of 1885. As Cree Chief Crowfoot expressed it: "We will follow the white man's trail, no matter how dim it may seem to us now."

Surrounded by wild tribes, the turbulent Crows of central Montana showed only passing interest in Wovoka's message. All too recently, in the summer of 1887, they had gotten their fill of prophets in the person of Wraps-His-Tail, a fanatic known to the whites as the Sword-bearer.

Far from indifferent, however, were neighbors of the Crows, the fierce, proud Northern Cheyennes. Close kinship ties and long association with the Arapahoes had alerted them to the ghost dance soon after the Arapahoes acquired the ritual. Porcupine, a prominent Cheyenne healer, was already advocating certain changes in the ancient medicine lodge ceremony to conform with the ghost dance.

Big Foot was deeply troubled. For long months he had waited patiently for the government to establish a school on Cheyenne River. But no move had been made by Agent McChesney to do anything about it. Not even the missionaries had set up an educational system there, much to Big Foot's growing disgruntlement.

"The agent, our father, gave me his word," Big Foot kept saying. "He shook hands on it."

But after a while it sounded as though he repeated the words to reassure himself as much as his listeners among the Minneconjous. The old chief earnestly desired to bring to his people all the bounty of the white man's civilization which he had seen on his journey to Washington. Yet the white man was doing little at Cheyenne River to bring it within the Indian's reach. Moreover, other forces were vigorously at work, nullifying McChesney's half-hearted effort to keep his charges satisfied and quiet.

Sioux Indians will long remember the summer of eighty-nine as one of their darkest hours. Suffering from hunger was intense. Indian-issue beef herds had been decimated by anthrax the previous year, and terrible drought and grasshopper plagues swept the plains. Like many another Sioux garden, Big Foot's little patch of corn withered to dust under the blistering July sun. Game had all but disappeared from the country, and empty Indian bellies had long been the rule rather than the exception.

Added to the ravages of nature were the white men's constant attempts to take the land. Since their "long-ago" victory over Custer at Little Big Horn in 1876 and their final surrender to the white men's army the following year, the Teton-Dakota or Western Sioux had been deprived of vast hunting grounds in Dakota's Black Hills, as well as in the Powder River, Tongue River, and Big Horn basins in Montana and Wyoming. By treaty they still held a great reservation—some 35,000 square miles in the area—in Dakota which included wide stretches of prairie and badlands between the Black Hills on the west and the Missouri River on the east.

During the seventies and eighties many attempts were made to dislodge the proud Sioux from much of this region, and the wild Teton bands were threatened more than once with whole-sale removal to Indian Territory. By 1889 the whites were ready for a final try.

A Sioux Land Commission was set up, chairmaned by a military figure of outstanding prominence, General George Crook. Known to the Sioux as "The Grey Fox" or "Three Stars," their old ad-versary in many a battle,[1] Crook was a choice well calculated to bludgeon the stubborn Indians into speedy compliance with the government plan to whittle down the great Sioux Reservation.

With an old Indian fighter's shrewd ruthlessness, the Grey Fox resorted to every conceivable trick to push through an outsized land cession. Strenuously opposed by such leaders as Sitting Bull, Red Cloud, and Two Strike, Crook simply shut out these chief-tains from his councils and set up rival chiefs in authority. He made outlandish promises to wavering leaders. He provided feasts and dances for Indians who would sign. As a final stroke, he had ballots favoring the sale printed in red, those opposing printed in black—fully aware that to the Sioux red symbolized happiness and long life while black was a color thought to bring bad luck if improperly used.

The commission was ultimately successful—but not until after Crook had skillfully padded his list of Indian signers to conform with an old Sioux ruling that three fourths of all adult males in the Nation must agree to a disposal of land before a cession was regarded as legal. By mid-August it was all over. Nine million acres of their best cattle range were lost forever to the Sioux.

Since his return from the Arapaho country and Pine Ridge, Kicking Bear had been constantly on the move, telling every Indian he met of the wondrous ceremony he had witnessed in Wyoming. From his own camp on Cherry Creek he rode to Bear Eagle's camp on the North Fork of the Cheyenne, then down-river to Big Foot's village at Deep Creek.

Big Foot was surprised to see his nephew-in-law, more aston-

[1] Soundly whipped at the Battle of Rosebud in June 1876, Crook trounced the Sioux that fall at Slim Buttes, Dakota Territory.

ished yet to learn of the younger man's apparent willingness to let bygones be bygones and side-step their old quarrel.

"What I have to tell you, Uncle, is of far greater importance than any small differences we may have had in the past," Kicking Bear said.

Big Foot listened with growing interest to the description of the Arapaho ghost dance and the rumored stories of an Indian messiah. It was fitting, perhaps, that new hope should spring almost from the very ashes of his disappointment in the white men and their failure to help his people. And yet the old chief's faith in the white men's promises lingered and held him back. And it was not Big Foot, but his medicine man, Yellow Bird, who showed the greater interest in Kicking Bear's tidings.

Kicking Bear moved on, preaching to the bands until word of the Wanekia was a whispering wildfire among the camps. He was visiting the down-river villages of Touch-the-Cloud and Hump, two of the Minneconjous' "scalp-shirt men" or head chiefs, when Wovoka's letter came from Nevada addressed to Chief Hump.

An educated Sioux just returned from an eastern boarding school read the letter to Hump. Backed by Kicking Bear's lively account, the letter from Nevada held out both hope and meaning to the Minneconjous. Calling in the various band chiefs, as well as the more powerful scalp-shirt leaders, Hump presided over an all-important council.

Like many another chieftain, Hump was angry over the land swindle. If all that was said in the letter and by Kicking Bear was true, he thought perhaps the land the Grey Fox had hoaxed away from the Sioux might be recovered through this Indian messiah. After much deliberation and some disagreement (two or three scalp-shirt leaders dissenting), it was at last decided to send delegates west into the sunset to seek out this holiest of persons.

"Thus we may see for ourselves what manner of person is this Wanekia," Hump told his fellow chiefs.

From the beginning Kicking Bear was a logical choice for one of the delegates. One man, the chieftains finally determined, was enough to go. As Big Foot himself put it: "My kinsman, Kicking Bear, has the brave heart of ten ordinary men; no others are needed." All through the summer Big Foot had looked with increasing favor on his niece's husband. Now, with all past bitterness forgotten, he almost fawned over Kicking Bear.

Word passed among the tribes—by runner, by letter, by communication known only to red men—as the delegates were selected and made preparations for a long journey into territory never before penetrated by the Sioux. Only in the far north at Standing Rock Agency did word fail to get through to the Hunkpapas, Blackfeet Sioux, and Yanktonnais. Due largely to the vigilance of Indian police and Agent James McLaughlin's policy of intercepting mail addressed to the leaders, these tribes seemed totally unaware of the ghost dance or the Wanekia until the following year.

Sitting Bull, head chief of the Hunkpapas, had grave presentiments of impending doom. After the breakup of the great Sioux Reservation in August, 1889, he announced to his followers that a bad year was ahead for all of his people.

"The sun will burn up everything," he told his tribesmen. "No crops can be raised in our land. And no rain will fall for many months to come."

At other agencies plans proceeded apace for delegates of the various Sioux tribes to meet and travel west in company to seek the Wanekia. The Brûlés sat in prolonged council at Rosebud Agency. With little deliberation they selected Short Bull, a medicine man from Lip's band on Pass Creek, as one of their delegates.

Their second choice was not so easily made. Finally, with some misgivings, the council picked Scouts Ahead. As a warrior Short Bull had fought bravely at Little Big Horn and in numerous intertribal wars. But Scouts Ahead was young and inexperienced in matters requiring keen judgment.

At Pine Ridge Agency the Ogalalas decided to send four delegates instead of two as suggested in Wovoka's letter to Red Cloud. The old chief blew hot and cold on the project, owing perhaps to his recent conversion to Roman Catholicism. After much palaver Yellow Breast (sometimes called Yellow Knife) was chosen to represent the Ogalalas near Pass Creek, Cloud Horse was picked from the Little Wound community, Good Thunder represented bands along Wounded Knee Creek, and Sells-a-Pistol-Butt was appointed as delegate for scattered bands along White Clay Creek.

At his Cherry Creek camp Kicking Bear made ready for the journey. Runners from Pine Ridge had brought word to him that the delegates would meet on Wounded Knee Creek and travel on together. Talking little now, Kicking Bear was a silent man of action as he staked out his favorite pony, the same buckskin he had ridden to the Arapaho country, and cleaned and oiled his old Winchester.

Woodpecker Woman accepted the coming absence of her husband with quiet resignation. Sensing that it might well be a long time before his return, she blinked away the tears from her large, dark eyes as she labored long hours on extra moccasins for Kicking Bear. Many years later the couple's surviving son recalled that the fall days before his father's departure seemed like a period of mourning, as though some dear one had passed away.

From Cherry Creek, Kicking Bear headed south alone after his usual abrupt leave-taking of his family. He stopped overnight at Big Foot's village on Deep Creek. Old Big Foot was friendlier than ever to his nephew-in-law, now renowned as the sole delegate to represent the Cheyenne River Sioux.

"It may be true about this Wanekia," Big Foot admitted. "In these troublesome times Wakantanka, the Great Spirit, may not have forgotten his red children after all."

Kicking Bear rode on south, following an old Indian trail that crossed the Bad Lands. He spent the second night out just north of White River, moving on the next morning to the mouth of Medicine Creek. From there it was an easy cross-country ride to the peaceful, sheltered little valley of Wounded Knee, some eighteen miles northeast of Pine Ridge Agency.

Good Thunder's camp was not far from the Wounded Knee store and post office run by half-breed Louis Mousseau. Here Kicking Bear rested, taking daily sweat baths in Good Thunder's sweat lodge beside the creek and purifying himself for the holy pilgrimage ahead. Word came from Rosebud Agency that the other delegates were on their way.

The Brûlé chiefs had offered six good riding horses to each of their two delegates. Short Bull carefully picked out three choice animals and returned the others to their owners. For such a mission as this one might do well to travel light. His two wives—they were sisters—prepared his packs and gear for the journey, making several extra pairs of moccasins in case his visit should be prolonged. Short Bull was a good-natured, sharp-faced man of small stature. He smiled approvingly as his wives worked to get everything ready. It was well to be thus equipped, for as yet no Sioux had gone into the sunset where he must now go. The morning of his departure his wives giggled a great deal to conceal their nervousness about his going. When one of them broke into tears, Short Bull had to get down off his horse to quiet her.

Near the head of Pass Creek, where the southward trail crossed one leading west from Red Leaf's camp on Black Pipe Creek, Short Bull met Scouts Ahead, who was weighted down with extra gear and had all six of his borrowed horses heavily burdened. Far from pleased, Short Bull tried to discourage Scouts Ahead from going. A few miles out he succeeded. Scouts Ahead grew so weary he was glad to turn back.

Short Bull reached Bear-in-the-Lodge Creek when he was overtaken by Scouts Ahead's replacement, a pugnacious young man known as Mash-the-Kettle (literally, Breaks-the-Pot-on-Him). Short Bull smiled broadly. Mash-the-Kettle was far better fitted for such an important mission. The two men rode on west together past Potato Creek to the Little Wound (now Kyle) post office and store on Medicine Root Creek. They were now well into the territory of their cousins, the Ogalalas.

At Little Wound they were joined by Yellow Breast and Cloud Horse. Another day's riding brought them all to Good Thunder's camp. They were all delighted to see that Kicking Bear was there, ready and waiting. Short Bull was especially gleeful. Kicking Bear was his brother-in-law which, among the Sioux, involved a certain playful camaraderie.

The assembled delegates carefully repeated their purification ritual in Good Thunder's sweat lodge. Then, with Kicking Bear leading out the procession of riders and pack animals, the chosen few quietly rode out of the serene valley of Wounded Knee.

There was some talk of stopping at Pine Ridge Agency to get the blessings of old Red Cloud. Two considerations finally ruled it out. Good Thunder explained that the old man had seemed to waver at the last councils owing to his joining the Catholic Church. Now he might even oppose the delegation.

Kicking Bear provided another reason for avoiding the agency. None of the delegates had thought to get passes from their respective agencies. If they rode into the agency obviously bent on some far-flung errand, Kicking Bear knew they might be arrested by the agent's Indian police.

One more stop was necessary, however: they tarried briefly on White Clay Creek to let Sells-a-Pistol-Butt join them. Now, at last, the group was complete. Often traveling under cover of darkness, carefully skirting towns and ranches, the delegates followed the way west and judged their path by the setting sun and the stars.

Never in all history had men set out on a stranger quest than this journey to seek the Wanekia. Fearless, the tiny party of Sioux rode far across the plains crisscrossed with ranchers' fences, cutting wire, slamming their mounts against the hated fence posts. Presently they reached the land of the Shoshoni, once the far limit of their raiding. Now the Shoshoni were their brothers in the search for an Indian Christ.

Beyond the Wind River ranges they pushed their ponies and themselves, seldom stopping, a tiring handful of strangers in a glistening winter world of shining mountains. Farther yet, they crossed a desolate plateau wilderness of mesquite and stunted cedars. Beyond that, surrounded by purple mountains, they came at last to the blustery sage plains of Nevada.

Kicking Bear looked wonderingly at the scattered tule-grass wickiups of the Paiute, this squat, alien tribe who gave them a friendly welcome. Their domed shelters were hardly larger than Sioux sweat lodges. Then, finally, the Sioux came face to face with the Wanekia. Although he seemed hardly more than a

heavy-set, placid-featured young man, they all fell prostrate before him and silently paid him homage.

All through the dark winter the tribes waited for the delegates'
return. While white men celebrated newly won statehood for
both North and South Dakota (as of November 2, 1889), the
starving Sioux hungered for word of the Wanekia. Although
some said it was foolishness, many already blindly believed. Remembering their former days of plenty, the people subsisted
mainly on the hope that the Indian messiah in the West would
save them.

While in Nevada, the delegates were joined by Kills-in-Water,
a Sioux who had been visiting the Northern Cheyennes in Montana and had come west with three Cheyennes and two Arapahoes to see the Wanekia.[2] Many tribes were now represented
among Wovoka's visitors. Many of them had never before been
encountered by the Sioux. All delegates mingled freely in a great
new spirit of Indian brotherhood few of them had ever imagined.

Language barriers quickly broke down. While only the plains
tribes spoke sign talk, the plateau and desert Indians seemed to
understand them readily as well as tribes from the rain forests of
the northwest.

All delegates looked in wonder and gasped at the sight of
Wovoka, who liked to appear before them emerging from clouds
of smoke or standing on high rocks above Walker River. And
when he would look directly at them, they were afraid and
would shut their eyes or turn away trembling. From time to time
he would raise his arms and fire seemed to be all around him.
The delegates would fall to the ground and worship him. When
they dared look up again, he would be gone from their sight.

One day they listened with amazement as Wovoka talked to
them in a willow grove by Walker Lake. He spoke Paiute, yet
in such a way that all the tribes could understand him. Even the

[2] The Northern Cheyennes were Porcupine, the healer, Tall Bull, a chief of
police on Tongue River, and Black Sharp Nose. The Arapahoes were Friday
and a medicine man named Sitting Bull (not to be confused with the Hunkpapa Sioux chieftain).

plains delegations knew exactly what he was saying to them. Porcupine, who headed the Cheyenne delegates, asked Short Bull in signs if he understood. Short Bull signed yes.

"A long time ago," Wovoka began, talking as though it hurt him now to remember such pain, "I came among the white people. But they did not like me. They rejected me. They crucified me."

He held up his hands and pointed to the palms. He showed his bare feet. Both hands and feet bore what seemed to be the marks of nails going all the way through flesh and bone. Then he bared his chest and revealed a scar where he had been stabbed to death. He smiled faintly.

"The white race did that to me long ago. But I no longer care about that. Now I come to bring you great news. A new world is coming—a new Indian world. Our dead will live again. They will share this new earth with us, the living members of our race. And the white men and their towering cities will be no more. I am truly the Son of God. I have come now to save my Indian children. The others I throw away. Many of you have fought the white men. Perhaps you want to fight them again and make war against them."

He paused significantly, looking sharply at Kicking Bear. This time Kicking Bear did not look away but returned the Wanekia's stare. After all, he felt no shame for having fought the white men.

"Now I tell you this is wrong," said Wovoka pointedly. "I want you to go back to your tribe and tell them all I have said. You must say that the white man and the Indian shall live together in peace. There may be trouble. Stamp it out like a prairie fire."

Kicking Bear's face darkened as he listened to this strange holy man talk of peace. This was not talk for a warrior. Kicking Bear had not come thus far to hear drivel. Seeming to sense Kicking Bear's growing antagonism, Wovoka turned to Short Bull, who sat raptly attentive.

"They may try to kill you, Short Bull. Even so, do not fight back. You must live in peace. Your children must go to the white men's schools and your children's children must grow to become the husbands and wives of white men and women. And then someday there will be no Indians and no white men. We will all be one people and there will be peace. And there shall be no night, no hunger, no cold, no death."

Then Wovoka showed them the robe he wore, a hip-length gown of pale muslin, shaped much like a Sioux war shirt save for its unique decoration. Instead of quillwork or beaded panels, it was covered with painted symbols as bright as fire: crosses, crescents, sun circles, and thunderbirds, all colored in brilliant hues. At last he taught them the strange, shuffling steps of the new dance.

"When you dance you must throw away your rifles and bows and war clubs. Live in peace and let the white man live in peace with you."

Kicking Bear's eyes gleamed savagely while Wovoka talked of peace. For the warrior Sioux these were empty words. Yet all else the Wanekia said held a bright promise. A strange power coursed through Kicking Bear as he conjured up a picture of the brave, clean Indian world that was surely coming. And in that moment Kicking Bear became a deeply dedicated man.

Accompanied by Kills-in-Water, the Sioux delegation returned to Pine Ridge while winter snow still lay banked along the pine-crested hills and ice clogged the prairie streams. In the minds of all eight of them the preaching of the Wanekia made a strange whirling. Not all of them were equally convinced. Cloud Horse was already expressing skepticism about things Wovoka had said.

"How can it be," he argued, "that the world can become Indian if we must share it with the whites?"

The delegates' return prompted a council among the Ogalalas. Presided over by Red Cloud, who still did not commit himself one way or another to the new beliefs, the assembled chiefs expressed profound wonder at the delegates' report. Normally reserved, Good Thunder was somewhat carried away by the excitement of the moment when called upon to act as spokesman for the others.

"My relatives," he said solemnly, "believe and cry no longer! Our dead are coming. Already they are marching toward us.

These eyes of mine have seen the Wanekia. He has come! He is no myth or legend that we may not believe in him with all our hearts and souls. Even now his feet are on the prairie!"

Acting with swift decision, the council unanimously approved Good Thunder's proposal that the delegates again be sent into the sunset to see the Wanekia once more and find out all they could about the new religion. Broken Arm, middle-aged and respected, was selected to replace the younger Sells-a-Pistol-Butt, who did not care about going to Nevada again. For good measure Sub-chief Flat Iron was also named to go. Without delay, without opportunity to visit their families, the eager delegates turned back west to retrace their journey into the sunset.

Spring 1890

THE Sioux sojourn in Nevada came to an end in late March, 1890, when the delegation split into two groups. Kicking Bear, Short Bull, and Mash-the-Kettle found their way to the Umatilla Reservation in Oregon, where they remained a short while discussing the new doctrine of the ghost dance with the hospitable Umatillas and their neighbors the Wallawallas.

The Pine Ridge contingent retraced their step to the Arapaho country in Wyoming, arriving back in Dakota early in April. Most of the delegates were firmly convinced that they had found a true messiah, only Cloud Horse holding to the prosaic idea that Wovoka was, after all, a mere man. After reporting to the chiefs, the delegates were given a chance to see their families while a council was called to hear all about the Wanekia.

A few days later Kicking Bear and the two Brûlés came through Pine Ridge and were persuaded to linger among the Ogalalas. They reported that the ghost dance was not yet in full swing among certain Oregon, Idaho, and Montana tribes. Good Thunder and the other Pine Ridge delegates, on the other hand, said the new faith was flourishing stronger than ever among the Arapahoes and Shoshoni. Known to other tribes as a keenly religious people, the Arapahoes had long been convinced of the truth of Wovoka's teaching. Some ghost dancers at Ethete claimed to have fallen dead and to have returned to life after flying to the Spirit Land, thus bearing out Kicking Bear's earlier observations.

William Selwyn, mixed-blood postmaster at Pine Ridge, had long been reading letters concerning the Wanekia to local Indians. Now, with a flood of fresh mail from points touched by the split Sioux delegation in their travels, Selwyn became alarmed

48

and reported his sudden concern to Agent D. H. Gallagher. Roughshod Irishman that he was, Gallagher acted with dispatch and ordered Kicking Bear, Good Thunder, and Yellow Breast arrested by his Indian police and thrown into the agency's cramped guardhouse jail.

For two days Gallagher tried to make the three Indians tell what lay behind their unauthorized visit to Nevada, but they steadfastly refused to say anything to this officious white man about such a sacred matter as the Wanekia. Even with his hands tied behind him with wet rawhide and a sharpened stick thrust into his mouth to make him talk, Kicking Bear kept silent as both agent and Indian police hammered away at him. Finally Gallagher gave up in disgust and turned the Indians loose.

The arrest of the three delegates prompted Red Cloud to postpone the council. Now that the men were free, however, the Ogalala chiefs decided to brave the agent's Gaelic fury and called a council to be held on White Clay Creek a few miles northwest of the agency. The delegates were assured of an eager audience. Everyone wanted to hear about the Wanekia and it was a big meeting.

Eagle Elk was in the milling throng that gathered on White Clay Creek before the talking began. He was nearly forty, almost the age of his old war companion, Kicking Bear. His heart sang to see Kicking Bear again, for long ago they had raided Crow camps for horses together or fought elbow to elbow against tough enemies. Many years had passed since Kicking Bear had gone to live among his wife's people, the Minneconjous, while Eagle Elk had traveled far across the great water with the white showman, Pahuska, "Long Hair," better known to the rest of the world as Buffalo Bill Cody.

Kicking Bear looked older now, but Eagle Elk knew him at once as he stood tall and travel-gaunted with people pressing close around him from all sides. Eagle Elk threaded his way through the crowd until he stood before Kicking Bear, who was so intent upon the preparations for the council that he did not seem to know his old friend.

"Cousin, I am Eagle Elk," said the younger man cheerfully

"Do you remember High Horse who died when we defeated Long Hair Custer? And Charging Cat and all those Crow ponies we got that time? And do you remember that fat old woman, how she bounced when her pony ran away with her?"

Eagle Elk laughed in recollection, thinking Kicking Bear would remember and laugh with him. But the other looked at Eagle Elk as though he were a stranger. His eyes stared cold and blank, and his face had a lean, whetted look that Eagle Elk had never seen before.

"Believe! Believe!" Kicking Bear cried. "For those who do not believe shall be lost!"

Then he strode away. Eagle Elk felt sick all over, for nothing seemed the same any more. He heard Kicking Bear's voice ring loud and clear as he addressed the people shortly afterward, but even the voice was not that of his old friend.

"My brothers," Kicking Bear was saying, "I bring you the promise of a day in which there will be no white man to lay his hand on the bridle of an Indian's horse, when the red men of the prairie will rule the world and not be turned from their hunting grounds by any man. I bring you word from your fathers, the ghosts of those who have gone beyond, that they are now marching to join you, led by the great Wanekia who came once to live on earth with the white men, but was cast out and killed by them and nailed to a tree when he tried to save them."

As Kicking Bear told it, the delegates had gone by horseback as far as the shining mountains (Rockies) on their second journey into the sunset. Coming to a railroad, they sat their ponies watching in wide-eyed wonder as a great smoke-belching monster came charging down the tracks. When the "iron horse" stopped, cowboys riding in the caboose of the train invited the Indians to ride with them and helped them load their ponies into a boxcar. They traveled far on the white man's train—almost to the land of the Wanekia.

At the end of the railroad they were met by two strange Indians who greeted them as brothers and fed them. Four days' travel brought them once more into the Wanekia's camp.

" 'Hau, my children,' the Wanekia greeted us," said Kicking

Bear, dramatizing his second meeting with Wovoka. " 'You have done well to make this journey to visit me again.' He led us up a great ladder of small clouds through an opening in the sky. My brothers, my tongue is straight; I cannot tell you all I saw, for I am no orator, but the forerunner and herald of ghosts."

He paused significantly, letting his words take effect on his listeners. All who heard looked upon Kicking Bear with new respect and considerable awe, for here was a man who not only had met the Wanekia twice, but was now about to tell of seeing even higher personages. His story carried deep conviction, and his listeners strained to hear every word. Indians who heard him that day long remembered his description of a visit to the Spirit Land itself, where the delegates found themselves prostrate before Wakantanka, the Great Spirit, and His wife who were dressed in Indian attire. Recovering from shock, the delegates looked down from great height at Wakantanka's bidding and saw all the countries of the world spread out beneath them. There they saw the old camping grounds and lodges and the dead relatives of all past generations. They saw vast herds of grazing buffalo and ponies fat from eating rich grasses.

For three days, Kicking Bear explained, the delegates watched, stupefied at such wondrous sights. Then Wakantanka had led them into a great tepee camp peopled by the ghosts of departed ancestors. They saw women cooking buffalo meat and stepped into a lodge to eat from a boiling kettle. Presently a great cloud settled upon the village. When it lifted, all signs of the camp and its ghostly inhabitants had disappeared. Not even a trace of the cook fires remained on the ground.

"A tall man with large joints and short hair all over his body and face came beside us and demanded: 'I want half of the people inhabiting the world,' " said Kicking Bear. "But Wakantanka said, 'No, I cannot let you have any—I love them all too much.' The hairy man insisted, asking a second and a third time. At last Wakantanka said, 'The Indians are my chosen people. I will not give them up. But you may have the white men.' This hairy man was a powerful evil spirit known to the whites as 'Devil.' With a wave of the hand he could make heaps of money or hundreds of spring wagons, freshly painted and ready to hitch horses to.

"Then Wakantanka said to us: 'I have neglected you Indians a long time. From now on you shall be under my special care. The earth is getting old and has become rotten in many places. So I will cover the earth with new soil to the depth of five times the height of a man. Under this new land will be buried all the white men, and the top of it will be covered with sweet grass and running water and herds of buffalo and wild ponies will stray over it. I will fill up the sea to the west so that no ships may sail over it; other seas I will likewise make impassable.' "

Kicking Bear talked on to an enthralled audience, now carried away by his recital of wonders. As Kicking Bear explained it, Indians need have no fear of the white men, for Wakantanka had promised that He would take away from the whites their secret of making gunpowder. When directed against Indians who performed the ghost dance and practiced the new religion, any gunpowder still in the possession of the whites would be rendered unusable. Moreover, believers would be lifted up and suspended in mid-air when the flood of new soil came over the earth. Indians who failed to believe, on the other hand, would be left in deep ravines and gulches from which it would take months to find a way out. The earth's rejuvenation was promised for the spring of 1891 with the coming of the young grass. Then all the ghosts of Indians long dead would rejoin their descendants and relatives among the living to reinhabit the new earth. Meanwhile, Wakantanka had sent His Son, the Wanekia, to help the Indians prepare for that time. His red children must carefully observe the Wanekia's teaching in order to be saved. With that, the delegates were returned to the world through the opening in the sky.

"My people, with these eyes I saw it, with these ears I heard it," Kicking Bear concluded. "The Wanekia who came long ago is again upon the earth, preparing for the end. He came before to help the whites, but they tortured Him and slew Him. Even they admit it! Are their hearts made over since they killed Him? I saw the white scars gleaming on His hands and the wound still fresh in His breast. The other time He came He was kind as new grass and spring rain. This time He will ride at the head of a whirlwind! The whites are greedy and faithless. Before the wrath of the Wanekia they will melt like winter snow in the moon when ponies shed.[1] He came to them once. Now He comes to us. Woe to those who fail to hear Him!"

Spellbound, Kicking Bear's listeners sat silent and gaping. Yet others were to be heard. While Kicking Bear stepped aside and hunkered down covering his face with both hands, Yellow Breast moved forward.

"My relatives," he began simply, not attempting to captivate his listeners but rather to convince them, "you all know me well. Many of you knew the boy I once was and the common way I grew up to be an ordinary man. Never in my youth did any vision come to me to give me power to behold all the hidden things. Neither am I yet old enough to be very wise. I have always believed only what my eyes saw or my ears heard. Sometimes I have heard lies and have been wrong in believing them. You all picked me to go into the sunset, knowing that I am but an ordinary person.

"Trailing an elk or a buffalo is one thing. A man may follow tracks; he may find meat or he may not. But who can trail a story of the dead returned to life and a new earth coming? I have said, 'It is far away and big and getting bigger every day. So are the hunger of the people and their sorrow. Here, perhaps, the empty belly of today and the fat promise of tomorrow have made up a lie.'

"You may think we all turned foolish on our way west to see the Wanekia. Yet I myself have seen. I must believe because of what I saw. In the Wanekia's land I saw no vision sent from heaven. I saw tall, gleaming mountains and winter sunlight on the clouds. But a growing strangeness lingered in the air—*something I could not explain!* Something like smoke lifted away and common things became wonderful and new.

"About twenty of us sat around a fire. The Wanekia sang a

[1] May.

sacred song four times, then prayed that I might again see my father. I sat and waited—as yet not knowing. All around me was a sort of singing—the sound of all the green living things the other side of death. Voices mingled with the bird song of new life. And great bison herds and wild, running horses sang with them—all one happy tribe rejoicing.

"Suddenly it became as still as death. Around me the night filled with the faces of people. But they were happy faces, and there with the others was my father, as alive as you or I! Many of you remember him well. Twelve winters ago I watched him die, floundering helplessly in the snow like a lung-shot buffalo with black blood bubbling from his lips, after Bear Coat [2] attacked us with his pony soldiers on Powder River.

"Now in the Wanekia's land my father came to me and smiled and laid his hand upon my head. 'Believe, my son!' he kept saying. Presently it was plain night again with a bright moon shining and all the faces gone, my father's gone with them. And only twenty of us sat there, staring at one another, words frozen on our lips. All had seen; none could doubt any longer. And now I can only tell you that I believe."

Yellow Breast stepped back from the center of the council circle and sat down beside Kicking Bear. The people stirred with tense expectancy as the other delegates spoke—Good Thunder, Flat Iron, and Broken Arm each adding to the ground swell of fervor that swept through the crowd. And finally yet another man stood before them, the slender, sharp-faced Short Bull, prodding them into decision with his words which snagged at their minds and gave them no respite.

"Kinsmen," he began importantly, waiting for the echo of his resonant voice to die, "this thing must be set going right away. All you have heard is true. I did not question this story of the Wanekia, for all my life voices have spoken to me. When I was young, the Great Spirit spoke to me with the tongue of birds. The dead often talked to me in some quiet place, and dreams showed me what things were to happen. I say this story did not

[2] General Nelson A. Miles.

seem strange to me because I dreamed it just before it came to my ears from living tongues. The Wanekia is the same as I saw in my dream. I even knew the words he would speak. There is no end to all He can do, this holy Son of Wakantanka, our Great Spirit. Birds and beasts come close to Him and talk to Him the same as people do. Trees and grass become greener as He passes near—just as they freshen in a sudden shower of rain.

"Now there is this sacred dance He sends you. It will make you see the world of light where care and trouble are no more. It will make you see your dead ones yonder in the Spirit Land. Every night and day you must dance until it becomes morning after the fourth night. Then you must bathe and go home until time for dancing comes again. The Wanekia has said it: 'Woe to men who hear not!' So be it!"

When Short Bull had spoken, all eyes turned to the chiefs and elders. Now that the delegates had reported it was up to the leaders.

His graying hair highlighted by the afternoon sun, feeble old Red Cloud sat musing like a leathery old mummy dressed incongruously in a rusty black suit and threadbare trade blanket. At last he got to his feet. Rheumy-eyed and decrepit, he seemed almost senile. In his drooping shoulders and shuffling steps there was no elderly spryness, no apparent spark of accumulated wisdom, no flicker of long-abandoned hope. And yet when he stood before the people he straightened and looked taller and more erect than any had seen him for many a year. The crowd caught a glimpse, perhaps, of their old fighting leader who had led the Sioux of an earlier generation against the white men's forts on the Bozeman Trail and had driven the soldiers from tribal hunting grounds in Montana.

"My people, you have heard this and it is good." Red Cloud's voice came low, and the people strained to hear him. "The passing seasons and the generations of our tribe and the succession of days are but moving shadows. The Light is Wakantanka our Great Spirit. When our feet are young, we see something and know it; we hear something and know it; we touch it and know it is true. For to be young is to believe and to act and accomplish. But when the eyes grow weary and one's flesh falls away from the bones, we know a silence wiser than any sound; we see clearer than the brightest sunlight. The earth is old now. Her blood runs in veins worn thin and her heart is getting cold. We, her children, mumble hungry at her withered teats. And the end is near. This is a good word we have come to hear. I believe it. You should begin this sacred dance."

And now more than ever the people believed, for Red Cloud had already forgotten he was a Catholic. The white men's beliefs seemed to fall away from him like shed hair and he was once more an Indian among Indians.

Other leaders similarly endorsed the new faith. Little Wound, an Episcopalian convert, stood tall and arrow-straight at fifty-five.

"My brothers, these are trying times for us all. I have given up hope for any good in this world. It will be far better for all of us when we go to the Spirit Land. The only way now for any of us to make a living is to work as the white men do. But who is to pay us when we work? No one around here has money to pay us for our work. If things keep on as they are, we will all starve to death and die as paupers. I do not know if the Wanekia can help us in this life. But if he can help us in the Spirit Land, then I see nothing wrong in this new dance."

A sub-chief, Yellow Bear, spoke next.

"All white men think all of us are bad. Our only hope is the Wanekia and His sacred dance!"

And so it went, all through that spring afternoon on White Clay Creek. Of all those present only Cloud Horse and an old man named Fast Elk were saying it was not true about the Wanekia and that the ghost dance could never help anyone, in fact might even bring on trouble. Their voices were lost in the chorus of those who approved. The ghost dance was formally launched among the Sioux.

Days of preparation and purification were necessary, however, before the ceremony could be held. It was agreed that Kicking Bear, assisted by Good Thunder, would lead the first Sioux ghost dance. A site was picked at the head of Cheyenne Creek just a half-mile or so north of Pine Ridge Agency. No one thought the agent or any other white men would interfere. Kicking Bear told believers that if soldiers came to harm him or stop the ceremony, all he had to do was to stretch out his arms to render these enemies helpless; the earth would open up and swallow them.

Wovoka's advice to the delegates to tell the Indians to go to work and send their children to white men's schools seemed all but forgotten. If Kicking Bear inwardly questioned the Wanekia's acceptance of this credo of work and education, he never indicated his doubt to any of his followers. Glossing over many of the Paiute's precepts, he readily accepted any idea that held out the promise of a restoration of the old tribal way of life. To Kicking Bear the dream of Indian supremacy and a revival of glorious warfare with honor were consistently of paramount importance—more vital by far than the bringing back of dead ancestors or the return of the buffalo.

A day or so before the dance Good Thunder went into a trading post at Pine Ridge, a store owned by whites but one where Indian customers could be waited on by Sioux clerks. As part of the preparation for the ghost dance, Good Thunder had to provide tobacco and bits of bright-colored cloth. He was surprised to find his nephew,[3] Black Elk, clerking behind the counter.

Black Elk was not yet thirty but he had already lived a full life. He had fought as a young thirteen-year-old warrior under Crazy Horse at Little Big Horn and had served Big Road's band of Ogalalas as seer and healer during their four-year sojourn in Canada with Sitting Bull. Since 1886 he had been traveling with Buffalo Bill's show, mostly in Europe. When the show had left England, Black Elk had accidentally been left behind. He could speak no English or any language other than Sioux, but he found a job with another smaller Wild West show that took him to

[3] Good Thunder was a first cousin of Black Elk's father; thus a relationship considered among the Sioux as that of uncle and nephew existed between Good Thunder and young Black Elk.

France. There he became desperately ill. For three days he lay stretched out like a dead person. A French girl nursed him back to health. At last Buffalo Bill came back to Europe and Black Elk rejoined the show until it returned to the United States in 1889. In order to eat and keep his old mother from starving, he had gone to work in the trading post.

Good Thunder had been away a long time and had not seen his nephew for a while. But he could talk of nothing now except the Wanekia.

"The Wanekia held out his hat for us to look into," Good Thunder solemnly declared. "And when we looked in we saw the whole world and all that is wonderful. Only Cloud Horse was unable to see it, and told us he saw only the inside of the hat. In the great Spirit Land where the Wanekia led us the people from every tepee sent for us to visit them. All of them were people who died many winters ago. Chasing Hawk and his wife, both long dead, were there and we went to his tepee. It was a buffalo-skin lodge—a very large one—and they wanted all their friends to go there to live.

"One of my own sons was also there and took us to his tepee. On the way we saw a herd of buffalo. We killed one. The Wanekia told us to take everything except the head and tail and four feet; then the buffalo would come alive again. We did as He instructed us. When we left that place, the buffalo came to life and ran off.

"The Wanekia gave me two eagle feathers. 'Receive these eagle feathers and behold them. My Father, the Great Spirit, will cause them to bring your ancestors back to you.' Later, when we were about to leave the Wanekia's land, He said to us, 'If you call upon me when you are tired, I will shorten your homeward journey.' This we did when we were tired. Night came upon us and we stopped and called upon the Wanekia to help us. We went to sleep. In the morning we found ourselves far from where we had stopped!"

Black Elk was himself a mystic, and such visions and wonders as his uncle described did not seem unreal or irrational. Yet his own great vision, experienced when a boy of nine, was unlike anything mentioned by Good Thunder. Black Elk was puzzled, hardly knowing what to think of the new religion.

From the beginning the Sioux ghost dance had unique features. Leaders and dancers fasted for twenty-four hours prior to the start of the ceremony. At sunrise of the day the dance was to begin men and women entered separate sweat lodges for the religious rites of purification.

The sweat lodge was a small circular framework of willow branches driven into the ground and bent over to form a low wickiup or round-top tepee. With an entrance left open to the east, the structure was covered with hides or canvas. Rocks were heated until white-hot at a nearby fire. A buffalo skull faced the lodge.

When all was ready, male and female participants entered their respective lodges. Women wore loose, gownlike coverings throughout the ceremony while men stripped to gee strings. In the men's lodge the entrance was sealed off with more hides save for a tiny space at the bottom through which heated rocks and water might be passed in from the outside. One by one the rocks were handed in to Kicking Bear by assistants who carried them from the fire with forked sticks. Water was then passed in to the medicine man, who poured it over the rocks until the interior filled with steam. Everyone inside was soon dripping with perspiration. Kicking Bear had to decide how long they all had to remain before they were sufficiently purified.

After the sweating ceremony, the dancers were painted by medicine men acting as leaders. Colors and designs varied with individuals, but nearly everyone wanted some of the sacred red paint that Good Thunder claimed had been given him by the Wanekia. So red was a predominant color. All the leaders kept busy painting crescents and sun circles and crosses and lightning streaks on the faces of the dancers. Since it was not to be a naked dance, only faces were painted. But dancers continually rubbed their bodies down with sweet grass and vernal while the painting process was going on.

As they were getting ready, the dancers would from time to

time approach a tall sacrifice pole placed near the sweat lodge. This was actually a dead tree. To its branches the participants would tie strips of bright cloth, tiny packages of tobacco, or other offerings suitable for Wakantanka.

Once painted, the dancers dressed in their finest native costumes and regalia. Since this was a purely religious ritual and not a time to display battle honors, war bonnets were not worn. Eagle feathers were prominently featured, however, in hair ornaments and dance bustles.

"No white men's clothing shall be worn," Kicking Bear decided on the spur of the moment, and the idea caught on. From that first day no article of white man's dress was worn by a ghost dancer.[4]

Since the sweating and painting rituals occupied the morning hours, it was afternoon before the dancers formed the great circle for the first Sioux ghost dance. In the center of the circle another dead tree had been planted. Colored streamers were tied to its branches. The leaders sat around the base of this tree. Standing within this group was a young woman known for her chastity. She held an elk-horn bow and four primitive arrows made with bone heads dipped in steer's blood. One by one she shot the arrows into the air, each toward a cardinal direction point. Then the arrows were gathered up; with the bows and a gaming wheel and sticks they were tied to the branches of the tree.

The young woman then returned to her place by the tree where she stood throughout the ceremony holding a sacred red-stone pipe toward the west, the direction from which the Wanekia and the ancestors' ghosts were expected to appear.

After a plaintive chant, the leaders passed around a vessel filled with sacred meat—actually beef but mythically the flesh of the vanished buffalo which would soon return in vast herds to darken the plains once more. The vessel was passed on around the circle of waiting dancers until all had partaken.

At a signal from the leaders, the dancers rose to their feet,

[4] Since beads came from the white men, no beadwork was worn. Heavy belts of German silver, favored by Sioux women, were also discarded.

joined hands, and moved, chanting the opening song, in the slow, shuffling steps of the ghost dance.[5] Over and over they sang shrill words:

> "The father says so—*E'yayo!*
> The father says so—*E'yayo!*
> The father says so,
> The father says so.
> You shall see your grandfather—*E'yayo!*
> You shall see your grandfather—*E'yayo!*
> The father says so,
> The father says so.
> You shall see your kindred—*E'yayo!*
> You shall see your kindred—*E'yayo!*
> The father says so,
> The father says so!"

As the dance continued through the afternoon and night, many fell in rigid trances, reviving minutes later to tell of seeing dead relatives in the Spirit Land.

And so the pattern was set at this first Sioux ghost dance on Cheyenne Creek. It fell on Sunday, the great medicine day of the whites, but the ceremony was like nothing any white man had ever seen. Other songs came spontaneously to the lips of leaders and dancers alike as the great crowd of onlookers and participants swelled with the dawning of each new day.

The ghost-dance camp broke up after the fifth day of dancing. The enthusiasm of the dancers guaranteed that the ceremony would be resumed with each full moon.

As the crowds dispersed, Kicking Bear slipped off to the north to start the ghost dance at Chief Hump's camp on Cheyenne River near the mouth of Cherry Creek. Woodpecker Woman met him there, accompanied by her uncle, Big Foot. The Minneconjous avidly took up the new ritual.

Short Bull and Mash-the-Kettle rode on east to Rosebud

---

5 Some tribes, e.g. the Shoshoni, called this a "drag step."

Agency, spreading word of the ghost dance as they went. The Brûlés listened eagerly, agreeing to obey Short Bull's imperious command to gather on a flat overlooking the west bank of Little White River some eight miles west of Rosebud Agency.

White authorities throughout the Sioux country seemed unperturbed by the ghost dance as spring wore on into summer. Indicative of official reaction was Agent Gallagher's offhand conviction that the new religion was harmless and would doubtless die out "as soon as the Indians find there is no truth to all these fantastic prophecies."

All might have ended quietly—sooner or later—had Charles L. Hyde, a citizen of Pierre, South Dakota, not written a letter dated May 29, 1890, addressed to Secretary of Interior John W. Noble in which he stated he had reliable information from a young Pine Ridge half-breed attending government school in Pierre that the Sioux were secretly planning an outbreak.

Summer 1890

THE Sioux in 1890 were hard hit. Bad times throughout the Indian country contributed greatly to the growing unrest of the tribes. The ghost dance also began to have a telling effect on the Sioux—particularly in the south.

Through late April and May Short Bull's preaching roused the Brûlés around Rosebud Agency to fever-pitch excitement. It was early summer, however, before Acting Agent E. B. Reynolds got wind of the new religion which was practiced under his very nose at the huge camp on Little White River. Reynolds at once sent word for Short Bull and Mash-the-Kettle to come in to the agency. Then he called Luther Standing Bear away from his schoolroom to interpret.

Young Standing Bear had been educated at Carlisle Indian School in Pennsylvania where his brother [1] was still learning to follow the white man's road. As a reservation schoolteacher and part-time storekeeper, Luther was considered a progressive by the authorities and was correctly thought to be disinterested in the ghost dance.

Once the three Indians were in his office, Reynolds fired questions at Short Bull, asking him to tell all about the new religion. With Standing Bear interpreting, Short Bull said:

"We heard there was a wonderful man in the far West. He was a Wanekia, so many tribes sent delegates to see Him. We went to the place where the sun sets, and there we saw this man. He told us we were going to have a new earth; that the old earth would be covered up, and while it was being covered up we were all to keep dancing a holy dance so that we could remain on top of

---

[1] Henry Standing Bear, late good friend of the author.

the dirt. The whites would all be buried, He said; even Indians who did not believe would be covered up.

"This man showed us great camps and visions of buffalo. All our late ancestors were there, dancing and feasting. This man hit the ground and made fire. He spoke to us all at once and the different tribes understood Him. He taught us the sacred dance and songs to chant during the dance. He showed us where the sun dropped down into the ocean and it boiled up and became hot!"

Luther Standing Bear snorted. "That is not so! The ocean never boils up with the setting of the sun."

And Short Bull looked straight at the young educated Indian, saying nothing. Hearing the meaning of the previous exchange, Reynolds laughed.

"Hardly anything to worry about in any of that," he told Standing Bear. "Warn them not to stir up the people any further and tell them to go back to their homes."

Both Short Bull and Mash-the-Kettle agreed to do as the agent ordered. Like Reynolds, they said polite things as they left for Little White River. For the moment the Brûlés were subdued.

At Standing Rock Agency far to the north the sun blistered the prairie, parching the earth to drifting dust. The Hunkpapas well realized the accuracy of Sitting Bull's ominous prognostication of the previous August. It had indeed been almost a full year of drought and untold hardship, just as the aging chief had predicted. No rain had fallen in the vicinity of Standing Rock since the day of his prophecy.

Now, in June, the sun was a dazzling white orb in the brassy sky. Yet Sitting Bull announced to his assembled tribesmen one ration day at the agency that it would rain that afternoon. Some scoffed, including Agent James McLaughlin and his mixed-blood wife who happened to be standing near. Even Mary Collins, one of the missionaries, was openly skeptical. Those closest to the chief were well aware of the powerful *wotawe*, or "war medicine," in Sitting Bull's possession and knew that with this talisman he could make it rain whenever he liked. Miss Collins, however,

felt that "creating" rain or even forecasting it without the benefit of proper scientific instruments was nothing short of "a heathen practice."

To the amazement—and chagrin—of white bystanders, Sitting
Bull chanted and prayed not far from the agency office, and soon
a fine thunderhead built up out of a clear sky in the north, followed presently by a light fall of rain.

In spite of his ability to foretell weather and perform wondrous feats, Sitting Bull found the Hunkpapas hopelessly divided, their natural loyalties split, their allegiance to him often
questionable. Crook's land cession swindle, agreed to by John
Grass and other progressive leaders, had alienated the Yanktonnai and Blackfeet Sioux from their more conservative Hunkpapa
cousins, while further disruption within the Hunkpapa tribe extended into normally harmonious family relationships.

Gray Eagle, Sitting Bull's brother-in-law, had long urged the
old chief to give up his Indian ways. Converted to Catholicism,
he pressed the issue past the usual limits of diplomacy.

"Brother-in-law, we are all now under the Government's jurisdiction. We must do what the white men tell us. We can no
longer go roaming around but should stay in one place and try
to follow the white man's road. You should give up your old
dances and Indian ways and join the Black Robes as I have
done."

Sitting Bull held his temper in check.

"What you say is fine for you. Go ahead and follow the white
man's road and do whatever the agent tells you. But I cannot so
easily give up my old ways and Indian habits; they are too deeply
ingrained in me. So I tell you just leave me alone."

Gray Eagle bristled with anger, frustrated in his futile attempt
to carry out Agent McLaughlin's orders and bring Sitting Bull
around to the agent's own way of thinking.

"If you don't obey and do as the white men tell you, you're
going to cause a lot of trouble and lose your life as well. I have
sworn to carry out the agent's orders. You and I have been
friends for a long time; in the old days we followed many trails

together. Now, if you refuse to obey the agent, we shall not be together any more."

After that Sitting Bull turned more and more to his old tribal ways, seldom visiting the agency at Fort Yates, a rough forty-five-mile journey north of his permanent camp on Grand River. Aside from issue days, when all Indians gathered at Fort Yates to get rations, the aging fifty-nine-year-old chief kept to the remote portions of the reservation.

Like other Sioux, Sitting Bull depended more than ever in these troublous times on government rations for subsistence. Since such rations were seldom adequate to feed his entire band, he further relied on the largesse of his well-to-do white admirer, Mrs. Catherine Weldon of Brooklyn, New York.

Mrs. Weldon was a field representative of the National Indian Defense Association, a benevolent group of citizens from Eastern states who sought to relieve—as well as reform—the entire Indian situation across the nation. Well-meaning, though largely inef-fectual, the association was headed by a retired minister, Dr. T. A. Bland, who held many unorthodox views on Indian policy, believing among other things that only he and his "brethren" in the group knew what was best for the Indians—no matter what the red men themselves desired. Catherine Weldon's iron re-solve to further the aims of the association had melted away since her first meeting with Sitting Bull in the late spring of 1889. From that time on she had been devoted almost solely to the chief's personal welfare.

For Sitting Bull it had turned out to be a complicating factor —one which widened the growing breach between the chief and Agent McLaughlin. Mrs. Weldon, in defense of the old Indian as well as her own views of propriety, had had harsh words with McLaughlin, who referred to her as "a female crank" and called Sitting Bull "a coward, a selfish man, no one's friend, of no im-portance, and a heavy burden on the younger men who are more progressive." Mrs. Weldon accepted this one-sided appraisal as a challenge to rush to Sitting Bull's aid.

Catherine Weldon was an attractive, somewhat overdressed

widow given to wearing showy jewelry and the latest styles. Her hair already streaked with gray, she was at an age when many women do the strange and unaccountable. And yet for all her flashiness, she had a genuine appreciation of solid values. Justice for Indians was her abiding passion. An artist, she was also absorbed in studying these American "aboriginals" at close range.

James McLaughlin, on the other hand, had no such aesthetic drives to disrupt the calculating ambition he shared with his mixed-blood Sioux wife. Preoccupied with the uninspired routine of running an Indian agency according to current government dictum, the McLaughlins were chiefly motivated by two factors. One was Mary McLaughlin's eternal striving to rise above the accident of her birth as a part Indian and to achieve what she thought to be her rightful place among the officers' wives who made up the exclusive social set at neighboring Fort Yates. Above all else, she wished to throw off the faint stigma which persistently clung to her husband as a "squaw man."

The other force activating the agent and his wife was their unrelenting hatred and contempt for Sitting Bull. The old chief's fondness for old Indian ways and natural conservatism stood like a stumbling block in the path of McLaughlin's program and possible future rise to prominence as an upcoming and aggressive official of the Government. Mrs. McLaughlin had long been irked at Sitting Bull's refusal in 1887 to join Buffalo Bill's Wild West Show which was going to tour Europe and appear in England at Queen Victoria's Jubilee. Since Mrs. McLaughlin had at times acted as interpreter for the old chief and had planned to go along in that capacity, she later felt that Sitting Bull had greatly hindered her social progress.

Catherine Weldon returned to the Standing Rock country in the late spring of 1890. In spite of—or perhaps because of—her former clash with "White Hair" McLaughlin and his beet-faced tirade against Sitting Bull, she was determined now to spend the rest of her life there if necessary to promote harmony between the old chief and the white "enemies" who surrounded him.

She visited Sitting Bull's camp on Grand River, ostensibly to paint a portrait of the chief, and lived with the rest of his family

in his sod-roofed, dirt-floored log cabin, a single room one end
of which was devoted to cooking and eating, the other to sleeping. Called Woman-Walking-Ahead by the Sioux, Mrs. Weldon
performed the most menial household tasks, sharing the work of
sweeping and cooking with Sitting Bull's two Indian wives, both
of whom soon grew jealous of the fair interloper.

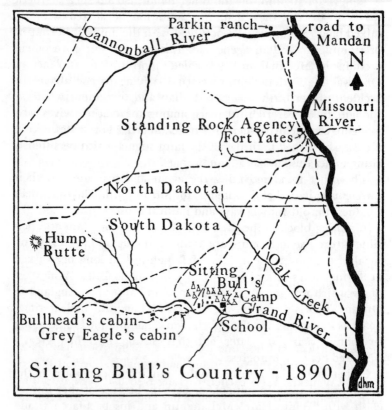

Sitting Bull's Country - 1890

For a time it seemed they may have had just cause. Mrs. Weldon's devotion to the old chief was obvious although its exact
character was long uncertain. Whites around Standing Rock
Agency and Fort Yates speculated that the lady from Brooklyn
was already Sitting Bull's third wife and was pregnant by him.

White women especially felt that Catherine Weldon had disgraced them with her "infatuation" for the old man.

Learning Sioux, Mrs. Weldon carried on long conversations with Sitting Bull, reciting tales of Napoleon and Alexander, great white soldiers whose exploits could have hardly failed to stir the old chief's dormant warrior instincts. She also acted as his secretary, writing to other Indians in his name and interpreting all sorts of documents for his benefit. Quite unwittingly, the prim Victorian lady managed to place herself in a position of excruciating embarrassment.

By performing acts of wifely service around the home of an adult Indian male, a woman subtly expressed her willingness to marry him. Since Sioux mating involves few preliminaries and it was not at all unheard of for an Indian to marry a white woman, the straightforward Sitting Bull took Mrs. Weldon at face value and offered to make her his bride. But when the old chief bluntly suggested a carnal arrangement between them, Catherine Weldon drew back in shocked amazement.

"Is this my reward for so many months of faithful friendship?" she asked the bewildered old man.

Counting the two still living, Sitting Bull had already had nine wives. Now here was this strange pale lady who would do all for him that a wife should do—save lying in his bed with him! There was little he could do in his perplexity other than to back away from this oddly chaste female.

Soon after Sitting Bull's unsuccessful courtship, the first rumors trickled north from Cheyenne River that Kicking Bear had made a long journey into the sunset and had actually seen and talked with the Wanekia. Years earlier, Kicking Bear had been a leading warrior among Crazy Horse's following and Sitting Bull remembered him well. But not until now had word of the new religion reached the isolated camp on Grand River. As expected, Sitting Bull was anxious to visit Kicking Bear at Cheyenne River and find out more about the Wanekia. He applied several times for permission to go, but each time Agent McLaughlin refused to grant him a pass. In his desperation, the old chief turned to Catherine Weldon for help in making a final appeal to the agent.

One morning in midsummer a wagon driven by Sitting Bull drew up in front of the agent's office. The lady from the East was sitting in the driver's seat beside the chief. News of their approach, flavored with the usual gossip, had already reached James McLaughlin, who came out on the office steps in vest and shirt sleeves, his shock of white hair bristling, before Sitting Bull reined up. Catherine Weldon eyed him coolly and got right to the point.

"Major," she announced, "I am going to Cheyenne River, and Sitting Bull is going to drive me there."

McLaughlin was equally distant in his response.

"Sitting Bull, as you may know, Mrs. Weldon, has no pass to leave Standing Rock. Furthermore, I do not think it advisable to grant him one."

The sharp exchange of words that followed has not been preserved, but there was some disposition on the part of Mrs. Weldon to argue the point, with the upshot that she was escorted by Indian policemen to the northern boundary of the reservation away from the southern side nearest Grand River, and told not to come back.

The Cannonball River bounded the reservation on the north and beyond it lay the Parkin ranch, inhabited at the time by a Mrs. Parkin and her sister, Mrs. Van Solen. The banished lady promptly appealed to them for advice and temporary shelter. Since the agent's jurisdiction did not extend beyond the reservation, there was little McLaughlin could do to prevent Mrs. Weldon's settling down in an unoccupied sod-roofed log cabin standing a mile or so below the ranch on the north bank of the Cannonball near its junction with the Missouri. Drab sand bars, muddy water, and stunted oaks and box elders provided little natural beauty for Catherine Weldon's eastern elegance, but here she bravely took up her abode. To add a sense of permanence and respectability, she sent East for her sickly young son, Christie, who made the trip alone traveling upriver on one of the old steamers that still plied the Missouri.

To this dreary place Sitting Bull drove once every two weeks after each issue day all through the summer, a round trip of one hundred forty miles from his Grand River camp. He was a common sight that summer, driving a half-wild team of loose-jointed cayuses hitched to the running gear of his old wagon, a few planks laid across the bolsters upon which he sat like an aloof old mummy, clad in a hot-weather robe and leggings of soiled white sheeting. Always riding with him was one of his wives, seated sideways in the manner of Sioux women, for thinking to keep the tongues of the soldiers' wives and ranch hands from wagging Mrs. Weldon had insisted he never come alone.

During Sitting Bull's summer idyll word came down through channels that the Sioux were planning an outbreak. McLaughlin and other agents in the Sioux country were requested by the Indian Department to file reports on the extent of the ghost dance and possible revolt among the tribes. Official concern obviously stemmed from Hyde's frantic letter in late May. This had been dug up and forwarded with circular instructions to the agents.

Agent James G. Wright at Rosebud answered that he knew of no impending trouble, while Gallagher at Pine Ridge reported the new messiah craze as nothing serious. Perrian P. Palmer, newly appointed agent at Cheyenne River, was not at all worried about ghost dancers. All was well in hand, he indicated, with military posts like Fort Bennett a stone's throw from the agency and Fort Sully only a few miles away.

Logically enough, more weight was attached to the report submitted by Agent McLaughlin from Standing Rock. Not only was he the ranking Sioux agent in length of service, but he was thought to be best qualified in terms of experience and ability. Reporting everything quiet on his reservation, McLaughlin attached no great importance to the messiah craze. According to his best information so far, not even the wild Hunkpapas on Grand River were doing the ghost dance. Nevertheless he took advantage of the outbreak rumors to submit a list of out-and-out non-progressive leaders it might be well to remove—removal meaning probable imprisonment in spite of the fact that the Indians in question had committed no crimes but simply "stood in the pathway of progress." The list was topped with the names of Sitting Bull, Big Foot, and Kicking Bear. From now on these would be marked men.

South Dakota in 1890 was a region of boom and bust. Midsummer marked the culmination of a brand-new political movement formed by communities of farmers led by pseudo-socialist agitators from eastern cities. Its high-sounding name, Populism, had the *honyockers*—or homesteaders—flocking like sheep to hear fire-eating tirades about poor crops and low prices. A spirit of genuine unrest was sweeping the state, bringing in its wake a fresh glut of bitterness against the Sioux who still held what were thought to be desirable areas for farming and cattle ranching.

No great friend of the Indian, James Henderson Kyle delivered the rabble-rousing Fourth-of-July address at Aberdeen which made him first a state senator, then a United States senator as a champion of the *honyockers*. Inevitably the Populists became involved in the women's suffrage movement. South Dakota had just adopted constitutional prohibition and it was felt that suffrage had a fair chance to win. Silver-haired, spare-framed old Susan B. Anthony hobbled onto the speaker's platform with Kyle and shared oratorical billing with him in Aberdeen's rickety old opera house, thus focusing national attention on the state.

The result was an unprecedented flow of immigration into portions of South Dakota still open to settlement. Half a century earlier artist George Catlin had pronounced the Dakota plains "a sea of grass, which is and must ever be, useless to cultivating man." Now the Great American Desert, just given up by the Sioux, was flooded with untold numbers of Scandinavian and German homesteaders. Soon farmers' "soddies" dotted the landscape where weeks earlier cone-shaped lodges had been clustered in old-time Indian village circles.

In other ways, too, the Sioux were feeling the white man's heavy hand. The Indian Office abruptly ordered a new cut in the beef issue, the second such cut in less than a year. Based on some federal efficiency expert's cost-trimming recommendations, the slash turned the tide of active Indian resentment against the whites. Moreover, Congress failed to pass Sioux appropriations before summer adjournment and funds for emergency relief measures were lacking. With their crops destroyed by drought, the starving Sioux turned increasingly to the Wanekia's promise.

A crowning blow came in the form of an order from Washington prohibiting the killing of wild game on Indian reservations. For years, even long after the settling of adjacent areas, this had been regarded as a natural right. A number of Sioux congregated at Hump's camp at the mouth of Cherry Creek on Cheyenne River to discuss this latest outrage. Only the sly, grim humor of Swiftbird, one of the leaders of the Minneconjous, prevented an outbreak then and there.

"My brothers," said Swiftbird solemnly, "you all have heard of the order made by our Great Father in Washington, prohibiting us from killing game on our reservation. Now this is a wise order. It must be or the Great Father would never have made it. I trust you all will carefully observe it.

"Of course, if you are riding across our reservation in your wagon, with your feet hanging over the tail gate and a deer comes up and bites your toes, you may feel at liberty to kick the deer, but otherwise you are not to disturb the wild game!"

Hungry as they were, the Indians went away laughing.

Things were not going so smoothly at Rosebud. Pushed to the limit, aggravated by the Government's failure to feed them or to provide adequate medical care for fresh outbreaks of scarlet fever and grippe, the Brûlés disregarded Agent Wright's earlier order and resumed the ghost dance with unprecedented zeal. All this while, Short Bull had been moving stealthily from band to band, preaching of the Wanekia's coming and the end of the world for all save those who believed. Ever at his side was the crafty young Mash-the-Kettle, as eager as Short Bull for prominence. Swiftly, almost overnight, Short Bull came out in the open as the leader of the cult in so far as Rosebud was concerned. Soon a majority of the Brûlés had joined in the ghost dance.

Dancing at the same flat on Little White River some eight miles west of the agency, band after band joined the ghost dancers. The swirl of dust from the shuffling feet could be seen all the way to Rosebud, and the all-night chanting and shrieking kept up until the dancers fell from exhaustion. Dead serious, they fully believed this new religion would rid them of the hated white men who had antagonized them so long.

Luther Standing Bear's father had moved to Pine Ridge with his family. Left in charge of his band at Rosebud were High Pipe and Black Horn, two of his brothers-in-law. As yet, the band had not joined the ghost dancers, but was camped some five miles from the agency, between the ghost-dance camp and Rosebud. Only three miles separated the camps.

As the excitement mounted during the summer, Agent Wright asked young Standing Bear to carry a message to High Pipe and Black Horn. Luther agreed without hesitation and Wright provided him with a team and driver to make the short journey. Since the driver was a white man, Standing Bear instructed him to drive into the center of the camp circle before stopping the wagon. It was a large camp nearly a quarter of a mile in diameter, made up of better than a hundred tepees. When the wagon came to a halt, it was quickly surrounded by curious, though as yet unexcited, Indians.

"I want to help you all, my people," Standing Bear said in stating the purpose of his unexpected visit. "Now the Government will soon put a stop to the ghost dance. It will not be right for you to join the ghost dancers and I know it is best that none of you be found in their camp. For it may be that the Government will call in soldiers to make them stop dancing."

The mention of soldiers disturbed them all. Luther hastily assured them there was no danger.

"If you feel afraid, my relatives, you can move your camp into the agency and set up your lodges around my house which is, as you know, less than a half-mile from the agent's office. There you will be safe."

The people readily agreed to come in the following morning.

His mission accomplished, young Standing Bear returned to the agency, happily reporting his success to Agent Wright who seemed quite pleased with the arrangement proposed by the young Sioux.

But morning brought no satisfaction to the agent or to Standing Bear. Some time during the night one of Luther's uncles, Hard Heart, had come into the camp from the Wounded Knee ghost-dance camp at Pine Ridge. When he saw the Indians breaking camp and getting ready to move in to the agency, he warned them not to go. He told them a new world was coming to roll on top of the old and that they must join the ghost dancers or perish with other unbelievers. Instead of coming into the agency, the band headed west to join the ghost dancers.

All through the summer there were hushed murmurs of impending outbreak, voiced in the booming Dakota towns under the tinkle of liquor bottles and the rasping sales talk of pimps lining up business for the joy girls who paraded around in little more than paint. In the settlements under the honky-tonk blare of gaiety, *honyockers* and miners and bullwhackers turned away from the looming specter of hard times to speculate on a Sioux uprising that seemed sure to come. In the new South Dakota state capital at Pierre, a lively town of seven thousand, rumors flew thick and fast of a steady Sioux demand for ever-popular .44 Winchesters, 1873 model.

One atrocity story after another went the rounds. One man told of finding a slain comrade staked out on the prairie, with eyelids, nose, and penis cut off and the latter stuck in the victim's mouth. Though doubtless untrue, the report was well calculated to keep the polyglot community of Cornish, Irish, and Chinese laborers well stirred up.

Hardly a word of alarm was heard over east in those sections of the state bordering Minnesota and Iowa, points from which most of the trekking *honyockers* entered. On the contrary, everything was done to keep them coming in without letup. As self-appointed booster for speeding up the development of the state, Colonel Pat Donan, writer, orator, and soldier of fortune, went all out in extolling the virtues of the fair land to the west.

"Dakota is a peerless bit of acreage, the world's true wonder-land," he would say whenever he could find an audience; "where no storms ever blow and where all the breezes are trained to sing pianissimo. Our wildest blizzards, as the down easters term them, are used by gentle mothers to lull their babies to sleep. The sun shines with a mellow splendor that recalls to mind the far-famed 'Happy Valley of Rasselas.'... This is the sole remaining section of paradise in the western world. Here no wave of trouble ever rolls across a happy people...."

Far to the west, in the Moon of Fatness (June), the ghost-dance circles grew with each passing day. Desperate with sadness and hunger, the Ogalalas swelled the throng that camped on Wounded Knee Creek until few members of the tribe had failed to take part or look on. Among the last to attend was young Black Elk, clerk-ing in the white men's trading post in Pine Ridge. For long months since his return from across the great water he had mourned for his father who had died during the time he had been ill in France. His heart was heavy with grief and melancholy. The thought of death outside of battle was increasingly hard for the young healer to accept. It seemed more and more unlikely these days that a Sioux could cover himself with glory as he went to the Spirit Land.

All the time he kept hearing talk of the *Wanagi Wacipi*—the "ghost dance." Though not yet a believer, he wanted to find out what lay behind it. All that spring, while the dance was building up, Black Elk had stayed away from the camp. Now, at last, he could keep away no longer. One day he got on his buckskin horse and rode across country to the ghost-dance camp on Wounded Knee Creek.

He looked on in astonishment at what he saw—a circle of dancers, men and women holding hands, and in the center a planted tree whose dead leaves had been painted a brilliant scar-let. It was exactly as Black Elk had seen it in his boyhood vision—a dying tree around which Indian men and women held hands to form the "sacred hoop of the universe," so seeking to make the tree bloom again. As he had seen in his dream, the sacred articles tied to the tree's branches were also painted scarlet. The dancers' faces were painted red. And even the sacred pipe and eagle feathers of his vision were part of this ceremony.

As he watched, so Black Elk recalled for the author's benefit many years later, he was both saddened and helpless. Then, suddenly, a feeling of great happiness swept over him. He saw that he had work to do. He would try to restore the lost power to the broken hoop that had not been whole since the summer the Sioux and their Cheyenne allies wiped out Long Hair Custer and his horse soldiers on Little Big Horn. Believing that this restoration could be accomplished in only one way, Black Elk asked Good Thunder and Kicking Bear, who shared the high priestship at Wounded Knee, to let him join in the dancing next day.

Regarded now by the Sioux as the founder of their ghost dance, Kicking Bear had started the Minneconjou bands of Big Foot, Hump, Eagle Bear, and others to dancing up along Cheyenne River. From time to time, however, he would return to Pine Ridge to look in on his own people, the Ogalalas. Now he was here at Wounded Knee Creek to get Big Road's band off to a fine start.

The next day as Black Elk, dressed for the ceremony, joined those who stood around the sacred tree, Good Thunder offered up a prayer for him: "Wakantanka, Our Father, behold this boy. Let him see your ways clearly!" After which words Good Thunder wept.

Presently Black Elk also began to weep, thinking of his dead father and overwhelmed by the deep despair of his people. Again he remembered the time of his childhood vision, how then the Indians had enjoyed a happy place on earth. He hoped now that the Sioux who had long wandered along the way of the white men could be brought back into the sacred circle once more.

With tears streaming down his cheeks, Black Elk knelt beside the withered tree and begged Wakantanka to give it life once again, as his vision had promised. Shivering as if he stood in sub-zero cold, Black Elk—with Good Thunder at one elbow and

Kicking Bear at the other—moved into the early phase of the ghost dance. Together they sang:

> "Who is it that comes to us now?
> One who seeks his father!"

All that afternoon Black Elk danced, praying for revelation, begging Wakantanka to let him see his dead father. But no vision was granted him that day.

The next day, before the dancing began, Kicking Bear offered the prayer: "Father, Wakantanka, behold these people! They are going forth this day to see their relatives. Yonder they shall be happy day after day and their happiness will never end."

Much happiness was in that dance, although many of those taking part wept and wailed as they shuffled through the great, slow-moving circles. From time to time a dancer would stagger about panting before he fell prostrate. Others lay as if dead. Supposedly it was these who were having the visions. All through the ceremony the dancers begged to be allowed to see their dead and to be permitted to live again as they once had.

Years later old, feeble, and blind, Black Elk recalled his own mystical experience that day:

"As I danced with Kicking Bear and Good Thunder, a queer feeling came over me. My legs seemed to be crawling with ants. Then I felt a strange power swinging me off the ground. I seemed to be gliding and swooping like a huge soaring bird, floating through the air with outstretched wings. Far in front of me I saw a single eagle feather dancing. The feather became a spotted eagle fluttering ahead of me, screaming for me to follow its dizzy flight. I floated over a high ridge. Beyond lay a beautiful green land where a throng of happy Indians lived in an old-time camp of tall cowskin lodges. On every hand meat racks were heavily loaded with fresh buffalo meat, while fat ponies grazed on neighboring hillsides. Off in the distance the wild game ran thick. From every direction came happy, singing hunters carrying fresh meat into camp. Everything glowed with a bright living light!

"Suddenly I found myself in the midst of this happy village.

Two men wearing strange painted shirts approached me. They said: 'It is not yet time for you to see your father. But he is happy. For you, much work is still to be done. We will give you a gift to take back to your people.' I was then lifted into the air again and came floating back to the camp on Wounded Knee Creek.

"Soon I found myself sitting on the ground with dancers crowding all around me, eager to know if I had seen a new vision. Knowing that the sacred shirts had been the gift for my people, I told the dancers of my dream and described the holy garments to them."

Of all who heard Black Elk tell of this vision, no one was more impressed than Kicking Bear. It reminded him of his own vision of the spotted eagle the time the sun died. Moreover, when Black Elk told of meeting the holy men who wore the strange shirts, Kicking Bear recalled that Wovoka far in the west had worn just such a garment.

"It is as the Wanekia said!" Kicking Bear exclaimed. "There in the far country I saw it with these eyes. It is the same! The Wanekia stripped to the waist to show us the scar on his chest where the white men had killed him with a spear long ago. Then he put on a holy shirt of unbleached cloth, painted all over with symbols such as my cousin here"—he indicated Black Elk at his side—"saw this day in his vision. Wearing this shirt, the Wanekia stood on a blanket while another of Those-Who-Wear-Rabbit-Skin-Robes fired a shotgun at him from a distance of only ten paces."

Kicking Bear clapped his hands twice to suggest the firing of a double-barreled shotgun, then paused dramatically to let the impact of his words have its effect upon his listeners.

"My relatives, you know me well. My tongue is straight. But I tell you this: *The shirt had not a single hole in it!* The Wanekia stepped away unharmed. All over the blanket upon which he had been standing were the scattered buckshot from the gun."

From his tobacco bag Kicking Bear brought out several tiny pellets of shot which he rolled around on the palm of one hand for the others to see.

"I tell you, my cousins, *that holy shirt has the power to turn away bullets!*"

All the next day Black Elk set himself to the task of making "ghost shirts" like those he had seen in his vision. There was no doubt in his mind after listening to Kicking Bear that the garments would be bulletproof. Of their power to guard the wearer against any danger he was certain.

Made of unbleached muslin or sheeting, the shirts were cut like old-time ceremonial war shirts, fringed and shaped alike but marked distinctively, each with an individualized pattern of symbols and markings. The picture of a young eagle with outstretched wings was painted in blue on the backs of most shirts, but crosses and sun circles and thunderbirds and crescents were marked in the sacred color—red. Eagle feathers were tied to a piece of fringe here and there along the seams.

Black Elk gave the first ghost shirt to Afraid-of-Hawk, while the second went to Big Road's son. Later in the day he painted a stick red and tied a spotted eagle feather to one end. This was for his own use in future ceremonies. Because of the remarkable vision he had experienced and his known power as a healer, he had already been asked to lead the ghost dance next morning.

Dancing the following day began with Black Elk's own prayer: "Father, Wakantanka, behold me! My nation is in despair. You have shown me the shining new world. Now let all my people behold it."

"That day I dreamed again," Black Elk told the author years later. "This time I flew once more to the Spirit Land. Now all the Indians who lived in the great camp were wearing the sacred garments—shirts for the men and loose dresses for the women. I decided that such holy dresses must be made for our women to wear during the ghost dance. These Indians in the Spirit Land were wearing white eagle plumes in their hair. I took this to be some sort of added protection that my own people must have so that when the new world came as the Wanekia had promised, Wakantanka would only need to glance down to know which people to save and which to destroy.

"From that time on the ghost dancers all wore 'ghost shirts' and 'ghost dresses' as well as eagle plumes in their hair. It was the first time our women had ever been allowed to wear feathers in their hair and it brought them a new sense of importance."

Presently Kicking Bear moved on to Rosebud Agency to see how the Brûlés were getting along with their ceremony. Good Thunder and Black Elk were left in charge of the ghost dancers at Pine Ridge.

Day after day the Ogalalas danced. Eagle Elk did not yet believe, for no vision had come to him. But his grandmother had seen his dead father during one dance on Wounded Knee Creek and the deceased was young and happy. When the old woman told about it, her face lit up strangely and she was so happy she wept and wailed for hours.

Many dancers claimed to have seen people long dead. Contrary to Sioux custom, names not uttered since the death of their owners were freely spoken.

Dancing at his grandmother's urging, Eagle Elk thought back to the old days of happiness and plenty, when he and High Horse and Kicking Bear had fought and hunted together. Now High Horse lay on a crumbling scaffold grave on a hill high above the Greasy Grass (Little Big Horn), and Kicking Bear was like a total stranger.

Most of all, Eagle Elk thought of the girl Her Eagle Robe, his long-lost childhood sweetheart who had fled into Canada with Sitting Bull's people after the Sioux rubbed out Long Hair Custer. In that far place known to the Indians as Grandmother's Land (after Victoria) she had finally married a Hunkpapa man. Hearing word of Her Eagle Robe's marriage, Eagle Elk had abruptly got himself wedded to Plenty White Cows. But their union was earmarked for tragedy. Plenty White Cows died several years back giving birth to a stillborn child.

It seemed to him that his whole life lay in the dead past now. Kicking Bear, once his best friend, was now an eerie, unfamiliar specter moving among the ghost dancers, preaching the return of old tribal ways and warning unbelievers. He was like an insane person whose mind had died but whose body continued to dwell among the living. And so Eagle Elk kept dancing and singing the sacred songs, his hopes for happiness in this life as dead as the past, his heart sick that no holy visions of the Spirit Land would come to him.

Some time in August many of the ghost dancers left Spotted Owl's place on Wounded Knee Creek to move twenty miles west to Sub-chief No Water's camp near the mouth of White Clay Creek. Here some two thousand Indians gathered, so far the largest assemblage of believers.

Now for the first time Agent Gallagher was alarmed. Until late summer the ghost dance had been taken up only by small groups according to reports that filtered back to the agent's office. Following McLaughlin's cool lead at Standing Rock where no dancing had yet been seen, Gallagher had consistently played down the ghost dance as long as he could. Now it suddenly appeared that things might be getting out of hand.

Gallagher was a rough-shod Irish "Hoosier" from Indiana who had risen to Colonel in the Union Army during the Civil War, later won an appointment as agent at Pine Ridge when the Democrats under Cleveland had cleaned house in eighty-six and removed former Agent McGillycuddy, a stanch Republican. No believer in leprechauns, Gallagher knew any real threat of trouble stemmed from more material problems than ghosts—no matter what Postmaster Selwyn or Captain George Sword, his Indian chief of police, had to say.

As far back as April, Gallagher had reported to the Indian Department that the monthly beef issue was down to 205,000 pounds, whereas treaty commitments called for 470,000. Department officials had answered that it was better to issue half-rations throughout the year than to give out full rations for two or three months, then cut them off entirely. Normally Gallagher might have shrugged off the matter of beef shortages, for he had no particular regard for his Indian charges. But now it spelled plain trouble.

This latest development was worst of all—the adoption of the ghost shirt which the Sioux believed made the wearer immune to bullets. As early as late June the agent had heard a firsthand account of the use of "bulletproof" garments from Mrs. Z. A. Parker, reservation schoolteacher. But the story she told then seemed too preposterous to believe.

Now, with a fresh flood of rumors flowing, Gallagher decided to check further into such phenomenal things as ghost shirts and dresses. When George Bartlett, deputy United States marshal and trading-post proprietor, volunteered to ride out to No Water's to investigate, the agent snapped up his offer. Since the ghost dancers were in no mood to brook interference from a white man, Bartlett was taking his life in his hands. Yet he was well liked by many Indians and was allowed to make the round trip safely. He brought Gallagher a report that the ghost shirts were indeed supposed to have bullet-repelling powers.

On the heels of this unfavorable news came word that the Indian Department was making even further cuts in the beef issue. Gallagher impetuously sent out a detail of Indian police to order the dancers to quit and go home. The ghost dancers flatly refused to obey, sending the cowed policemen back to the agency under a hailstorm of abuse. The police reported that among the prominent Indian leaders supporting the ghost dance at No Water's camp was Jack Red Cloud, ambitious son of the old chief.

Forced to take further action, Gallagher called all white men at Pine Ridge Agency into emergency conference. They eventually agreed with his plan that he should go personally to No Water's camp with a police force and break up the dance.

"It won't work, Colonel," Philip Wells, half-breed agency interpreter insisted. "Take your police out to No Water's now and there'll be a massacre for sure. If you have to go out there, take me and old Red Cloud and maybe Young-Man-Afraid-of-His-Horses. But no police and no weapons, or you're in trouble. Then we'll have a little friendly palaver with these ghost dancers and bring them to terms."

Gallagher knew that Wells was the only man present who had seen the Sioux back in their old fighting days. Yet the agent was not a man for talk where action seemed indicated, so he stuck to his original plan. Taking Wells and Lieutenant Fast Horse with thirty armed Sioux policemen, he set out for No Water's camp on Sunday, August 24.

They met an Indian en route who warned them that the ghost dancers at No Water's were spoiling for a fight. By the time the agent and his party reached the camp, however, not a person was in sight other than a few frightened Sioux women and children. The scattered log cabins of the settlement had an empty look and the whole area seemed deserted.

Suddenly Wells caught sight of an old Indian he knew, hiding below the creek bank, only his head and shoulders visible above a leveled rifle. Wells pointed him out to the agent. Gallagher at once snapped an order to Lieutenant Fast Horse to arrest the old man for daring to flourish his rifle under the agent's very nose. Wells translated the order into Sioux so Fast Horse could understand it. At the same time the interpreter took advantage of the situation to add a sharp warning to the Indian police.

"Don't obey this order!" he told them. "That creek bed is full of ghost dancers just waiting to gang up on us. But the agent doesn't know it yet, he doesn't see we're in a trap."

Turning to Gallagher, Wells said in English:

"Let me go out and get that old man, Colonel—without any gunplay."

Gallagher hesitated. He wanted no bloodshed, but here was this aging subordinate Wells trying to take over authority when the agent himself should be in command. It galled Gallagher to think his office was being usurped in the slightest degree, but he reluctantly agreed. Then, just as the interpreter had the old Indian talked into laying down his gun and coming out of hiding, Gallagher changed his mind and moved in.

The old man swung his rifle around sharply, forcing the agent to step back. Not until Gallagher had retreated several paces would the Indian set down his gun and climb up the bank.

By that time the agent had spotted some three hundred armed ghost dancers crouched along the creek bank. As Wells talked, Gallagher took stock of the situation. His police were outnumbered at least ten to one and an open clash could end only one way. Gallagher's immediate action, however, was not influenced by this realization, and when a handful of leaders headed by Jack Red Cloud finally climbed out of the creek bed and agreed to a parley, the agent insisted they put a stop to the ghost dance and return to their homes.

But now the ghost dancers knew their strength and sensed the power of their "bulletproof" shirts. Leveling rifles at Gallagher and his policemen, they refused to disperse or give up their dancing. They were ready, they said, to defend their religion with their lives. It was a bitter pill for Gallagher to swallow, but he knew his bluff had failed. Resorting at last to the rule that discretion outweighed valor, the agent and his retinue withdrew while the ghost dance continued.

As the summer waned, Kicking Bear, Short Bull, and Mash-the-Kettle led a new Brûlé ghost dance on Cut Meat Creek some twenty-five miles northwest of Rosebud Agency, where the new faith flourished with unprecedented fervor. When the dancers occasionally flagged from sheer fatigue, the three leaders opened the eyes of the believers all over again to the wonders of the Wanekia. Often this meant only a simple repetition of the details of their far journeying into the sunset. But at times something more startling was indicated.

Short Bull resorted more than once to a contrivance he called a "bird stick"—a "magical" staff which mysteriously gave off thick smoke but failed to burn even when placed in the hottest flame. Mash-the-Kettle used an even more impressive attention getter. His equipment consisted of an iron kettle, a new knife, and a rock —said to have been given him by the Wanekia. When the kettle was ceremoniously handed to him, Mash-the-Kettle would set the rock inside it, showing his audience that nothing else was in the kettle. Then he would stab into the rock with the sharp blade of the knife, after which the kettle miraculously filled with cool, fresh water that apparently came from the rock. Completely mystified, the people drank from the kettle, convinced that the liquid was sacred and that many blessings would come to those who drank.

Late summer breezes were rolling out of the distant Nebraska sand hills off to the southwest when Black Elk journeyed to the camp on Cut Meat Creek. With him he brought six of the holy ghost shirts like those he had made at Big Road's camp on Wounded Knee Creek. Dancers at Wounded Knee and White Clay Creek had kept Black Elk busy all summer leading their dances and fashioning "bulletproof" garments for them. Now he had brought immunity from bullets to the Brûlés. While leading one important ceremony with Kicking Bear, Black Elk fell into another trance and came out of it strangely troubled.

"A spotted eagle soared ahead of me as before," he told Kicking Bear. "But this time he kept screaming, 'Remember this! Remember this!'—yet would tell me nothing more. I do not know what this may mean, Cousin. I fear it is some sort of warning I lack the power to understand."

Kicking Bear was unable to suggest a meaning to this vision, however, portentous as it seemed. The two Ogalalas turned to matters closer at hand. And as the winds sharpened and the plains became brown with the advent of autumn, the Brûlés, like their Ogalala cousins, took time out from dancing only to fashion the muslin shirts and dresses that would make them "bulletproof."

Fall 1890

TENSION steadily mounted among Indians throughout the West.
From the Canadian line to the Wichita Mountains in Indian
Territory the tribes were in turmoil. Unrest fermented in a
witches' cauldron of starvation, dire poverty, and broken treaties.
It was brought to the boiling point now by the belief in a red
messiah.

In northeast Montana Chief Calf Child of the Assiniboins felt
moved to devise some supernatural means of dissipating the
hordes of whites who were crowding his people off the open
range. Enacting a sacred vision, he called his tribesmen to their
first ghost dance. Few Assiniboins doubted that between Calf
Child and the Wanekia they had the power to cause the entire
white race to melt away.

The ghost-dance cult stretched tentacles in all directions. Paiute runners from Mason Valley were making fresh incursions into
the far southwest, inciting the Walapai and Havasupai of Arizona
Territory to dance in order that hurricanes and storms might
destroy the whites. Ghost dances at Fort Whipple had already
been going on for several months, each dance lasting at least four
successive nights.

Navaho around Fort Wingate were dancing, too, accepting a
belief that "old men long dead," together with certain mythical
heroes, would soon return to help living tribesmen drive out all
Americans as well as Mexicans from their old domain.

In September, High Wolf, an Ogalala sub-chief, carried the new
religion south to Indian Territory. During the summer a Kiowa
delegation under Poor Buffalo had visited the neighboring Southern Arapahoes and Cheyennes, who, through contact with their
northern relatives, had heard of the Indian messiah. Poor Buffalo

had returned with quantities of the same "sacred" red paint that Wovoka had given to visiting delegates. Sparked now by High Wolf's report that the Sioux had accepted the ghost dance, the new religion was formally inaugurated among the Kiowa at their agency at Anadarko, Poor Buffalo assuming leadership of the ceremony.

Before he left to return north, High Wolf invited a young Kiowa named Apiatan, or Wooden Lance, grandson of a captive Ogalala woman, to come up to Pine Ridge to visit his Sioux relatives. Then thirty years old, Wooden Lance had recently lost a child to whom he had been closely attached. Since love for one's children was a deeply ingrained force in Indian life, the young Kiowa listened eagerly to the new doctrine which promised believers an early reunion with deceased relatives.

Vague reports indicated to the Kiowa that the Wanekia was somewhere in the north. From the lips of such a holy personage, Wooden Lance was sure he might hear if it were possible for him to talk again with his lost child. Kiowa chiefs decided to send him as a delegate to locate the Wanekia and find out if all the reports were true. Accompanied by High Wolf, Wooden Lance started north on his long quest in mid-September.

Back on the northern plains trouble seemed imminent at Camp Crook near Tongue River Agency, Montana. The Northern Cheyennes had been holding ghost dances for months and, expecting the worst, Lieutenant E. W. Casey was whipping his troop of Indian scouts into shape for any emergency. Big Red Nose, as his Cheyenne scouts called him, had a lot of faith in his little company and knew they would soon be ready for anything.

Since securing the Government's permission to enlist a troop of scouts in the winter of eighty-nine, Casey had encountered little difficulty in finding recruits. The Army fed well and the Cheyennes were perpetually and desperately hungry—often to the point of starvation. Casey regretted that the authorities would allow him only fifty men. Many more than that tried to join up every month—fine, stalwart youths who always made excellent scouts.

Casey was justly proud of his tiny unit. Even Frederic Remington, the artist-author who accompanied General Nelson A. Miles on an inspection tour of nearby Fort Keogh that fall, said that Casey's Scouts could "fill the eye of a military man until nothing was lacking." Miles himself said he would be a friend of the scouts until he had "white hair, a white beard, and was bent double with age."

Hunger was only part of the problem of the Northern Cheyennes. Wolf Voice, Casey's trusted right hand, laid much blame on the ghost-dance excitement, which since spring had caused growing unrest throughout the tribe. Through the summer Porcupine, the healer, had kept his people stirred up by a prediction that the end of the world would come by early fall.

"We must dance!" he exhorted them. "If we do not, we will get crazy and poor."

By September, when his prophecy failed to materialize, Porcupine suffered considerable loss of face. Just as the fervor of the dancers began to flag, however, a party of visiting Arapahoes and Shoshoni from Wyoming reported that during their journey to Tongue River they had encountered a group of Indians who had been dead for thirty or forty years, now miraculously resurrected by the messiah. With this startling news, the Cheyennes resumed their dancing with accelerated zeal. Porcupine even made up a song for the occasion:

> "Our father has come,
> Our father has come,
> The earth has come,
> The earth has come.
> It is rising—*Eyeye!*
> It is humming—*Eyeye!*"

Added to the renewed faith in the ghost dance was yet another factor—growing friction between the Cheyennes and their white neighbors in the Tongue River country. As Porcupine put it after General Miles' visit:

"All whites who live near us are cattlemen, and when they meet the Cheyennes we are cursed; they wish us Indians to be far away. We are afraid that those white people living along the river will fight us and whip us. If General Miles would arrange it so the cowboys would be moved away there will be no trouble."

Suddenly violence flared. Tim Boyle, a young homesteader, was found dead. Moccasin tracks in a nearby ravine and empty cartridge shells of an outmoded type indicated he had been murdered by Indians.

The culprits were soon uncovered. Two young bucks, Head Swift and Young Mule, confessed to their families that they had done the killing. After age-old custom, the entire Cheyenne tribe offered to settle property on the homesteader's family, thus atoning in full for the murder. Agency authorities, however, demanded that the murderers surrender. Although the Cheyennes bid up the price in ponies and other valuables to a high amount, the stubborn whites demanded that the young men submit to trial and probable death by hanging—a fate which, in the Indian mind, prevented a red man from entering the Spirit Land.

After much haggling, Agent James A. Cooper learned with alarm that on September 13 the two murderers would ride armed into the agency at Lame Deer, attack the troops stationed there, and thus be shot down by the soldiers! Fearful lest a full-scale outbreak occur, Cooper was forced to agree to these startling terms.

The unequal duel took place as scheduled. Carefully dressed and painted for war, the two bucks charged into the agency settlement at Lame Deer even as a full troop of the First Cavalry reinforced by Indian police formed ranks and prepared to carry out their part of the spectacular tragedy. All around the agency Cheyenne ghost dancers watched from surrounding hills as the two impetuous youths rode at top speed toward the waiting troops. A shrill death chant rose from the throats of the two warriors:

"Man dies. . . . The mighty buffalo dies.
Only the earth and mountains last forever!"

Once within range both of the young bucks began firing their Winchesters, more to draw the soldiers' fire than to kill. The troops answered with blazing carbines, shooting Young Mule's mount from under him in the first volley. Head Swift charged on, shooting wildly until the soldiers' bullets chopped him down a bare handful of paces from the foremost troops.

Young Mule had been thrown twenty feet or more when his pony fell. Now he jumped to his feet and charged in on a racing zigzag course while a hundred carbines blasted away at him. Caught by a fatal slug, he crawled off into a dry wash to wait for death, hearing the mournful keening of the Indian women rise from the pine-topped hills around the agency. Then everything grew quiet. The execution was done.

"We crawled through the brush toward Young Mule," the First Cavalry's Lieutenant Robertson later reported, "not aware that he was yet dead and suddenly stumbled upon his body. I was startled, awe-struck by the weird beauty of the picture he made as he lay in his vivid costume with his painted face and his red blood crimsoning the yellow of the autumn leaves."

At Rosebud Agency a number of Brûlés known to Agent Wright as "progressives" gathered at the old home of Spotted Tail, late friend of the white man. It was a large house given to the pacifistic chief long ago in exchange for much of northern Nebraska which he traded off to the whites without his tribesmen's knowledge. Nine years had passed since Spotted Tail had been killed by Crow Dog for taking another man's wife. But the old place on the hilltop overlooking the agency buildings was still known as "Spotted Tail's house."

Below it on the hillside stood Luther Standing Bear's cabin, bought from a Catholic missionary soon after Spotted Tail's death. From its windows the young schoolteacher watched as a group of important chiefs trudged up the hill. Finally he decided to see for himself what the meeting was all about.

His brother-in-law, Chief Hollow Horn Bear, was talking when Luther reached the open doorway and paused to listen. Not yet a believer, the chief was speaking strongly against the ghost dance. His talk was punctuated every now and then by a chorus of *"hau's,"* signifying the approval of his listeners. It was an imposing address and everyone was carried away by it.

Hollow Horn Bear was still talking when hoofbeats pounded up the hill. Luther turned to see an Indian on a white horse galloping toward the building. Leaping from his jaded mount, Brave Eagle burst into the meeting without ceremony, interrupting the speaker and causing a flurry of excitement among the audience.

"*Hohey!* What are all you men doing here? White soldiers have taken all our women and children from Cut Meat Creek! Why do you all sit here doing nothing?"

Since many in the council had relatives among the ghost dancers on Cut Meat Creek, this sudden alarm broke up the meeting. Several Indians headed at once for the agent's office. On their way downhill young Standing Bear and his brother-in-law stopped briefly at Luther's house, just long enough for Hollow Horn Bear to spot Luther's Winchester rifle and fifty rounds of ammunition in one corner of the cabin.

"Let me have it, and I'll go up to Cut Meat Creek and see what this is all about," he told Standing Bear.

When Luther arrived at the agency office a few minutes later, Agent Wright was in a dither, walking the floor and nervously rubbing his hands together.

"I can't understand this," he told Luther. "If anything's gone wrong, I should have sent a telegram to Fort Niobrara."

Indian police were arriving on the double from nearby cabins and the leaders who had been sitting in council were now mounted and impatient to get going. Once the police were assembled, Wright swung into an empty saddle, ordered Standing Bear to hold down the office until he returned, then led out toward Cut Meat Creek.

Little work was done the rest of the day by the agency employees who remained behind. Everybody stood around, waiting and wondering what might happen next. Toward evening the riders came straggling back, their horses fagged to a slow walk, fatigue showing on the face of every rider. Yet they brought good news.

The agent announced that he had found the ghost dancers on Cut Meat Creek stripped and painted for war; that a few stray shots had been fired when they mistook the agent's party for troops; but that he was later able to convince them that no soldiers were yet on the reservation. For some obscure reason, he said, Brave Eagle had apparently gone out of his way to give out false alarms to both factions.

Chief Hollow Horn Bear did not return to the agency. Reversing himself completely, he had joined Short Bull and the ghost dancers. Members of his band also defected, and young Standing Bear never saw his rifle again.

Next day Isaac Bettelgeau, a mixed-blood scout working out of Fort Niobrara and Standing Bear's distant kinsman, stopped by to give Luther some frightening information.

"In one night, Cousin, the soldiers will surround all the Sioux agencies. I do not know when this will happen but it is coming soon."

That same afternoon Agent Wright unaccountably quit his post, leaving Rosebud Agency in the inexperienced hands of Acting Agent E. B. Reynolds.

The situation at neighboring Pine Ridge Agency was going from bad to worse. Through September Indians not formerly sympathetic with the ghost dancers were demonstrating against recent beef-issue cuts by staying away from the issue grounds. One by one the bands were moving away from the agency to join the ghost-dance camp on White Clay Creek.

Old Red Cloud, whose true convictions were still somewhat in doubt, took this opportunity to urge his people to go on dancing. Little Wound was no friend of Red Cloud but for once saw eye to eye with him. Said he:

"My people can dance all they like. If the new religion is good, I am happy. If it is bad, then it will fall to the ground."

Agent Gallagher made a final attempt to deal with the ghost-dance leaders who now included many of the reservation's foremost chiefs. In a spirit of compromise, Gallagher told the leaders that the Sioux at Pine Ridge would be permitted to dance three days a month provided they spent the rest of the time making a living as white men did. When pinned down, however, he could offer no suggestions as to how the Indians were to go about caring for themselves. Nevertheless, the leaders agreed to the proposal.

A few believers even trickled back to the agency on issue day to butcher the handful of travel-gaunted steers just trailed up from Texas.

But for Gallagher it was a losing fight and he knew it. Seeing a chance to extend local patronage, South Dakota's Senator R. F. Pettigrew used his influence with the Indian Department in Washington and had Gallagher removed from office. A new agent, D. F. Royer, was slated to take over at Pine Ridge the first of October.

Every night the half-dozen whites at Cheyenne City's new townsite could hear the shrill yelling and wailing of ghost songs upriver at Hump's camp in White Thunder Bottom. At the mouth of Plum Creek across Cheyenne River from the Cherry Creek subagency the Robinson brothers, Harvey and Charlie, decided to put in an Indian trading post. It was a fine location and the Robinsons were certain they would soon be doing a brisk business—both with Hump's Minneconjous and the whites that were sure to pour into Cheyenne City. Plans called for a store twenty feet square, so all summer long members of Hump's band had been cutting and hauling in cedar logs for construction at the going rate of fifty cents a log. Edwin Phelps, a part-time preacher, had been hired to cut hay, and everything was working out fine until Kicking Bear had showed up again at Hump's camp in midsummer and roused the band into starting a ghost dance.

Since then the wild Minneconjous would cross the river in their bull boats and would trade regularly at the store and were all right as long as they were in the trading post. But once away from the townsite, they would not speak to whites and kept their heads and faces covered with blankets. Silent and sinister figures, they prowled restlessly along the opposite riverbank with rifles cradled across their arms as though waiting for some sort of signal. With close to a thousand Sioux ranged within thirty or forty miles of their store, the Robinsons began to feel uneasy. Down in Pierre one week they stocked up on life insurance: Winchester .73's, ivory-handled Colt .45's, and plenty of ammunition.

Agent Palmer at nearby Cheyenne Agency was not only alarmed

but provoked at Kicking Bear's activities. Until now he had not regarded the ghost-dance excitement as a serious danger. Yet he had always felt that Hump with his soldier band and control of the Indian police was a big question mark. And since Kicking Bear was encouraging Hump's people to dance, Palmer persistently urged the commanders at Fort Bennett and Fort Sully to bring their garrisons up to full strength. Hump was "a most dangerous character" and would bear surveillance.

Big Foot was also considered formidable in spite of his long record of friendship with the authorities at Cheyenne Agency. It was reported that his disillusionment over the Government's failure to establish schools near his village had caused him to welcome Kicking Bear and the ghost dance with open arms.

One solution seemed clear to Palmer: Kicking Bear must be arrested and removed permanently from the reservation. A single obstacle lay in the agent's path. For those offenses of which Kicking Bear might be guilty, only an Indian court could try him. No way seemed open to get him before a white judge, and the local Sioux court was completely under Hump's domination.

All though September Kicking Bear had kept the ghost dance going full swing along Cheyenne River. Bands controlled by Hump, Big Foot, Touch-the-Cloud, Bull Eagle, and White Swan were all dancing. Only one prominent Minneconjou leader held out: White Bull, one of the eight scalp-shirt men (or head chiefs), and a hero of Little Big Horn and earlier Sioux triumphs. Although White Bull acknowledged that the ghost dance was *wakan* (holy), he consistently opposed the new religion as one fraught with danger for his people.

"This can only lead to your destruction," he warned Big Foot solemnly. "Those who take part will be killed."

But Big Foot was of no mind to relinquish what he felt sure was the last hope of the Sioux. Moreover, the idea of returning to the old, free tribal way of life now had considerable appeal. The old man's mouth fairly watered at the picture of plentiful buffalo meat conjured up in a ghost-dance song Kicking Bear had been teaching the crowd. Composed by Short Bull, the song promised believers that if they saw themselves eating pemmican (buffalo meat pounded into a mixture of berries) in a vision trance, they were sure to awaken with pemmican in their hands. The words forecast an early return of the vast bison herds and with them a favorite Indian recipe. Kicking Bear sang:

> "*Hey-a-hey!* Joyous feast we now,
> *Hey-a-hey!* Joyous feast we now,
> Eating pemmican,
> Eating pemmican!"

Such reminders of past pleasures were well calculated to maintain a high degree of fervor among the aged, sick, and downhearted. Strangely enough, however, it was usually the young women who were first affected, then the older women, finally the men.

Kicking Bear maintained an impressively high following among the young men, youths who would have been full warriors but a few years back. They admired him both for his past battle record and his present acumen, for they did not believe the white men's injustices should go unchallenged.

This lack of docility on the part of the Minneconjous was soon interpreted by the whites along Cheyenne River as an open desire for war. Talk of a coming outbreak spread among traders and settlers from Pierre to Cheyenne City and troops at Fort Bennett and Fort Sully began to regard themselves as the chosen antagonists of Kicking Bear and his followers.

Tension mounted daily. Booming Pierre had always boasted one of the busiest red-light districts in the West. A house or two there had consistently catered to full-blood Sioux. Now the city fathers clamped down. Whorehouses were declared out of bounds to all Indians. Redskins were also impolitely shoved off the horse-drawn streetcars, long favorite conveyances of Indian visitors of all ages. The tribes were discouraged from entering town, and many emporiums were cleaning up, selling whites the government stores sidetracked from needy Sioux families on the reservation. Indian Department-issued overcoats sold like hotcakes for a quarter each while wool blankets were only a dollar.

With whites buying all the I. D.-issue shoes intended for them,

Indians were forced as cold weather approached to wrap their feet in rabbitskins over which they wore outsize moccasins. Indian ponies, carrying I. D. brands and deliberately stolen from Sioux herds, were openly sold to *honyockers* in the Pierre horse market for as little as two dollars a head.

Late in September Agent Palmer ordered Kicking Bear's arrest. The prophet submitted calmly—much to the surprise of the Indian police who apprehended him at Hump's camp where the agent had expected resistance. Kicking Bear was expeditiously turned over to an Indian court for immediate trial under the vague charge of unauthorized absence from the reservation. Palmer's gravest fears were borne out when the Sioux judges promptly released the prisoner.

Since midsummer rumor had had it that Sitting Bull, on the Standing Rock Reservation to the north, wished to see the prophet. Soon after Kicking Bear's release, he quietly dropped out of sight in the Cheyenne River country. Most Indians knew that he had departed on a "sacred errand" to see the most important leader in the Sioux Nation, Sitting Bull, chief of the Hunkpapas.

Early in October Kicking Bear and six Minneconjou ghost dancers came riding into the Grand River Valley and proceeded to Sitting Bull's camp, a scattering of tents and cabins dominated by a two-room log house in which the chief lived with his younger wife, Four Times. Another cabin for his first wife, Seen-by-Her-Nation, stood near.

Here was no pretentious residence such as the two-story frame dwellings the Government had provided for Red Cloud and Spotted Tail, friends of the white man. Sitting Bull's place was hardly better than the camp of the poorest Indians in Dakota. For Sitting Bull was no meek proselyte to whom the Indian Department could point with pride. His fierce independence and reluctance to accept the ways of white men had earned him only enmity among government officialdom. His old foe, Agent McLaughlin, had long since branded him "a polygamist, a libertine, an habitual liar, an active obstructionist, and a great obstacle in the civilization of his people." But as Sitting Bull himself had put it years earlier:

"God Almighty made me; He did not make me an agency Indian. I'll fight—and die fighting—before any white man can make me an agency Indian."

Animated by this spirit, Sitting Bull maintained his camp a remote forty miles southwest of the agency at Fort Yates, North Dakota. The place was accessible only by a rough wagon trail known throughout the reservation as Sitting Bull's Road which meandered across hills and streams and threaded through cottonwood groves to the relative serenity of Grand River.

Spurred as always by his restless sense of destiny, Kicking Bear lost no time in seeking out Sitting Bull. Seen-by-Her-Nation was working around a cook fire which blazed cheerily before an open brush-covered "squaw cooler." After greeting her, the prophet followed her pointing finger to the large tepee standing behind the log house. While weather permitted, the old man preferred to spend both waking and sleeping hours out-of-doors or in his lodge rather than under the confining roof of the cabin. Kicking Bear lifted the door flap and stooped to enter the tepee, saying respectfully:

"Father, I am Kicking Bear."

With gentle courtesy, the chief greeted his visitor. "I am glad you are here. You and your companions must be hungry. When you have eaten and are refreshed, we will talk."

Sitting Bull had changed little in the fourteen years since Little Big Horn when Kicking Bear had last seen him. A trifle fleshier perhaps, the old bowlegged limp a bit more pronounced—these were only surface differences. The thinning hair was still carefully oiled and plaited and the broad face with its good-natured, thin-lipped smile was, as usual, painted red for good luck. Great strength still showed in the massive jaws and piercing eyes as yet unfaded by age or defeat. It could truthfully be said, as Kicking Bear well knew, that no man, red or white, had ever defeated Sitting Bull. Only the wanton destruction of *pte,* the sacred buffalo uncle of the Sioux, had brought starvation and surrender to the great chief after four hungry winters in Grandmother's Land (Canada). Not even the terrible years of captivity spent at Fort Randall down the Missouri River had been able to dim the old fighter's look of calm courage. His clothing remained typically Indian: fringed shirt, leggings, moccasins—all made of smoke-tanned buckskin; and a trade-cloth blanket draped around his waist.

Around the camp, Kicking Bear noticed little that smacked of the agency Indian. In the smaller house but seldom displayed was Catherine Weldon's full-length oil portrait of the old chief. Other gifts from the white widow lay scattered about as though discarded by the recipient. White influence was at a minimum here. Agent McLaughlin's right-hand man in the district, John M. (Jack) Carignan, ran a government school three miles down-river but the presence in camp of several school-age children showed that Carignan carried little weight with Sitting Bull's followers. As though in repudiation of Carignan's school, Sitting Bull had sent his son, Crowfoot, to Reverend Theodore L. Riggs' YMCA seminary for Indian children at Oak Creek, twelve miles away.

As Sitting Bull listened to Kicking Bear describe the new cult, it was obvious that the old man wanted, perhaps more than any other Indian, to accept the ghost dance and all its promises. He was still mourning the passing of his beloved young daughter, Standing Holy,[1] and nothing would have pleased him more than to see her and talk with her again. And yet he doubted.

"It is not possible for a dead person to live again," he insisted after hearing Kicking Bear's prophecy that the Wanekia would soon come leading a horde of Indian ghosts from the Spirit Land.

Kicking Bear countered that if the tribes united and cast out all that was of the white man, if the Indians prayed and purified themselves, then the old happy world they had once known would surely exist again.

"And all the dead ones of our race will return driving the buffalo before them!" Kicking Bear added.

Sitting Bull pointed out that the white invaders were hopelessly

[1] Sometimes given as Standing Holly.

strong, that whites had devoured great forests to the east and made corn grow where once only trees had been. The whites were now more numerous than the buffalo ever had been and all the combined tribes of the plains could never hope to defeat them. Sitting Bull himself had given up war only because it was foolish to fight against such overwhelming odds.

Kicking Bear called the old chief's attention to the fact that the forerunners of these white men had once faced situations similarly desperate. Their Holy Book was full of such troubles. And when everything had seemed to go against them and they despaired of weapons and war, they had simply prayed to their Great Spirit and He had sent unseen powers to help them. Even the strongholds of their enemies had crumbled to dust at the sound of a trumpet. Now the tribes must look to Wakantanka and beseech Him to turn His face toward His chosen people, the red race. Then the enemies of the Indians would melt away before them.

Proof lay in the fact that many ghost dancers had already been able to "leave" their bodies by performing the new ritual. They had ridden after buffalo as in the olden days and had even eaten pemmican.

"Let us dance!" Kicking Bear urged. "Proof will soon come."

But Sitting Bull was still skeptical. He wondered how the destruction of the whites would come about. Kicking Bear explained that when the new earth came rolling over the old, white men and unbelievers would be submerged in a sea of mud and turned into fishes. On the other hand, the believers, recognized by Wakantanka from the white eagle plumes worn in their hair, would be lifted high above the flood and saved.

"Before this happens the soldiers may come to put a stop to our dancing," Sitting Bull suggested. "As they did nine years ago when they stopped the sun dance." [2]

"You need not fear the soldiers," Kicking Bear said calmly. "The white man's gunpowder is harmless. And believers among our people to the south have devised sacred garments which will protect all dancers against bullets."

[2] The last time the Hunkpapa Sioux danced the sun dance in the nineteenth century was on Grand River in 1881.

Suddenly Kicking Bear's eyes seemed to glaze over. Deep in their limpid irises a strange light glowed.

"Father, the tribes are dancing—all the nations, all the red people!" he wailed. "The Blue Clouds [Arapahoes], the Shahiyelas [Cheyennes], the Brûlés, the Ogalalas, the Minneconjous, the Sansarcs. I bring a true message. Hear me!"

Then he began a high falsetto chant—the opening song of the ghost dance. Presently the Minneconjous joined him in the mournful wailing cries that seemed to melt the hearts of all who listened. As he sang, the prophet began to shake and tremble; he flung his right arm about as though it were a war club; at last, like a person having a fit, he fell stiffly to the ground.

Sitting Bull got to his feet and crouched over the prostrate body of Kicking Bear. Now the old man was more curious than ever. One of the Minneconjous warned him not to touch the prophet, who was "even now in the Spirit Land."

For a long time Kicking Bear lay as if dead. No one, not even Sitting Bull, dared disturb him. At last the old chief sat down beside the outstretched body and lighted a pipe. This was indeed a fit time for prayer and contemplation.

After a while Kicking Bear began to stir, then slowly sat up, staring around him with slitted eyes. Sitting Bull watched him quietly, waiting for him to speak.

"I have just seen Our Father, Wakantanka," [3] Kicking Bear announced, his face shining, "and He has given me a sign of power. He has made my left hand stronger than the strongest man. Behold!"

He held out his left hand and one of the Hunkpapas gathered near reached out to touch it. At first contact the man jumped back, flinging the hand away from him, crying out that it made his muscles twinge and his flesh sting as though thorns were thrust into him.

A fanatic gleam grew in Kicking Bear's eyes. He began to sway through the movements of the dance again, chanting mournfully. Stopping suddenly, he reached down for a white china cup

---

[3] Apparently Kicking Bear no longer felt he required the intercession of the Wanekia in approaching the Great Spirit.

lying in the dirt, one of the many discarded gifts showered on Sitting Bull by Catherine Weldon.

"Behold!" Kicking Bear thundered, grinding the cup to bits against his palm. Shards of china fell to the ground around his moccasined feet.

The Hunkpapas danced for five days that first time, led through the ceremony by Kicking Bear and his Minneconjou assistants. Sitting Bull danced with the others, hoping eagerly, desperately, that a vision would appear to him. He had seen many visions in his time, such as the long-ago dream of earless enemies falling into camp that had foretold the great Indian victory over Long Hair Custer at Little Big Horn. Now it was no use. No dramatic trance would come, no magic revelation would appear. Sitting Bull thought ruefully that he was getting too old to dream any more.

Others were more fortunate. Looking Eagle, an old man, went into a trance the third day. Stretching his arms before him, he cried out:

"I see it all—the new land! I see the buffalo feeding. It is spring and the grass is new. My father stands before the door of his lodge. He calls with his hand. My mother is there. *Ho!* I come, my father!"

Then he fell to the ground.

Kicking Bear and the Minneconjous made up a new song:

> "The whole world of the dead is returning, returning.
> Our nation is coming, is coming.
> The spotted eagle brought us the message,
> Bearing the Father's word—
> The word and the wish of the Father.
> Over the glad new earth they are coming,
> Our dead come driving the elk and the deer.
> See them hurrying the herds of buffalo!
> This the Father has promised,
> This the Father has given."

Soon the Hunkpapas joined in the chant and all around the dance circle their bright painted faces glistened with sweat and shone with fervor. Presently the dance became violent and fast as the dancers made leaping motions leftward, their muscles jerking, their tongues lolling, their lungs heaving in panting gasps. And Kicking Bear moved everywhere within the circle, his mouth gaping, his hooded eyes set in a dreadful fanatic stare.

Tiring, Sitting Bull watched from the side lines, smoking gravely, his trembling hand showing his profound agitation. He plainly was longing to believe, but he could not. Some unseen power, as great as that which moved Kicking Bear and the dancers, held him back.

The most convincing argument so far in favor of the new religion was Looking Eagle's coming out of his trance with what appeared to be a handful of pemmican. Several Hunkpapas tasted it and swore that it was made with buffalo meat. But Sitting Bull wondered if, after all, it might not have been only beef.

Agent McLaughlin got wind of the Grand River ghost dance a day or so after it began on October 9. On the thirteenth he sent a detachment of thirteen Indian police headed by a captain and a lieutenant, with orders to arrest Kicking Bear as "an unauthorized intruder" on Standing Rock Reservation.

Next day the detachment returned empty-handed and in a dazed condition—rendered completely incapable of carrying out their orders by the "power of Kicking Bear's medicine." At first the police would not even say what had happened. But presently recovering, they explained that they had heard Kicking Bear talking of the Wanekia and preaching the new religion; that, during the ensuing dance, they watched several Sioux "fall dead" in the dance circle and come to life again, describing ecstatic visits to the Spirit Land. The amazed police heard minute descriptions of their own long-dead friends and relatives the dancers claimed to have just seen. Finally they had simply left Grand River without attempting to carry out the agent's orders. They were still in a sort of trance after the forty-mile ride back to Fort Yates.

McLaughlin was shocked and angry. He knew better than to question the loyalty of these police, most of whom were hand-

picked from among the friendly Yanktonnais and Blackfeet Sioux
—tribes unencumbered by any traditional fealty to Sitting Bull.
The agent selected Lieutenant Catka, well known for his fearlessness and determination, and sent him back to Grand River that
same day with Crazy Walking and One Bull, both of whom were
highly dependable.

The following morning Kicking Bear was giving further instructions to the dancers:

"Think hard of that which you wish to see in your sleep, and
it will be given to you. The old shall be made young and the sick
shall be made well. Turn your thoughts to the Wanekia in the
West who listens to all His children."

At that point Catka and Crazy Walking burst into the circle.
Confronting Kicking Bear, Catka announced sternly that Agent
McLaughlin demanded the immediate departure of the prophet
and his Minneconjou friends. Crazy Walking then ordered the
dancers to stop, whereupon Sitting Bull came up to him.

"Leave my people alone," the old chief said. "Their dancing is
not the most important undertaking. Eventually they will stop."

Kicking Bear, however, quieted the dancers with a wave of his
hand.

"My relatives, you see how it is. The white man is jealous of
our religion. Now he would even deprive us of our dreams. Nevertheless, I will go—for my mission here is fulfilled. The dance belongs to you. Do not forget it!"

As if in response to an unseen signal, the six Minneconjous
came abreast of Kicking Bear, one by one, until all seven men were
standing in line facing west with outstretched palms. After praying silently a moment, they began to chant in unison:

> " 'My children, take this road!
>   My children, go this way!'
>   Says the Wanekia.
>   'It is a goodly road,'
>   Says the Wanekia.
>   'It leads to a joyous land!'
>   Says the Wanekia."

When they turned to go, the ghost dancers began to cry out, "Stay! Stay! Tell us more!" But Kicking Bear seemed deaf to their voices. Looking neither to right nor to left, he led the way out of camp.

Catka and his detail made a sorry spectacle, traipsing along behind Kicking Bear and his companions, feeling foolish instead of brave as they put on a show of bravado by lashing the rumps of the Minneconjous' ponies with their quirts. Catka and Crazy Walking both confessed later to One Bull that they were trembling inwardly at "the sacrilege" they were forced to commit in escorting Kicking Bear's party across Grand River and over the reservation's south line.

Indian Summer

INDIAN summer had come to the plains. All across the hazy land the indolent warmth of October lay like a tawny blanket, while the whitish brassy blue of the cloudless sky was a gigantic up-turned bowl holding in the scintillant brilliance of the autumn sun. As far as the eye could see, the ocher-tinged uplands stretched their carpeting of short grass; and in the nearer hollows of undulating landscape glinted the gold and purple of cornflower and bluejoint. No red man could look upon such a beauteous land and withstand the compulsion to believe the Wanekia's promise that it would soon revert to its proper Indian owners.

Even in the minds of those Sioux who did the white man's bidding and served as hated policemen there may well have been doubt. All that Kicking Bear preached, in spite of its unique rituals, was no more incredible to most Indians than what the Christian missionaries were teaching every day in their mission schools and churches. The credo of salvation and revelation had been the standby for years of the Black Robes and White Robes and Long Coats and all the other sects and denominations represented throughout the Sioux country. Now it was presented here to Indians by members of their own race in terms they all might understand. Surely the Wanekia in the West who had actually been seen and heard by trusted tribesmen was more believable to many Sioux than Jesus Christ of far-off Nazareth who was merely described in the white man's Holy Book.

Sitting Bull had been a pagan all his life. Never having accepted the missionaries' doctrine of Christ's First Coming, he was disinclined to believe in a Second Coming, even though the Saviour was to be an Indian this time. However, he resented White

Hair McLaughlin sending policemen to tell him what he could or could not do.

Three days after Kicking Bear's departure, McLaughlin learned that while Sitting Bull had stopped dancing, he had publicly announced that he would deny hospitality to no man, whether ghost dancer or white missionary. Moreover, he would do nothing to prevent his people from worshiping Wakantanka in any manner they pleased.

The agent angrily dispatched a policeman, One Bull, who was a nephew and adopted son of Sitting Bull, to Grand River with a message demanding that the old chief come in to the agency for a talk. Fearing arrest, Sitting Bull refused to go. When One Bull reported back empty-handed, McLaughlin discharged him as untrustworthy. Apparently the agent considered it improper for One Bull to feel any loyalty toward his uncle.

As the ghost-dance excitement grew on Grand River, McLaughlin decided to enlist other members of Sitting Bull's own band into the agency police force. Until now most of the police had stuck by the agent. However, he feared the ghost dancers would never allow Yanktonnais or Blackfeet Sioux to arrest Sitting Bull. There was little doubt that such an attempt would depend largely on the agent's success in persuading some of the chief's own tribesmen to go against him.

Black Fox, Two Crows, Old Bull, and several other Hunkpapas from Grand River volunteered for police duty and drew their blue coats and rifles and shiny badges before they learned that the agent expected them to kill their own people, if need be, in order to carry out his wishes. They promptly turned in their guns and equipment and quit.

Now McLaughlin realized he must take drastic steps, for his entire police force was falling apart. He authorized Lieutenant Bullhead to enlist Hunkpapas whose loyalty and courage were unquestionable but whose fondness for Sitting Bull was in doubt.

"I'll get men who'll stick," Bullhead promised.

Overnight Sitting Bull unwittingly became the archvillain of the ghost dance, now branded in the nation's press as a fanatic

Indian conspiracy to wrest former Indian territories away from the whites. Nearly every newspaper in the land viewed the situation in South Dakota with growing alarm. Moreover, the extent of the new religion and the resulting Indian "nationalism" was vastly exaggerated in the public mind. Generally uninformed newspaper editors hungrily latched on to the aging chief of the Hunkpapas as the best available material for reams of copy.

On the surface, Sitting Bull seemed highly qualified for a "heavy's" role in the unfolding drama. The Battle of the Little Big Horn and its humiliating defeat of American arms fourteen years earlier were still the outstanding *cause célèbre* of the age. Buffalo Bill Cody had augmented Sitting Bull's notoriety in eighty-five by taking the old man on tour in his Wild West Show and billing him widely as "Custer's Killer." Although the chief proved to be too affable by nature to be convincing as a murderer, the general public soon forgot the quiet old bowlegged Sioux and remembered only the promotional build-up put over on them by Cody's press agents.

Renewed agitation against Sitting Bull and his cohorts stemmed from Agent McLaughlin's October report to Indian Commissioner Morgan in Washington. News releases from the Indian Office and Department of the Interior echoed McLaughlin's harsh demand for the chief's "early removal."

Rumors circulated freely in the press to the effect that the old chief was apparently stirring up tribes all over the country. Reports from Darlington, Indian Territory, some seventeen hundred miles south of Standing Rock, stated that Sitting Bull had led a great ghost dance on the South Canadian River about two miles below the agency. Some three thousand Indians had participated, including almost all the Southern Arapahoes and Cheyennes as well as many Kiowa, Caddoes, and Wichitas.

Not until later was it determined that this ceremony in mid-October had been led by Sitting Bull of the Arapahoes, who had come all the way from Wind River, Wyoming, to bring the new religion to his people in the south. Although the identity of the Arapaho apostle was confused with that of the Hunkpapa chief, one aspect of the doctrine as it was believed on the southern plains caused added alarm among whites the country over. The new earth, according to Sitting Bull of the Arapahoes, as it advanced over the old, was to be preceded by a wall of fire which would drive the whites across the great water to their original countries in Europe, while the Indians would be able to surmount the flames until after they were extinguished by a twelve-day rainstorm.

Newspapers grabbed up the report as an indication that the ghost dancers were now including mass arson in their sinister plot against the whites. Many editors clamored for immediate and stern measures on the part of the United States Army. One particularly vicious criticism of the new religion was published editorially in the Chicago *Tribune*. John Daylight, an educated Sioux then living in the Windy City, promptly answered as follows:

You say "If the United States Army would kill a thousand or so of the dancing Indians there would be no more trouble." I judge you are a "Christian" and are disposed to do all in your power to advocate the cause of Christ. You are doubtless a worshiper of the white man's Saviour, but are unwilling that the Indians should have a Messiah of their own. The Indians have never taken kindly to the religion preached and practiced by the whites. Do you know why this is the case? Because the Good Father of all has given us a better religion —a religion that is adapted to our wants. You say if we are good and obey the Ten Commandments and never sin any more, we may be permitted eventually to sit upon a white rock and sing praises to God forevermore, and look down upon our heathen fathers, mothers, brothers, and sisters who are howling in hell. It won't do. The code of morals as preached by the white race will not compare with the morals of Indians. We pay no lawyers or preachers, but we have not a tenth of the crime that you have. If our Messiah does come, we shall not try to force you into our belief. We will never burn innocent women at the stake or pull men to pieces with horses because they refuse to join in our ghost dances. You white people had a Messiah, and if history is to be believed nearly every nation has had one.... You are anxious to get hold of our Messiah so you can put him in irons. This you may do—in fact, you may crucify him as you did that other one, but you cannot convert the Indians to the Christian religion until you contaminate them with the blood of white men. The white man's heaven is repulsive to the Indian nature, and if the white man's hell suits you, why, you keep it. I think there will be white rogues enough to fill it. . . .

Lieutenant Henry Bullhead, a Yanktonnai Sioux known to the Hunkpapas as "Afraid-of-Bear," was doing a thorough job for Agent McLaughlin. With deliberate care he selected brave men from Sitting Bull's band on Grand River to serve as "Metal Breasts," the agent's Indian police. It was a strong force made up of such courageous fighters as Running Hawk, Weasel Bear, Iron Thunder, and White Bird,[1] men who would never quit. Sergeant Red Tomahawk was foremost among them, but the spine of the entire outfit was First Sergeant Shave Head.

Charlie Shave Head was one of the fiercest and most hard-boiled scrappers anywhere in Sioux country and was McLaughlin's special pride and joy. Long idolized by the agent, he had come to McLaughlin's particular attention years earlier when, as ration chief at the beef issues, he had fallen into a dispute with a Sioux named Crooked Neck.

Some beeves were naturally fatter than others and Crooked Neck accused Shave Head of taking the meatiest animals for himself, whereupon Shave Head angrily pumped fifteen shots into Crooked Neck at point-blank range. The dead man's relatives laid Crooked Neck to rest on a burial scaffold opposite Standing Rock Agency near the mouth of Cat Tail Creek. They made no attempt to retaliate on Shave Head—possibly because he was a policeman. But Indians around the agency began whispering that the dead man's ghost haunted Shave Head, terrorizing him day and night. Shave Head was so affected by the "curse of the dead" that he was even unable to drink from a tin cup—always he saw Crooked Neck's face staring up at him from the cup's shiny bottom. To try to rid himself of the curse, he got a cup made of buffalo horn.

[1] A late friend of the author, White Bird died in the early 1940's.

Still Shave Head was haunted by the dead man. Every payday he would spend all his money on cartridges at the agency trading post, then cross the Missouri with his Winchester and go to Crooked Neck's grave. All day long the agency people back at Standing Rock could hear the firing as he pumped bullet after bullet into the body of his old victim. Only when the dead man's remains disintegrated and fell through the scaffold did Shave Head cease his monthly pilgrimages to the grave.

In keeping with his name, Shave Head disdained the customary unshorn locks of his tribe in spite of the fact that long hair was traditionally sacred to the Sioux. This personal habit, borrowed from the whites, appealed to McLaughlin, who promoted Shave Head to first sergeant, second only to Bullhead, and decreed short hair for all members of the police force. After that no Indian dared taunt Shave Head for not wearing a scalp lock. His flaring temper was no longer to be roused and behind him now lay not only the power of the police but the tacit support of the agent. Building his force around Shave Head, Lieutenant Bullhead gravely prepared his Metal Breasts for the grim task for which they had been reorganized: the arrest of Sitting Bull.

Spurring McLaughlin was the fact that through the country at this time the newspapers were lampooning most agents in the Dakotas for "losing control of their Indians." Owing to his long experience and much-touted ability as a minion of the Government, James McLaughlin was castigated more than the others. Recalling the earlier success of former Agent Valentine G. McGillycuddy, who had prevented several outbreaks in the early eighties at Pine Ridge when Red Cloud and other recalcitrants got out of hand, the press was hammering away constantly at McLaughlin and building the ghost-dance scare into outsize proportions.

While McLaughlin privately felt that the ghost dance was basically harmless and would die out once the Indians discovered "the futility of such nonsense," he was officially committed to a course of action which would put down the new religion—at least at Standing Rock—once and for all.

Adding greatly to the agent's discomfiture was the stand taken against the dance by local missionaries. Failing to see the new faith as an Indian brand of Christianity, they were horrified at some of its pagan characteristics which seemed as dreadful and uncivilized to them as the old self-torture features of the long-banned sun dance.

In all the chorus of white protest around Standing Rock no voice was louder or more shrill than that of Catherine Weldon. From her retreat across the Cannonball she bombarded McLaughlin with reams of correspondence, pleading with him to "have pity on Sitting Bull and the Hunkpapas who have been under the evil influence of Kicking Bear." [2]

At the same time she wrote voluminous letters to Sitting Bull in which she tried to persuade him not to have anything further to do with the ghost dance. (These letters were translated and read to the old chief by his educated son-in-law Andrew Fox.) Not since late summer had she had frequent contact with him, and she was growing worried about his reported participation in what she called "this absurd new religion." Lacking sufficient stationery to pursue all her correspondence, she resorted to sending hurriedly scribbled messages on old calendar memoranda which had lain around the Parkin ranch for nearly a decade. In a brief note to McLaughlin she wrote:

> .... Have pity on him [Sitting Bull] and do not send the police or soldiers and I will induce him to come to you of his own accord. S. Bull will surely accompany me to the agency; but please do not detain him; his brain has suffered, but his heart is good. He will be all right now that Kicking Bear has gone. My heart is almost breaking when I see the work of years undone by that vile impostor. . . .

Without waiting for authorization to return to the reservation, Mrs. Weldon took it upon herself to travel all the way down to Grand River, arriving at Sitting Bull's camp during the third week in October. She plunged at once into an impossible task.

She had already prepared a long sermon in English which she proceeded to translate into Sioux. This, along with other care-

---

[2] In her correspondence, Catherine Weldon referred to Kicking Bear by his name as it is given in Sioux: "Mato Wanahtaka"—"Bear That Kicks."

fully worded speeches, was completely wasted on the ghost
dancers. She might as well have been reciting gibberish.

Desperate, she offered to debate the new religion point by
point with Kicking Bear, should the ghost dancers succeed in pre-
vailing upon him to return to Standing Rock. She shrieked out a
defiance of his power to strike her dead. She painstakingly explained to an indifferent audience that there was nothing new or
mysterious about hypnotism which Kicking Bear obviously practiced on his converts. A Frenchman named Mesmer had practiced
it many years earlier in Europe. Kicking Bear was deluding the
Indians, she insisted. She even warned them that the white men
would surely use the ghost dance as an excuse to wage war against
the Sioux, an eventuality that could only prove disastrous for the
Indians.

The Hunkpapas listened to her heated arguments. It was poor
manners not to hear a speaker out, although it was unconven-
tional among Indians for a woman to address a group which included men. After listening, the ghost dancers went on dancing.
There is no indication that her words had the slightest effect on
any Indian who heard her.

Sitting Bull was in a quandary. After the voluble white widow
had addressed the whole camp, several ghost dancers insisted that
her talk of a coming war was cover up for her own plot to destroy
the chief. Yet, for all her standoffish prudery and present ve-
hemence, the old man could hardly believe she meant to have
him killed.

"Perhaps," he said sadly, "since you are no longer my friend,
you want me to be put in prison."

Catherine Weldon's harsh laughter puzzled him further.

"Do you suppose," she retorted, "that I have spent all these
years working for you and your people—ready to share your every
danger and tribulation—and am *not* your friend? Are you foolish
enough to believe that I am your *enemy?*"

That night the Hunkpapas sang and shrieked louder than ever
as they shuffled in the great dance circle. Unable to sleep for the

racket, Mrs. Weldon fearlessly sought out Sitting Bull among the dancers and upbraided him mercilessly.

"If you do not stop the dance at once," she said testily, "I will leave this camp at daylight—forever!"

That broke up the dance—at least for that night.

The next morning the widow pleaded with Sitting Bull to have no more dances, as troops were almost certain to come and many people—both Indian and white—were sure to be killed.

"If the soldiers kill me, I will be glad," said the old chief solemnly. "Our old Indian way of life is almost gone. Now I want to die."

Catherine Weldon sniffed impatiently.

"If you want to die, kill yourself. Don't bring other people into your trouble."

And Sitting Bull said nothing, his thin-lipped mouth twisting into a half-smile as he wondered at the woman's strangeness.

A few days later Mrs. Weldon met Gall, a Hunkpapa chief and long-time rival of Sitting Bull. Under McLaughlin's tutelage, Gall had been blown up by the press as the real military genius behind the Indian victory over Custer at Little Big Horn. Not on the best of terms with Sitting Bull, he saw a good chance to further his own ends by weaning the white widow even further away from the old chief. He offered to take Mrs. Weldon back to the Cannonball after convincing her there would soon be trouble at Grand River. Fearing that Sitting Bull would think she might betray certain council secrets to his rival, she confronted the old man with her plan to leave the camp.

"Do as your heart dictates," he told her. "If you want to go with Gall, go; but if your heart says 'stay,' remain, and I will take you to the Cannonball myself."

Resignedly, her spirit broken, Catherine Weldon at last permitted Sitting Bull to take her back to the Parkin ranch in his wagon. He walked far ahead of the vehicle as they passed Fort Yates, for he feared that if any soldiers tried to take him Mrs. Weldon might be harmed. Having utterly failed to persuade the Hunkpapas to give up their dancing, the widow was not disposed to face McLaughlin and they drove on through the agency without paying their respects.

Save for the fact that it was the last time the old chief and his "white squaw" ever saw each other, the journey was uneventful. Three agency Indians, jealous of Sitting Bull's power, waited in ambush for him at Long Soldier Creek. By a fluke the old man took a different route on his return trip to Grand River—foiling this first assassination attempt.

Catherine Weldon was crushed at her own failure to stop the ghost dance at Grand River. Her disillusionment complete, she unaccountably poured out her woes in a letter to Agent McLaughlin. She wrote:

> ... I have turned my former Hunkpapa friends into enemies, & some feel bitter toward me. Even Sitting Bull's faith in me is shaken, & he imagines that I seek his destruction, in spite of all the proofs of friendship which I have given him for many years. In fact his brain is so confused that he does not know friend from foe.... Poor misguided beings, so earnestly desiring to seek God, groping blindly for the true light & not finding it. If I had known what obstinate minds I had to contend with, I would not have undertaken this mission to enlighten and instruct them. It was money, health & heart thrown away....

One statement in her message to the agent substantiated profound fears in the Indian Department when McLaughlin relayed the letter on to Washington. She had written:

> I believe that the Mormons are at the bottom of it all & misuse the credulity of the Indians for their own purposes....

The federal government at once stepped up pressure on Mormons in Utah and elsewhere to the extent that not only did the Church of Latter-Day Saints in Salt Lake City ban the ghost dance among its membership, but it outlawed polygamy as well.

Sitting Bull was apparently unaware of the growing gulf between himself and the few white friends he had left. On a rare visit to Grand River, Father Bernard Strassmeier, Catholic priest at Fort Yates, was greeted cordially by the old chief. Even then, late in October, Sitting Bull was having little to do with the ghost dance.

He was not so friendly, however, to White Hair McLaughlin who unexpectedly showed up in his camp after Father Bernard had made sure a white man would be safe there. Still, the old chief submitted to an interview with the agent in which he disclaimed all responsibility for the new religion.

"But I am willing to be convinced," Sitting Bull told him. "Let us go together to the Indian nations from which this dance came. If they cannot produce the real Wanekia, if we do not find the dead coming our way, then I will return and tell the Sioux it is a lie. And that will be the end of it. If, on the other hand, these things are true, you will let the dance go on."

It was a fair proposition—except in McLaughlin's mind. The agent said he had neither time nor money for such a journey. He invited Sitting Bull to come to the agency for further discussion of the matter. But, fearing for his life, the ghost dancers refused to let the old chief go.

A few days later Sitting Bull wandered through the breaks along Grand River looking for his favorite mount, the old gray circus horse Buffalo Bill Cody had given him in eighty-five when he left the show. Almost at the old man's elbow a meadowlark burst into song; but rather than plaintive melody, Sitting Bull heard ominous words:

"Your own people will kill you!"

Deeply troubled, the old chief took his nephew and adopted son, One Bull, into his confidence. As always, they talked of many things, including the ghost dance.

"There's nothing to it, Nephew," the old man decided. "Our own religion is best for us, no matter what Kicking Bear and the others say. This new religion belongs to tribes far to the west. They should have kept it over there."

After that he publicly renounced his faith in the Wanekia. But at the same time he tolerantly told his people they were free to dance as long as they liked.

"The sun will shine warmly on you," he predicted. "The weather will be fair, and you can dance all winter long."

In spite of this favorable prediction, Sitting Bull's disclaimer of the ghost dance cost him followers. A large group of Sioux accompanied Male Bear, a young rabble-rouser, to a new camp site on Oak Creek eighteen miles away. Once again all was quiet on Grand River.

From the day he took over as agent at Pine Ridge, D. F. Royer was in trouble. General Nelson A. Miles had stopped by the agency on his way west on a routine tour of inspection and told Royer he thought there was little danger in the ghost dance. He had met with various Ogalala chiefs in council, had heard them say the Sioux intended to keep dancing, had given them a stern lecture warning them to stop, and let it go at that. Equally unruffled about the situation at Pine Ridge was the agent's mainstay, a progressive chief called Young-Man-Afraid-of-His-Horses who picked this inopportune moment to go off on an extended hunting trip in Wyoming.

His courage bolstered, Royer went out to No Water's camp on White Clay Creek to order a halt to the ghost dance. To impress the Sioux with his authority, Royer carried a Colt revolver in plain view. When the agent arrived, a lone Indian broke away from the dance and accosted him. Royer demanded that the dancing stop at once.

"White men dance when they please," said the dancer defiantly, "and so will we Indians."

Then he asked the agent what he meant to do with the revolver he carried.

"Did you ever kill an Indian with it?" the red man asked. Then he raised his ghost shirt, baring his belly and bare chest. "Here, white man, kill me! For I am going to dance!"

Dreading violence, Royer took his departure—fast. From that time on he seldom ventured far from the agency. Soon the word got around that he had backed down. He was no longer referred to by the respectful title "Father," but became known throughout the reservation as "Lakota-Kokipa-Koskalaka"—Young-Man-Afraid-of-His-Indians!

Before he had been in charge a full week, half-a-dozen roisterous Indians raced up the agency guardhouse and forced the release of a prisoner named Little, a troublesome ghost dancer recently arrested and jailed by Indian police.

Royer was so unpopular and ineffectual that responsible chiefs and head men of the Ogalalas began casting about for someone to take his place. They had few friends now among the whites, few men they could trust. Dr. Valentine McGillycuddy had served them fairly and well in years past when the agency had first been started. But now McGillycuddy was out of government service, working on his own in banking, construction, and other projects at Rapid City, the growing "Gateway" metropolis of the nearby Black Hills.

Late in October a number of chiefs and leaders including several of the ghost-dance faction paid a visit to their old friend James H. Cook, former scout and cowboy, who had a ranch near Agate, Nebraska. Somewhat under protest, since an agent's pay was small, Cook agreed to let his name be submitted on a tribal petition requesting that he be appointed agent in place of Royer. Many whites in the surrounding country joined in supporting Cook's appointment, but no action was taken. Authority remained in precarious hands.

Royer grew increasingly panicky. On October 20 he telegraphed the Indian Office demanding troops and stating that at least six or seven hundred soldiers were needed to restore order at Pine Ridge. Since no particular emergency was noted in Washington, however, no troops were yet ordered into the field.

Locally, the situation was viewed with growing alarm. The Rapid City *Journal,* which had been devoting considerable space to the fatal mauling of Charles Jones by a large silver-tip grizzly at the Etta Mine at neighboring Hill City, ran a front-page account of Will Zoekler's report that fully two hundred Pine Ridge Indians had jumped the reservation and were camped on nearby Battle Creek. From this base of operations, according to Zoekler, the Sioux were running off stock belonging to white ranchers and committing numerous other depredations. One cowboy, when confronted by twenty Winchester-armed Indians, had been forced to give up his saddle horse. True or not, the report indicated that trouble between cattlemen and Indians was imminent.

Ugly news also came from Rosebud Agency. Short Bull was leading a fresh outbreak of dancing at Red Leaf's camp on Black Pipe Creek. Acting Agent Reynolds' attempts to put a stop to it had met with failure. Indian police details had been sent out to stop the dancing but had barely escaped with their lives. Two Strike, strongest of the Brûlé chiefs, was openly considering taking his band into the ghost-dance camp. Most ominous of all, however, was the report that the Brûlés were spending every available dollar on brass cartridges and were even swapping ponies for ammunition wherever they could get it.

On the last day of October Short Bull harangued the dancers.

"My relatives," he began, "I will soon start this thing running. I have told you a great dust storm would bury the whites in two seasons, but since the whites are interfering so much, I will advance the time from what Wakantanka told me, so the time will be shorter. You believers need not be afraid of anything, but some of my relations have no ears and I will have them blown away. . . . We must dance the balance of this moon, at the end of which time the earth will shiver very hard. Whenever this thing occurs I will start the wind to blow. . . ."

It was plain to his listeners that Short Bull was taking on certain powers heretofore ascribed only to the Wanekia. They began to believe that Short Bull, with his professed power to hasten the destruction of the entire white race, must surely be a messiah in his own right.

Swelled with new importance, Short Bull urged the ghost dancers to desert their homes and follow him to Pass Creek which marked the boundary between the Rosebud and Pine Ridge jurisdictions.

"There a sacred tree is sprouting, and there all the members of our religion must gather to await the coming of our ghost relatives. You must not take any earthly things with you. The men must take off all their clothing and the women must do the same.

No one shall be ashamed of exposing his person. Only our sacred shirts shall be worn if danger threatens. My Father, Wakantanka, has told us to do this, and we must do as he says.

"You need not be afraid of anything," he went on. "The guns of the white men are the only things we are afraid of, but they belong to Wakantanka. He will see that they do us no harm. . . . "

With a Dakota winter coming on, the Brûlés had not counted on running around naked—even in the fine new Indian world now approaching! They readily abandoned their cabins and other belongings as Short Bull had ordered, but piled their wagons and pony drags high with winter robes and heavy clothing as they prepared for the westward trek to Pass Creek.

Woodpecker Woman, wife of Kicking Bear, accompanied by her eldest son,[3] a wiry boy of seven, was searching for firewood in the cedar breaks along Cherry Creek when the crier's voice sang out in the camp half a mile downstream. The crier had been well picked for his lung power and even at that distance the words rang clear and sharp.

"Kicking Bear has come home! Kicking Bear has come home!"

In his haste to get back to camp the boy dropped his load of dead sticks and dashed off downstream, for it had been months now since he had seen his father. Sighing wearily, Woodpecker Woman stooped to gather the kindling, then followed along slowly.

In some ways, she reflected, her husband had almost become a stranger to her now. It had always been his way to ride off somewhere unexpectedly and stay away long days at a time. But during the past year—since the beginning of the ghost-dance rumors —he had been away from home more than ever. Still, whether from her old longing or force of habit or a sudden new hopefulness, her heart leaped when she saw him hunkered down in front of the family lodge saying fatherly things to the wide-eyed boy who stood before him.

[3] The boy was Frank Kicking Bear, the author's long-time good friend, who now lives near Manderson, South Dakota, on Pine Ridge Indian Reservation.

Kicking Bear had aged since his family had last seen him. His sunken eyes wore a haggard weariness and his hollowed cheeks and knotted jaws seemed gaunter than ever. His greasy old buckskins were in tatters, making him look like some white rancher's wind-blown scarecrow. Yet there was still that great majesty in his bearing that set him apart from other men and made his wife beam with pride. He stood as she walked toward him, then waited quietly while she set down her load of wood by the cook fire.

"Your clothes need mending," she said, touching his arm gently as she lifted aside the door flap and entered the lodge.

He followed her inside, wordless, his eyes seeking hers. And the boy looked after them, wondering how long it would be before his father would go away again.

"It is a small thing I ask, my husband," Kicking Bear's wife said to him as they sat, content for the moment, staring at the dying embers of the fire that warmed the lodge and made the children drowsy. "Give up your wandering. Let others carry the new religion among our people."

Kicking Bear was silent. Dimly highlighted in the glow of the fire, his lean features took on a moody cast.

"The whites will kill you for it," she warned him. "Not understanding, they will stop at nothing. I fear for you!"

Kicking Bear gazed steadily at the last flickering flame dancing among the embers.

"I am chosen," he said simply.

His wife kept her eyes downcast as she prepared to give him what she felt would surely be unwelcome news. Then at last she spoke, telling him that since he had gone away to the north among the Hunkpapas and Blackfeet word had spread among the tribes to the south that Short Bull, his own brother-in-law, had suddenly risen to great power. No longer was Short Bull a mere disciple of the Wanekia—he was himself now the Wanekia!

"The Wanekia is not one of us!" Kicking Bear almost shouted the words, and on their animal-skin pallets by the entrance the children stirred into wakefulness. "The Wanekia is far from here —beyond the sunset."

"Let Short Bull lead the believers if such is his wish." The woman gave emphasis to her request by reaching for one of his strong, bony hands and tenderly bringing it to rest between her breasts. "My heart asks this little thing of you: stay here among your family. This is your place now, my husband. You belong to us."

With sudden purpose Kicking Bear jerked his hand free of her touch. Standing in the near darkness of the lodge he was a tense, looming figure spurred into propulsive action. Years later the eldest son often recalled the shadowy silhouette of his towering father as the man quietly announced:

"I cannot stay."

Then Kicking Bear stooped to grab up his blanket and push through the door flap into the outer darkness.

His family heard him out in the brush, taking the hobbles off his fastest horse and fitting the rawhide jaw rope into the animal's mouth. Then they heard a brief thunder of hoofbeats that died away in the night, while the woman sat where Kicking Bear had left her, her hunched shoulders convulsed with silent sobbing.

Kicking Bear found Short Bull in full control of the great Brûlé camp on Black Pipe Creek. More and more Indians were coming in daily from outlying portions of the reservation to swell the teeming hundreds already camped there. One chief after another paid homage to Short Bull, adding to his growing influence. Few men could now doubt his power. He was cordial but a little condescending when he greeted Kicking Bear.

With cool reserve and steady determination Kicking Bear took Short Bull to task for claiming to be a messiah. All that was said during this meeting was not later recounted. Nor did the Indians ever know exactly how a compromise was effected in Kicking Bear's own mind; his true feelings on this point were never told. It is certain that no open break occurred between the two men and, while Short Bull never retracted his supernatural claim,

Kicking Bear continued to profess belief that the Wanekia dwelt in the West beyond the sunset.

Pine Ridge Agency was bleak and desolate and windy that day early in November when Dr. Charles A. Eastman arrived just ahead of a South Dakota dust storm. Eastman was a Santee Sioux, one of the more advanced eastern branches of the Nation, and he had been educated as a physician at Dartmouth and the Boston University School of Medicine from which he had just graduated the previous June. Although he was entirely Sioux by blood and had inherited the Indian name Ohiyesa—"Winner"— he was far removed in upbringing, manner, or outlook from any of his western cousins, the Ogalalas. A product of the white man's schools, he looked on in wonder at these wild Indians, strangely stirred by the tumultuous character of their present striving for peace of soul as well as body. At the same time he sensed a deep, rumbling undercurrent of danger for his people in the new ghost-dance cult, and he feared for them.

He was then thirty-two, but with his short haircut and breezy, vigorous manner he appeared much younger. His boundless enthusiasm and his eagerness to practice medicine among the members of his own race and nation were like a breath of fresh air in the fetid, apathetic atmosphere of the agency. Other physicians had been stationed at Pine Ridge for brief periods in the past, but a "white doctor" of Indian blood was a great novelty to red men and whites alike.[4]

As was customary for new employees or casual visitors, Eastman reported to the agent upon arrival.

"I tell you, Doctor," said Royer, after an exchange of greetings, "I am mighty glad you came here at this time. We have a most difficult situation to handle, but those men in Washington don't seem to realize the facts. If I had my way, I would have had troops here before this. This ghost-dance craze is the worst thing that has ever taken hold of the Indian race. It is going like wild-fire among the tribes, and right here and now the people are

---

[4] Any doctor is referred to in Sioux as *wasicun wakan*—"holy white man."

beginning to defy my authority; even my Indian police seem to
be powerless. I expect every employee at the agency to do his
or her best to avert an outbreak."

Eastman assured the agent that he could count on him. Then
the young doctor was shown to his quarters—two unfurnished
rooms for himself, plus an office and dispensary, all in a continuous one-story barrack which also included the agent's offices
and quarters for the police. Like that of most buildings in the
settlement, the construction was crude and makeshift of warped
cottonwood lumber through which the prairie winds whistled
incessantly; everything, inside and out, was coated with fine
Dakota dust.

In addition to his dismal lodgings, Eastman's meals consisted
of unappetizing dishes served up to unmarried employees by the
German cook at the agency mess. The only bright spot in the
gloomy haze of that stormy November at Pine Ridge was the
presence of another educated Indian, a Yankton Sioux who
served as the Episcopal missionary, the Reverend Charles Smith
Cook.[5] Knowing he was at the agency, Eastman looked forward
with keen anticipation to a tea party at the rectory to which
Cook invited him.

The tea was a prim, sedate affair, singularly out of key with
the storm of elements and emotions which raged all around it.
Cook's young wife was a gracious New Yorker, a trained musician
with a sweet, dulcet voice who had endeared herself to the entire Dakota community. She trilled an eloquent rendition of "I
Dreamt I Dwelt in Marble Halls" which set the pace for an
entrancing afternoon.

Several young ladies from the teachers' staff at the agency
boarding school, accompanied by two or three awkward swains
from nearby Nebraska towns, were in the select group of guests.
But for Eastman, the dominant personage was Miss Elaine
Goodale, white supervisor of Indian schools in the Dakotas and
Nebraska, then at Pine Ridge on a tour of inspection.

Miss Goodale made a lasting impression on the young doctor.

[5] Not to be confused with white rancher James H. Cook, mentioned elsewhere in this book.

Back in Boston he had read her slim volume *Apple Blossoms* as well as several of her authoritative articles on Indian education. Now, as he met her at last face to face, Eastman realized his life would be woefully incomplete without this sparkling blond woman at his side. Her obvious sincerity in her work for the Indians bound her to him all the more, and he felt no barrier of race between them. To his private dismay—for he had never given due weight to the possibility—he knew he was in love.

His wooing began gently, subtly, yet persistently. Well chaperoned by the Cooks, Eastman saw a great deal of Elaine Goodale in the weeks that followed. Gradually he became aware that she returned his affection. Moreover, she was keenly interested in his work.

Eastman inaugurated a series of lectures on physiology and hygiene at the government boarding school as part of a medical program which met with the highest approval of his superiors including Agent Royer. And once the Indians discovered that they had for the first time a doctor with whom they could discuss their health and ailments in their own language,[6] the young physician enjoyed unprecedented popularity.

All the while, however, there were ominous skirlings of impending outbreak. One night after seeing Miss Goodale to her quarters from an evening musicale at the Cooks', Eastman found a visitor waiting in his dusty office. Captain George Sword, dignified and intelligent head of the Pine Ridge Indian police force, was a man in his early forties. He was a product of the old McGillycuddy regime and had been police chief since the organization of the agency. Though close to the intricate balance of power maintained among the chiefs of his tribe, Sword had sufficient knowledge of the white man's world to appreciate what Eastman was trying to do for his race.

"*Kola*," [7] he began presently, "the people are very glad that you have come here. You have begun well; we are all your friends. Your reputation has already traveled the length and breadth of the reservation. You treat everybody alike, and your

[6] Allowing for a few dialectal differences between Santee and Teton speech.
[7] The Sioux word for "friend."

directions are understood by the people. No government doctor has ever gone freely among them before. It is a new order of things.

"But I fear you came at a bad time, *kola*. The ghost dancers have not heeded the agent's warning. They pay no attention to us policemen. The craze is spreading like a prairie fire and the chiefs who are encouraging it do not even come to the agency any more. They send after their rations and remain at home. It looks bad."

Eastman was incredulous. Cook, as well as other local missionaries, had openly discussed the matter and were more or less agreed that, as long as no attempt was made to stop it by force, the ghost-dance craze would die out before long.

"Do the dancers really mean mischief?" asked the young doctor.

"They say not," Sword answered. "All they ask is to be let alone. They say the white man is not disturbed when he goes to his church. But I must tell you that the agent says he will send for soldiers to come here and stop the ghost dance. The agent says the Great Father in Washington wishes it stopped. I fear the people will not stop. I fear trouble, *kola*."

The Little Wound settlement some forty miles northeast of Pine Ridge Agency was a model community.[8] Subsidized and equipped by the estate of Mrs. John Jacob Astor, it was thought to represent a tremendous forward stride on the part of the Sioux along the white man's road. It lay some thirty miles west of Short Bull's destination at Pass Creek and soon came under the influence of the ghost-dance mania.

Many of the Little Wound "friendlies," however, stood firmly opposed to the ghost dance and loyally served the agent and his government. Next in importance to old Little Wound himself, the most prominent leader was American Horse. He had befriended former Agent McGillycuddy in the thick of Red Cloud's threatened outbreaks in the early eighties; he had helped McGillycuddy's successor, Gallagher, over some rough spots; now he was doing what he could to support Royer's policies. Since

[8] Now the Indian town of Kyle, South Dakota.

Royer's weakness was all too apparent, American Horse volunteered to go to No Water's camp on White Clay Creek and personally try to stop the ghost dance.

While American Horse was away, Short Bull and a Sioux named Little Gun (probably another name for Sells-a-Pistol-Butt) came over from Rosebud and started a dance in the very heart of the Little Wound settlement. Cloud Horse, a member of the Little Wound band, tried to discourage it and reminded the Indians that he had always felt there was nothing to the new religion. His efforts were fruitless.

Old Little Wound and his followers had been strong Episcopalians and had been rated as progressive for years. But the old chief rapidly succumbed to the craze after falling "dead" during a dance, "visiting his relatives in the Spirit Land," and reviving to speak and act like an old-time wild Sioux. His veneer of civilization had apparently been rubbed away by ghosts!

Chief American Horse's eldest son, known to the whites as Tom, had been left at the settlement by his father to look after the family stock. Attracted by all the excitement, he soon became a regular onlooker at the ghost dances—watching one day, taking part the next. Barely twenty-four, Tom was far more interested in all the pretty Sioux maids who congregated around the camp than he was in any of the ritual. Nevertheless, he decided that the people were being misled. Even such converts as Little Wound, he thought, were being sucked in by crazy tales of men who rode eagles to far-off places and saw Indians long dead.

One day in a spirit of daring young Tom faced a group of lusty fellows his own age and told them they were all being foolish to believe in the ghost dance. They accused him of siding with the whites, and for a while it was touch and go until Indian police showed up and put a stop to the dancing.

With Little Wound's "defection" early in November, Agent Royer frantically ordered all white and mixed-blood employees in the reservation's outlying camps to abandon their schools and farms and come with their families into the agency. Many whites in government employ were so alarmed, however, that they did not stop at Pine Ridge but kept on going south until they reached *honyocker* settlements in northern Nebraska.[9]

At the same time the agent sent word throughout the reservation instructing "friendly" Indians to leave their farms and gather in one large camp on White Clay Creek, at the very edge of the agency settlement. Like so many of Royer's other actions, this move was ill advised, for such a large gathering of Indians inevitably included many Sioux who were in sympathy with the ghost dancers and acted as their spies in relaying news of the activities of the agent and his police back to the ghost-dance camp.

Two hundred maddened ghost dancers swarmed into Pine Ridge Agency on November 12, virtually taking over everything but the agent's office. Royer quailed at the sight of all the "naked painted savages" and sent a frantic appeal to the Indian Office, again begging for troops.

The message eventually was called to the attention of President Harrison. With characteristic aplomb, the unruffled chief executive merely commented that the Army was already investigating the Sioux ruckus. Until the War Department's findings were complete the agents should "limit their activities" to separating the friendly Indians from the ghost dancers and should "avoid action which might cause irritation." On November 13, however, Harrison directed the Secretary of War to assume military responsibility to prevent an outbreak.

In a frenzy of terror, Royer sent another telegram on November 15 which read:

> Indians dancing in the snow and are wild and crazy. I have fully informed you that employees and government property at this agency are at the mercy of these dancers. Why delay for further investigation? We need protection and we need it now...

[9] Such towns as Rushville, Gordon, Chadron, and Crawford each had their full share of white refugees from Pine Ridge Agency and vicinity during this first ghost-dance scare.

Impelled by hunger rather than bent on mischief, thousands of Indians crowded into the agency on ration day, November 17, the same day that troops under the command of General John R. Brooke were ordered to Fort Robinson, Nebraska, and other nearby army posts. Flooding onto the Pine Ridge issue grounds located on a wide flat about two miles east of the agency settlement, the Indians arranged themselves as usual into bands of thirty for the running of the steers—an exciting monthly reminder of the old free life back in buffalo-hunting days.

One by one the steers were turned out of the government corrals as an official Indian haranguer called out the name of the band for which each animal was intended. Young Sioux riders, armed with bows and rifles, headed the animal down the flat in a whirlwind chase accompanied by the frenzied yelling of the "hunters" and loud cheering from the side lines. Once in proximity of the band for which the beef was earmarked, the steer was brought down with arrows or bullets.

Far short of enough to feed the swelling multitude, only ninety-three scrawny, trail-weary steers were run through the chutes and turned loose for the Indians. Before the last steer was down the raw flesh and steaming viscera—known as the "fifth quarter"—of most of the animals were already in the mouths of the starving Sioux. And before the hide was half off the quivering carcasses the "feasting" was almost done. Little but hide, hoofs, and horns escaped the Indians' ravenous stomachs.

This meager issue was far from sufficient to stave off a fresh spate of trouble for Agent Royer. The ghost dancer, Little (also known as Charging Hawk), took advantage of the shortage to harangue the crowd at the issue grounds. Royer immediately ordered his arrest. In a storm of protest an infuriated Indian mob swarmed into the agency and surrounded the barrack where the police were assembled. Spotting Little at the head of a group of fanatical ghost dancers, the police rushed out to seize him. At once the enraged dancers closed in on them with leveled rifles and drawn knives. One policeman was hurled aside. A wild Indian stood over him, ready to crack his head open with a stone war club.

"Hurry up with them! Finish them off!" someone shouted.

Just then American Horse shouldered through the mob and took a stand in front of the embattled police. Back from his unsuccessful mission to stop the ghost dancing at No Water's camp, he well realized his danger in a group that opposed him almost to a man. He was tall—every inch a proud chief in spite of the cheap, shabby castoff citizen's clothing given him by the Government. With his long braids and craggy face and flashing eyes he was still an imposing figure. His voice came clear and steady.

"Stop! Think! What are you planning to do? Kill these men of your own race? Then what? Kill all these helpless white men, women, and children? And then what? What will these *brave* words and *brave* deeds lead to in the end? How long could you hold out? Your country is surrounded by railroads. Thousands of white soldiers could be here within three days. What ammunition have you? What provisions have you? What will become of your families? This is a child's madness! Think, my brothers, think! Let no Sioux shed the blood of a brother Sioux!"

It was an impassioned appeal for peace and was not without effect upon the crowd. But a moment later Jack Red Cloud, power-hungry son of the old chief, burst through the press and thrust a cocked revolver into the face of American Horse. Long a troublemaker, he had openly sided with the most tempestuous elements among the ghost dancers, hoping to rise to the leadership once enjoyed by his father.

"This is the one who betrayed us!" he shouted. "Here is the man who sold us out! Here is the one who brought on this trouble by selling our land to the whites!"

Jack was referring, of course, to the land cessions of eighty-nine. But his words were worse than ill advised. After the sale of the Black Hills to the whites back in the seventies by old Red Cloud there was hardly room for talk from his upstart son. Jack's own tongue tripped him up and turned the tide. As the crowd subsided and stood back to allow the police to withdraw, American Horse merely ignored his rash accuser and turned on his heel to walk away. For the moment bloodshed had been averted.

That night American Horse and his wife, Captain Sword,

Lieutenant Thunder Bear, and most of the Indian police force of Pine Ridge Agency gathered informally in Dr. Eastman's quarters to seek the young physician's advice as to what might be done to prevent further strife among their people. After handing out tobacco and waiting respectfully for the chief to say a few words, Eastman said:

"There is only one thing for us to do and be just to both sides. We must use every means for a peaceful settlement of this difficulty. Let us be patient. Let us continue to reason with the wilder element even though some hotheads may threaten our lives. If the worst comes to the worst, however, it is our solemn duty to serve the United States Government. Let no man ever say we were disloyal!"

This seemed to satisfy the police. After another ceremonial smoke they trooped out and went back to their quarters. Only Sword and American Horse and his wife remained. The police captain explained to Eastman that certain young men had threatened to kill American Horse while he was asleep in his tent. His friends had persuaded him and his wife to ask the doctor's hospitality a few days until things quieted down. Eastman at once showed Mrs. American Horse to the dispensary and told the couple they might sleep there. At that moment three strokes of the agency office bell sounded, summoning the doctor to the office.

Royer had also called in the Reverend Mr. Cook. And the chief clerk, second-in-command to the agent, and a visiting inspector were already on hand. The three white men viewed the day's events with the utmost alarm.

"You see, Doctor," Royer said, addressing his remarks to Eastman, "the occurrence today was planned with remarkable accuracy, so that even our alert police were taken entirely by surprise and readily overpowered. What will be the sequel we cannot tell, but we must be prepared for anything. I shall be glad to have your views."

Eastman told him that he did not believe there was any widespread plot or deliberate intention on the part of the Sioux to make war upon the whites. On the other hand, he argued, if troops were called in the ghost dancers would almost certainly accept their arrival as a challenge to fight. Once placed on the defensive, members of the cult might be tempted to commit warlike acts.

Cook agreed with the doctor's analysis.

But Royer seemed caught in a turmoil of indecision. Impulsively he called in Captain Sword, Lieutenant Thunder Bear, and Chief American Horse. Their opinion was in accord with that of the officials: the lives and property of government employees, as well as friendly Indians, should be safeguarded by calling for soldiers without delay.

As it turned out, Royer's conference had been a needless formality. The agent had telegraphed earlier to nearby Fort Robinson for troops before making a pretense of consulting the Indians. The Army having at last decided on positive action, soldiers were even now on their way to Pine Ridge Agency.

Old-time Sioux still recall with amusement the headlong flight on the following day (November 18) of "Young-Man-Afraid-of-His-Indians." They tell gleefully of his mad dash in his buckboard across the reservation's south line into Nebraska and the disappearance of both man and vehicle in a great cloud of dust.

Other eyewitnesses in neighboring Rushville, Nebraska, have filled in on that end of the story. Agent Royer's dramatic whirl through the town's wide dirt main street with his team at a dead run and coated with lather is remembered to this day. All the way south from the agency, he is said to have shouted to everyone he met that the Sioux had "broken loose" and all whites would surely be murdered.

A day later he rode back up to Pine Ridge Agency with the troops from Fort Robinson. On paper he was still the agent. But actual control of the reservation had passed into the less tenuous hands of the Army, a move which plunged the maddened Sioux into a final desperate war against the whites.

Winter 1890

THE winter of 1890 was a time of flaring passions and raging violence, but it was also a time of stark despair. With the waning of autumn, death was close at hand.

All through the dark fall days, while storm clouds gathered across the Dakotas, Catherine Weldon clung desperately to her tear-dimmed little dream of a better world for the Sioux. Isolated at the Parkin ranch, she grew increasingly discouraged. With his life in dire peril, Sitting Bull no longer dared risk a visit to the Cannonball. Not even the friendliest Blackfoot Sioux or Yanktonnai would bother now to come and see "the lady from the East" who had no further part in the grim struggle that McLaughlin had fostered among the tribes. Mrs. Weldon had only her young son, Christie, at her side to give her a small boy's meager comfort.

The end came unexpectedly. On one of his many rambling solitary excursions along the riverbank, Christie stepped on a rusty nail which pierced shoe leather to lacerate and infect his right foot. The wound stubbornly refused to heal. Mrs. Parkin and other neighbors tried to help but the injured foot grew worse. At the urging of the white women, Mrs. Weldon reluctantly gave up her last toehold in the Indian country and took Christie out to the Cannonball landing to catch a down-river steamer for Pierre where she might get medical attention for the boy.

On board the boat Christie went into spasms of lockjaw poisoning. The steamer went aground on a sand bar opposite Pierre, and neither mother nor son could reach land. There, on an antiquated river craft stranded on the wide Missouri, the boy died.

Catherine Weldon's grief was obsessive. She wrote copiously of her sorrow to Sitting Bull on black-bordered stationery:

> If he had died on the Cannonball, I should be more content; for then I would have buried him there & remained near my Indians. . . . Now I am far from all my Dakota [Sioux] friends, & from you, and my only child gone too. Nothing left to me. . . .

Alone, no longer affluent, in fact reduced to poverty, the widow confessed she wished to live no longer. In another grief-laden letter to Sitting Bull she implored him:

> And if your prayers to the Great Spirit are heard, pray to him to give me a speedy death, that my heart may find peace. . . .

Death was often on Sitting Bull's mind as the days grew shorter and a wintry haze settled over Grand River. The old chief sincerely grieved for the dead white boy, but he felt even deeper sorrow for Catherine Weldon—his last friend among the whites. She had long been his only link with the white man's world and now she, too, was gone.

An even greater blow was word brought by Grasping Eagle that McLaughlin was conspiring with his Indian police to arrest Sitting Bull. With so many men involved, the agent's plot had been an ill-kept secret. The old chief heard the startling news and was silent awhile before he spoke.

"Why should the Indian police come against me?" he said at last. "We are of the same blood, we are all Sioux, we are relatives. It will disgrace our Nation, it will be murder, it will defile our race. If the white men want me to die, they ought not to put up the Indians to kill me. I don't want confusion among my people. Let the soldiers come and take me away and kill me wherever they like. I am not afraid. I was born a warrior. I have followed the warpath ever since I was able to draw a bow."

It was no surprise to Sitting Bull to learn that Agent McLaughlin had been planning to eliminate him for some time.

"White Hair wanted me to travel all around [with Buffalo Bill] and across the sea, so that he could make a lot of money. Once was enough; after that I would not go. Then I would not join his church. Ever since then he has had it in for me." The old man's thin lips twisted into a scornful smile. "Long ago I had two women in my lodge.[1] One of them was jealous. White Hair reminds me of that jealous woman.

"Why does he keep trying to humble me? Can I be any lower than I am now? Once I was a man, but now I am a pitiful wretch —without country or horses or guns worth having. Once I was rich; now I am poor. What more does White Hair want to do to me? I was a fool ever to come back down here. I should have stayed with the Red Coats in Grandmother's Land—even though I starved."

Among Sitting Bull's listeners there sprang again a long-cherished hope. Back in the early eighties, soon after the Hunk-papas had been settled permanently at Standing Rock Agency, a strange white man had visited them. While he had worn ordinary civilian clothes and was in no way conspicuous, he openly declared to the Sioux chiefs that the United States Government was cheating its Indian wards.

He went on to promise that within a short time—he did not specify the number of months or years—the Red Coats of Canada would come to the relief of the Sioux and reconquer all the lands stolen from the tribes by the Americans.[2]

"Be ready," he had said, "expect us in the Black Hills. We will restore your hunting grounds to you."

And so the Sioux leaders had waited through the years. The hope that help might yet come from the Red Coats to the north flared brighter than ever during the ghost dances. Yet Sitting Bull put little stock in the idea of any whites—even Canadians—doing much to help his people. Moreover, he lost added faith in the new religion.

"I did not start this ghost dance," he told the Hunkpapa leaders.

---

[1] Neither of these women was Sitting Bull's wife in 1890.

[2] Although this white man's identity is now uncertain, he may have been an emissary from Louis Riel whose abortive rebellion in 1885 had many Canadian Indians and half-breeds up in arms against the whites of Saskatchewan and Alberta.

"Kicking Bear came here of his own accord. I told my people to go slow, but they were swept into this thing so strong nothing could stop them. I have not joined in the sacred dance since I was told to stop."

A year and a half earlier, in the summer of eighty-nine, the old chief had told his nephew, Chief White Bull of the Minneconjous:

"Great men are usually destroyed by those who are jealous of them."

There was some precedent even among the Sioux for Sitting Bull's sense of foreboding. Both Spotted Tail and Crazy Horse had been the victims of assassins and the old chief was well aware that many of his own people as well as McLaughlin were jealous of him.

When troops marched into Pine Ridge Agency on November 19 alarm spread like wildfire among the Ogalalas. On the same day a mixed-blood government employee at Rosebud Agency sent out a secret warning that soldiers were on their way there. Within hours a majority of the Rosebud Sioux were swept into the ghost-dance camp on Black Pipe Creek.

Two Strike and his band followed by Long Mandan and his Two Kettle Sioux from Little White River quickly came under Short Bull's growing influence. Many of these Indians were not ghost dancers nor even active sympathizers but had fled their farms and cabins in panic at the thought of soldiers marching into their domain. They realized all too well how little the white men and their armies were to be trusted. Once they heard the report of troops coming to Rosebud Agency was untrue, most of them might have returned to their homes had not certain ghost-dance fanatics threatened to kill them if they attempted to leave.

Driving great herds of ponies and cattle before them, their wagons and pony drags piled high with tepees and winter clothing, several thousand Brûlés and Two Kettle Sioux began the move west to Pass Creek. The time was close at hand, Short Bull kept telling them, for the coming of the new earth and the long-promised destruction of the white race.

The presence of soldiers at Pine Ridge Agency had a disquieting effect throughout the reservation. Many Sioux who had obeyed Royer's instructions to camp near the agency now struck out across the hills to join the so-called hostile camps. Actuated by fear of the troops rather than by any outright hostility toward whites in general, the majority of the Ogalala tribe was "out"—beyond the present control of the agent.

Of the various chiefs whose bands remained camped close to the agency only American Horse was an open ally of the authorities. No Water, He Dog, Yellow Bear, and Four Bears were siding with the ghost dancers, while old Red Cloud and Red Shirt were ostentatiously on the fence and not taking sides.

American Horse's loyalty to the Government meant little at this point. His life had repeatedly been threatened and he seldom ventured away from the accommodations provided for him in Eastman's quarters.

Plenty Bear, an old-time friendly Indian who lived at Wounded Knee twenty-five miles northeast of the agency, came in with an alarming report for Agent Royer. Some three hundred and sixty-four lodges, representing more than two thousand Sioux under Chief Big Road, had resumed the ghost dance with many warlike accompaniments. Armed with rifles, their muslin shirts crisscrossed with full cartridge belts, the dancers were decreeing vengeance upon the whites for conspiring to stop the dances. As Plenty Bear described the ceremony, it was much like an old war dance with many of the dancers vowing to resist further interference even if it "cost the last drop of their heart's blood."

Wounded Knee was dangerously close to the great Brûlé camp on Pass Creek. Acting on a tip that Short Bull was at Wounded Knee inciting Big Road's followers to violence, fifty Indian police marched up during one cold November night and began an early-morning search of the camp.

Short Bull had not been there. But in one of the lodges a policeman found Black Elk, inventor of the ghost shirt, and Good Thunder, both still prominent ghost-dance leaders. Until the weather grew cold, Black Elk had been visiting the Brûlés and there was little question that his recent arrival here at Big Road's camp had helped to spark the new outbreak of dancing.

"We are looking for Short Bull now," the policeman said. "But for your own good I will tell you what I have heard—that soon they are going to arrest you two."

That evening Black Elk and Good Thunder saddled their horses and started for the Brûlé camp. On the way they met Brûlé scouts foraging for stock cattle abandoned by friendly Sioux now encamped at Pine Ridge Agency. With such a large following and so many mouths to feed, Short Bull kept riders out every day, scouring the country for stray livestock. Joining the Brûlés, the two Ogalalas rode back with them to Pass Creek.

Few of the ghost dancers planned on all-out war against the whites. Assured by their prophets that the new earth was close at hand, they intended to hold out somewhere on the reservation until joined by their ghost relatives, at which time all white men would presumably be swallowed up in a great sea of mud or destroyed in a gigantic dust storm. And so, for all their warlike preparations, they actually believed there would be no need to fight the whites.

The matter of food, however, presented an increasingly acute problem. As soon as they left the agencies the ghost dancers cut themselves off from free government rations, inadequate as they were. Forced now to live off of stolen cattle and abandoned crops, the Indians were almost as hungry as ever. Only the dream of the returning buffalo herds kept them content.

One of General John Brooke's first official acts after setting up headquarters at Pine Ridge Agency was to increase the beef ration for Indian families who remained "friendly." And while a number of Sioux professed to be friendly or at least neutral, outriding scouts from the ghost-dance camps were visible daily on the surrounding hills, watching every move made by the troops and on the alert to spread the alarm if soldiers were seen on the march.

The military establishment at Pine Ridge was extremely unsettling and demoralizing to the Indians. Never had white soldiers come into their territory without trying to start a fight. Many

Sioux who otherwise might have remained near the agency were thrown into the hostile camp simply by the proximity of troops. During the first day or so of army occupation hundreds of Indians who had obeyed the agent's instructions to come in and camp at Pine Ridge Agency hurriedly struck their lodges and headed northeast to join the ghost dancers. Still fresh in their minds were attacks by soldiers on peaceful Sioux camps at Killdeer Mountain and Little Big Horn and Slim Buttes. Now they were taking no chances on the troops again moving against them.

The Reverend Mr. Charles Smith Cook, as Indian by blood as any ghost dancer, was sorely troubled. Since the Indian exodus already included many members of his own congregation, the rector used every available means to persuade his Episcopal families to remain at the agency. Other missionaries were busy at their respective churches, making similar efforts among their own converts. But one after another these Christian Indians turned deaf ears to the pleas of the churchmen. Nothing the missionaries said seemed to have much effect. Bishop W. H. Hare, Episcopal head of the diocese which included Pine Ridge, was on hand to lend his support, but neither rector nor bishop was able to persuade many Sioux into staying on.

Lone Eagle's daughter Lucy was a convert of whom Cook was especially proud. Although both her parents had been swept into the ghost-dance cult, the young girl had come faithfully to church and had been confirmed the previous summer by Bishop Hare himself. When it was apparent that her life among her own people was becoming increasingly difficult, other Indian members of the congregation hinted that a white man might have something to do with the situation, for the girl, delicately pretty, never failed to draw stares from storekeepers, agency employees, and other whites around the settlement.

Then Cook heard a rumor which explained much—if true. Lone Eagle's lodge in the ghost-dance camp was often a rendezvous for the men and women who fashioned the mystic shirts. At first Lucy had protested. Then she had attempted to join in the work. But now that her father's people were flocking to join the Brûlés, Lucy's mother took a firm stand against her daughter.

"My daughter," she said solemnly, "you must not join in the ghost dance. You belong to the white man's church; you believe in the white man's religion. The ghost dance belongs only to the Indian way of life. It has nothing to do with the white man's church. You cannot dance with us. You must not come."

And the girl had obediently folded up the unbleached muslin she was making into a ghost dress and put it away. . . .

Then came the day when the Indians about to leave the agency filed into the rector's study behind the Episcopal church to bid Cook a fond farewell. Under the influence of the ghost-dance doctrine, many believed that the rector would perish with the whites when the new world came and that they would never see him again.

With Mr. Cook's visitors Lucy entered the study unobtrusively, carrying a small rag bundle. Calmly deliberate, she opened the package. Taking out her crucifix and prayer book and laying them on the rector's table, she quietly renounced the white man's faith. Before the rector or Bishop Hare could say a word she was gone— to rejoin her people.

Bishop Hare was inclined to be indulgent—even in the face of such bitter failure on the part of the mission to hold its converts. "You expect too much of them," he told the downhearted Cook. "The Indians must come to it slowly. After all, it took three thousand years to civilize Europe. We can't expect to civilize the Indians in ten."

Overnight the ghost dance became an all-absorbing topic among Indians and whites alike. Mention of the cult was on the lips of people everywhere, and various newspapers across the country referred to it ominously as "The Dance of Death to Come." Unjustifiably regarded as a prelude to war, what little was known of its history was jammed into a jumble of accounts of previous raids and massacres of whites by Indians. Bloody tales of the Minnesota outbreak of 1862 and Custer's stand on the Little Big Horn were revived to keep the journalistic pot boiling.

One enterprising reporter had it that the alleged Indian messiah was really a Ute named Johnson who had fomented a rebellion of his tribesmen in 1878 and had precipitated the "bloodiest massacre ever perpetrated west of the Missouri—the Meeker massacre in Colorado." Such stories were well calculated to create panic among whites the country over, but particularly in regions bordering Indian reservations.

On Thursday, November 20, the Rapid City *Journal* blatted out the alarm that the Sioux had broken loose and were now on the warpath. After reporting an interview with a friendly Indian visitor from Pine Ridge, however, the newspaper rationally editorialized that "there is hardly a possibility of the Sioux crossing the Cheyenne River. It is possible the present outbreak will be entirely subdued within a few days. . . ."

Other sources were less optimistic. While few Rapid City residents actually feared invasion, Sioux raids elsewhere in the Black Hills were expected daily, giving rise to rumors of redskins on the warpath from every quarter. Late in November one of Charley Fargo's wood haulers brought word of having seen Indians riding furtively through timber near Deadwood. People at Hermosa were badly frightened at a report that some one hundred and fifty Sioux were camped close by on Battle Creek, and ranchers and settlers in the area were flocking into Rapid City for protection. All over western South Dakota people were hurrying to safety. Those who lived near towns were driving their stock ahead of them, while many who lived far out were leaving everything behind in order to make the utmost speed.

Fort Meade, fourteen miles northwest of Rapid City, was the effective guardian of the Black Hills, and most Dakotans felt much comfort in its existence. But many citizens privately wondered if Fort Meade and its cavalry would prove adequate if all the hostile tribes between the Missouri River and the Big Horn Mountains were unleashed.

"If Fort Meade ever falls," said Judge Bennet, who along with Judge John H. Burns and Sheriff Seth Bullock represented law and order in Deadwood, "there'll be nothing between us and the Sioux."

In all the hubbub and excitement only a handful of experienced
men foresaw the real-danger in threatening to use force against
the Indians. From the outset the foremost advocate of caution had
been former Agent Valentine G. McGillycuddy, tall, handsome,
mustachioed, and so lean flanked that Rapid City townsfolk accused him behind his back of wearing a corset.

McGillycuddy had just been appointed assistant adjutant general by South Dakota's Governor Mellette, and was the logical
choice to head a "home guard" company mustered up in front of
Rapid City's Lakota Bank on Saturday morning, November 22. He
made a brief public statement, duly noted by the press, but hardly
calculated to stir the volunteers.

"The Indians are greatly excited," said McGillycuddy calmly,
"and any attempt to stop the ghost dance—or to disarm them—
will result in serious trouble."

While towns in the Black Hills were organizing militia, settlers
in northwest Nebraska were going to greater lengths and "forting
up." Such outposts as Fort Robinson and Fort Niobrara did not
seem handy enough for comfort in case of an all-out Indian attack,
so the homesteaders built a civilian stronghold called Fort Nendle
because of its location on Will Nendle's quarter-section spread.

Situated fifteen miles south of Pine Ridge Agency in the Wolf
Creek region of Nebraska's Sheridan County, the soddy "fort"
was actually an enlarged cyclone cellar used for storing potatoes.
Cut through with gun ports and roofed over with logs and sod,
the earth walls rose only a few feet above ground level, providing
a huge cave into which many people could be crowded. *Honyocker*
women and children could thus be safely sheltered while their
menfolk blazed away at marauding Indians through the gun ports.

Needless to say, no Indians ever came near such an impregnable
structure, although it was occupied almost nightly by homesteaders and their families all through the winter of 1890–91. One
moonlit night a general alarm went up and settlers flocked in
from miles around when a flighty *honyocker* on night watch mistook a clump of trees for a band of stealthy redskins.

Such Indian scares were frequent these days throughout the

frontier. An influx of some six hundred thousand homesteaders to Nebraska alone between 1880 and 1890 brought in many impressionable people who readily blamed the once warlike Sioux for countless acts no Indian would have been foolish enough to commit.

Sarah Finch, wife of a homesteader in Custer County, Nebraska, was often left alone on an isolated ranch. When an unaccountable blight caused her flock of chickens to lose their feathers, she made up a wild story that a Sioux war party had raided the farm with the express purpose of picking her fowl clean. Knowing that Indians often had a sweet tooth and craved sugar, anxious homesteader Finch helped his wife prepare a box of sugar well mixed with strychnine. Sarah Finch, ready at an instant to offer it to some unsuspecting Sioux, carried the box on her person for nearly three years!

Indians sometimes rode through the Nebraska sand hills, usually hunting for the rare prongbuck or deer that might have escaped the *honyockers'* guns. Normally the errand was fully authorized by the agent, but an exception was the case of No Flesh, an aging Ogalala chief, who occasionally strayed off the reservation and inspected the homesteads out of simple curiosity.

John Peterson, shoemaker turned rancher, was out rounding up cattle when No Flesh paid Peterson's young bride, Mathilda, an unexpected visit. The girl was busily making doughnuts for her husband and failed to notice No Flesh's soundless entrance into the farmhouse kitchen. She was so startled to see the old chief sitting comfortably in her home that she dropped a hot doughnut which rolled, sizzling, across the floor to No Flesh's moccasined feet.

Thinking it a novel way to offer him food, the chief bent over and reached for the doughnut, drew his hand back in a flash of pain, and crammed his fingers into his mouth to ease the burn of hot grease. Suddenly he found that this strange white farm woman was offering him a new, untried sort of culinary excellence. Intrigued by the taste, he kept touching the doughnut and licking his fingers.

New to the prairie and frightened by the old Indian's appear-ance, the young bride kept feeding the hungry chief as long as she had flour and lard. When Peterson returned to the ranch late that afternoon, No Flesh was still sitting there in the kitchen, eating Mathilda's delicious doughnuts.

No Flesh seriously made John Peterson a proposition: the chief would trade his own three wives for Mathilda. The rancher jok-ingly agreed and, as the chief departed, dismissed the matter.

Several days later No Flesh, accompanied by half-a-dozen war-riors and three downcast elderly Indian women, returned to the Peterson homestead. A frightened glimpse of the Sioux convinced Mattie that the chief was determined to carry out his end of the bargain. Dashing madly out of the house, she sprinted, terror-stricken, to the nearest neighbor's half a mile away. His ardor sharpened by hunger pangs, No Flesh kicked his pony into a lope and chased Mattie across the open prairie.

"Make trade!" he shouted, "Make trade!"

The terrified girl arrived at the neighboring homestead bare seconds ahead of the old chief and his strung-out followers. It re-quired a lot of palaver on the part of hastily summoned John Peterson to talk No Flesh into keeping the wife situation *status quo;* and only after Mattie agreed to make lots of doughnuts and had passed them around to all the Indians was the old chief paci-fied.

Citizens of Mandan, North Dakota, thirty-five miles north of the Cannonball River which marked the northern boundary of Standing Rock Reservation, were so fearful of an Indian attack that they took over a large coal mine as a place of retreat. Only a mile or so from town and well stocked with provisions and am-munition, the mine was considered a public refuge to which the residents were ready to flee at the first onset of the dreaded Sioux. Tension mounted at Standing Rock Agency when Stewart, the agency saddler, visited a nearby camp and witnessed his first ghost dance. A throng of painted Indians at once surrounded Stewart's buggy, dragged him from the vehicle, and, while vigorously shak-ing him, pointed to the blazing sun.

"See! See! There he is now! The Indian messiah is coming! See!"

Compelled to look at the sun, Stewart was not released until he acknowledged that he actually was able to see the messiah—a statement which greatly pleased the ghost dancers. Free at last and badly frightened, the saddler returned to the agency as fast as his team could take him.

South Dakota was continually having scares. Attending a Thanksgiving Day dance at Pierpont in Day County, a greenhorn *honyocker* was frightened nearly out of his wits by a gang of white roustabouts masquerading as Indians. Firing a few wild shots into the dance hall, the jokers sent the young fellow rushing home to his parents at nearby Bristol. Remembering all too clearly the days of horror back in Minnesota in the sixties, when Little Crow and Inkpaduta had led the Santee Sioux on the warpath, the old folks babbled out an alarm. For several days local newspapers printed stories of outrage and destruction all over the county. Nearly a week went by before the hoax was discovered and the gang arrested for their misguided sense of humor.

Alarms were frequently false. True or not, Indian scares practically put a stop to the further settling of the great plains. As James M. Allen put it:

"News of this Indian difficulty will travel all over the country and we cannot expect any more immigration this way for years to come. . . ."

Rapid City residents had cause to be grateful on Thanksgiving Eve when one hundred and fifty stands of arms and five thousand rounds of ammunition arrived from Pierre for the "home guard." Reports of pitched battles between Indians and soldiers at Pine Ridge kept the town at fever-pitch excitement. Due to "the Sioux troubles" no theatrical troupes were permitted to come into the Black Hills area, and a Thanksgiving Day charity ball was indefinitely postponed.

Guns and ammunition were stored in the Lakota Bank. Requests for rifles and bullets were refused, however, pending the return of Colonel McGillycuddy, who had been ordered by the governor the day before to go to Pine Ridge Agency to "ascertain the probability of danger from Indians to the settlers in Dakota." For the time being, at least, the home guard was without a commander. Stubbornly fearless, McGillycuddy had refused to allow any of the militia to accompany him as he rode off alone across country to the reservation.

News of McGillycuddy's arrival at Pine Ridge spread rapidly through the camps, word of his coming even reaching the ghost dancers. Indian leaders called a council and requested that their old agent be present to explain to them why troops had taken over the agency. As a matter of form, McGillycuddy had to present his credentials to General John R. Brooke, who, as commanding officer of the Platte, had brought in a thousand soldiers in answer to Royer's frantic plea for protection. Somewhat reluctantly, Brooke granted McGillycuddy permission to attend the council, providing a full report was subsequently submitted to him personally.

Most of the Ogalala chiefs were on hand, including Little Wound, who had come in from the Medicine Root ghost-dance camp. Old Chief Red Cloud first addressed the assembly, pointing to the former agent.

"That is Little Beard," [3] he announced. "We know him well. Seven winters he was our agent. I did not want him for the agent then and there was bad feeling between us. But when he went away four winters ago, he said, 'Someday you will say that my way was best for the Indian.' I will tell him now that he spoke the truth. If we had listened to him then we would not be having this trouble now. We did many worse things when he was our agent, but he never sent for soldiers. We always settled our troubles among ourselves.

"These soldiers have stolen in here in the night. It looks as

[3] McGillycuddy's name among the Sioux, because of his sweeping mustaches. He was also known to them as *wasicun wakan*—"holy white man"—the Sioux term for doctor. McGillycuddy had been an army surgeon prior to his appointment as agent at Pine Ridge in 1879.

though they came here to fight us. If so, we must fight. But we are tired of war. We think of our women and children, of our property, our homes, our little farms, and the cattle we are trying to raise. Little Beard, we ask you to take these soldiers away. We promise that one sleep after they have gone everything here will be quiet. We will give you twenty-five of our young men as hostages until all is settled."

McGillycuddy said:

"My friends, I am no longer your agent. I have no power here now. I only represent the governor. But I will take your words to the soldier chief at the agency."

That night McGillycuddy went over the council's proposals with General Brooke. A pompous sneer showed through the general's beard as he listened.

"Do you think you could settle this matter?" he asked.

"I might be warranted in the belief," McGillycuddy replied evenly, "since more serious troubles were settled here when I was agent—without the aid of troops."

Brooke visibly bristled at what he assumed was a veiled slur at the Army.

"You have an exalted opinion of your influence over these people," he said with a touch of sarcasm.

"Possibly, General, but I know these Indians. I have known them for more years than you have days; seven of the best years of my life have been spent among them. They have my confidence, and I have theirs. It is now November. A cold winter is coming. This is not the time Indians go on the warpath.

"I took charge of these people in seventy-nine. I organized the Indian police, had the troops removed, and for seven years we had no soldiers near us—sometimes during harder propositions than we have today—and I won out. These Indians are no fools. I cannot but regard it as a mistake to have run troops in here. Were I still the agent I would let the ghost dance continue. After all, if the Seventh-Day Adventists get up on the roofs of their houses arrayed in their ascension robes, to meet the Second Coming of the Saviour, the United States Army is not rushed into the field to prevent them from doing so. Why shouldn't the Indians have the same privilege?"

The next evening Young-Man-Afraid-of-His-Horses, back at last from his Wyoming hunting trip, came to McGillycuddy's quarters for a friendly smoke.

"Father,[4] fourteen years have passed since our fight with Long Hair Custer at Little Big Horn," said the chief. "The children of those days are now our warriors. They do not know the power of the white men as we older people do. They think they can hold their own—even now that troops have come here to take over. Unless the soldiers are taken away, we chiefs will not be able to control our young men."

It was the consensus among the Indian leaders. At their urging, McGillycuddy arranged for them to meet with General Brooke to discuss the matter further. McGillycuddy was already *persona non grata* around the general's headquarters but nevertheless accompanied the chiefs to the agent's large frame house which the general had taken over.

Red Cloud spoke first, reiterating past events.

"We have not behaved half as badly as we did when Little Beard was our agent," the old chief told Brooke. "Why have these soldiers been brought here, coming in the night with their big guns? We want you to take the soldiers away. Once that is done, we will give no trouble to anyone."

The other chiefs present approved the request with a chorus of *"hau's."* Representing the ghost dancers, Little Wound rose to speak. Before he could speak, however, Brooke broke in.

"Are you a ghost dancer?" he asked bluntly.

"My friend," Little Wound answered calmly, "I am too old for dancing. Whether the story of the Wanekia is true or not I do not know, but it is the same story the white missionaries have told us —that the Messiah will come again. I gathered my people together and told them, 'If it is a good thing we should have it. If it is not a good thing it will fall to the earth of itself. Therefore learn the

---

[4] Agents were usually addressed respectfully as "Father"—*Ate*—by the Indians.

signs and the dances, so that if the Wanekia comes in the spring he will not pass us by.' "

Little Wound turned to McGillycuddy.

"If the Wanekia is not coming, or by his coming will not make us a great people again and return to us the land which Wakantanka gave us for our home, why have the white soldiers come here to stop our dancing?"

McGillycuddy said nothing. After the chiefs had gone, he told General Brooke that Little Wound's remarks "gave the key to the whole situation." The Indians would go on dancing through the winter; when spring came and the Wanekia failed to appear, the matter would readily adjust itself.

"If the troops remain," McGillycuddy continued, "trouble is sure to come. The troops have the Indians badly frightened. But now you are here, I suppose your presence will have to be justified. If so, you are going to have the biggest ruckus you have ever seen on your hands."

At that Brooke blew up. Had McGillycuddy not been representing Governor Mellette, he undoubtedly would have been forcibly removed from the reservation on the general's order. Brooke told him to get out, then sent for Agent Royer. At the general's insistence, Royer sent the following telegram to the Indian Office in Washington, demanding that an investigation be instituted at once:

> McGillycuddy is here abusing the administration, inciting the Indians to disturbance, and doing me dirt. I want him removed. . . .

Next day Little Wound, bitterly disillusioned after the unsuccessful conference with Brooke, left the agency to return to Medicine Root. Discouraged and wavering, old Red Cloud called again on the general, requesting that McGillycuddy be sent to the ghost-dance camps to advise with the leaders. Brooke's antipathy for the governor's representative was now so pronounced that he flatly refused. He would, however, send another emissary—a man of his own choice.

McGillycuddy was in Ed Asay's store when Agency Interpreter

Frank Merrivale wandered in and told him the ghost dancers were asking continually that McGillycuddy come out and talk with them. The two men discussed the situation at length. McGillycuddy explained that he had asked Brooke for permission to go to the hostile camps, but that the general had refused outright.

That afternoon the interpreter was called over to Brooke's headquarters. With Royer's stamp of approval, the general had just picked Merrivale himself to ride up to the ghost-dance camp at Wounded Knee and talk the hostiles into coming into the agency.

Overnight Pine Ridge Agency had become an armed camp. Patrols of soldiers moved constantly through the dusty streets and the nickering of cavalry mounts sounded all through the settlement from the picket lines behind the enclosure of eighteen-man Sibley tents—which the Sioux called "white man's war tents." Two twelve-pound howitzers were included in the armament brought in by troops. One stood on a knoll in front of the camp enclosure, pointing north up White Clay Creek. The other was located behind the agency building, pointing toward the friendly camp of Blue Horse, a one-eyed old Ogalala band chief.

Learning that Little Beard was at the agency, Blue Horse sought out McGillycuddy and asked him to use his influence to have the howitzer pointed in another direction.

"There is no trouble in my camp," he insisted. "That big gun might go off and hurt someone."

McGillycuddy went to General Brooke's headquarters and made the request to change the gun's position, but Brooke shrugged off the matter and the howitzer remained where it was.

The next evening, Sunday, storekeeper Ed Asay entertained high-ranking officers Agent Royer and McGillycuddy at dinner. Wine flowed freely from bottles sent up from Fort Robinson marked "With the compliments of the Messiah." Much gaiety attended the occasion and, interspersed with frequent toasts, were eagerly concocted jokes—most of them at the expense of the ghost dancers, whose chants and gyrations Agent Royer cleverly mimicked.

McGillycuddy sat stone-faced and silent through much of the hilarity, contributing little to the merriment. Unamused by the agent's parodies, he was about to step in and put a damper on Royer's absurd clowning when a knock sounded at the door. Captain Sword wished to speak to the agent.

Only snatches of the conversation could be heard in the hushed dining room: "Gone away!" "Bad Lands!"

Returning to the table, Royer was apoplectic with fear.

"It's come!" he blurted. "War's come! The ghost dancers at Wounded Knee wouldn't listen to Merrivale. They shot bullets over his head. Now they've struck out for the Bad Lands!"

That was not the worst of the bad news that night.

Indian police riding in from Medicine Root reported that Little Wound's followers in the model community were leaving everything behind and rushing to join Big Road in the Bad Lands.

Rocky Bear, a former chief of Buffalo Bill's show Indians, arrived after a hard day's ride from Pass Creek to report increasing restlessness among Short Bull's Brûlés. Having eaten all available food in the district, they were ready to break camp and move west to meet the Ogalalas.

A telegram from Cheyenne River Agency further advised the Pine Ridge authorities that a large band of a thousand Minneconjous and Sansarcs were striking southeast "as if to join the Pine Ridge and Rosebud malcontents." Within hours the various ghost-dance camps would be consolidated into one huge force, so formidable that no army then in the field would dare tackle it.

The most disturbing piece of news, however, was brought to Agent Royer that night by William D. McGaa, former scout and now a wealthy rancher who lived near Buffalo Gap, South Dakota, a few miles beyond Pine Ridge Reservation's west boundary. Traveling alone on horseback across country, McGaa had accepted the hospitality of an Indian family near Cedar Bluff where he spent the preceding night in a tepee full of bronze-faced Sioux. Although the Indians were fully armed, the rancher had blithely ignored rumors of outbreak and settled down for a safe and secure rest among his Sioux friends.

Familiar with the Sioux language, McGaa feigned sleep out of curiosity to see what the Indians might say. After he had lain quiet awhile, they began whispering excitedly about a fiendish trap the ghost dancers were setting for General Brooke and his troops.

The plan of the hostiles, as McGaa heard it, was to continue the ghost dance until the troops tried to stop it. The place where their murderous design was to be carried out was near the confluence of White Horse and Wounded Knee creeks. Here, in a natural amphitheater, the ghost dance would be started. Hidden in dense timber on all sides of a narrow trail leading into the hollow, the Indians could easily shoot down any soldiers who followed General Brooke into the trap. Within minutes every soldier now stationed at Pine Ridge could be wiped out.

While nothing more was ever heard of the plot, McGaa was so shocked at what he had heard that he raced his horse all the way back to Pine Ridge Agency to warn Royer and the soldiers.

Next morning McGillycuddy found Merrivale and learned an item that Royer had not repeated. While shooting over Merrivale's head, Big Road's warriors in the Wounded Knee camp had shouted:

"Send McGillycuddy to us! We will counsel with *Little Beard!*"

The Bad Lands—*makoce sica* as the Sioux call them—comprise one of the most desolate and fantastic regions on earth. Here, between the Cheyenne and White rivers in South Dakota, a great trough some one hundred and ten miles long from northeast to southwest and nearly forty miles wide has been eroded out of the plains by centuries of rain and ice and wind. A chaotic jumble of buttes, alakali flats, precipitous cliffs, and gloomy rattlesnake-infested gorges, the area was long deemed uninhabitable—even impenetrable—by Indian and white man alike.

Some three hundred feet below the surrounding plain the floor of the Bad Lands provides to this day startling glimpses of the prehistoric past. For here, preserved in multicolored strata of clay deposits, are fossilized skeletons of bulky titanotheres—rhinoceros-like creatures eight feet high with tremendous shovel-shaped horns—and tiny three-toed horses and deer with antlers growing from their noses.

Although this mysterious region had long been part of the territory claimed by the Sioux, only a single Indian trail crossed it from north to south, linking the Ogalalas and Brûlés with their northern cousins at Cheyenne River and Standing Rock. Not until the Sioux country was cut up into reservations, however, was the trail widely used. Prior to the eighties and nineties these horrendous wastelands were given a wide berth by the tribes, who often traveled miles out of their way to avoid the area. In 1874, during his gold-seeking expedition to the Black Hills, George Armstrong Custer had called the Bad Lands "a part of hell with the fires burned out." Had the Sioux believed in a hell they might well have agreed.

Now, in 1890, the Sioux were at last finding a use for their hated *makoce sica*. Remote from the agencies, far from white settlements, the rugged, barren land had been carved by erosion into great islands and peninsulas. These high mesas or tables provided almost inaccessible fastnesses where, given sufficient food and water, a wild, free-roving people might subsist indefinitely.

One such elevated plateau was known to the Sioux as the Oonagazhee—"sheltering place" or, as it was commonly known, the "Stronghold." Several square miles of level grassland watered by two springs, the Stronghold had precipitous sides which rose hundreds of feet above the floor of the Bad Lands. The only means of ready access to this formidable fortress was a narrow neck of land connecting it with a larger mesa since locally known as Cuny Table. Barely wide enough to admit a wagon, this tiny isthmus could easily be defended against any enemy.

Pressed more than ever into finding some sort of sanctuary where they could await the day of their millennium, the ghost dancers retreated en masse toward the Stronghold. The Ogalalas under Big Road and Little Wound joined forces near the confluence of Wounded Knee Creek and White River. Before they moved on into the Bad Lands, however, they were overtaken by

Father Craft, one of the Roman Catholic priests from the Drexel Catholic Mission four miles north of Pine Ridge Agency.

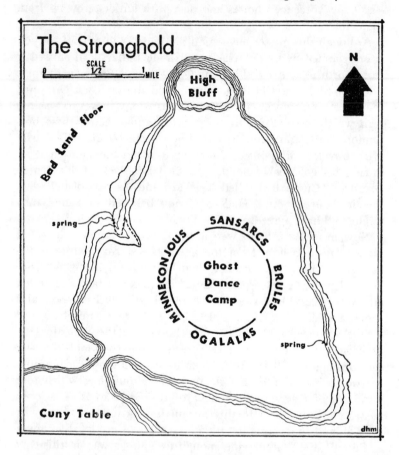

The Stronghold

SCALE 1/2

0 ————— 1 MILE

N

High Bluff

Bad Land floor

spring

SANSARCS

MINNECONJOUS

Ghost Dance Camp

BRULES

OGALALAS

spring

Cuny Table

dhm

Alone and unarmed, the doughty priest took his life in his hands to approach the ghost dancers. With infinite patience he tried to coax the Indians into returning to the agency, but his plea was answered to the effect that a white man's promises were no good. Only a handful of Ogalalas turned back with Father Craft.

The ghost dancers made camp in the Bad Lands that night just south of Cuny Table, where they were joined by nearly a hundred lodges of Minneconjous and Sansarc Sioux from Cheyenne River. Accompanied by Black Elk and Good Thunder as well as several Brûlés from the Pass Creek camp, a number of Brûlé families from Medicine Root and Porcupine creeks caught up with the others. The chiefs were increasingly confident of their growing strength and camp moves were now accomplished in leisurely fashion. The Indians spent another night at Highpocket's place just southwest of Cuny Table.

Next day they climbed two hundred feet up to Cuny Table's grassy plateau—called Top of the Bad Lands by the Sioux. At Black Feather's place near the northwest rim of the table they made camp for the night.

Scouts were constantly out watching for any movement of troops from the direction of Pine Ridge. Shifts of men stayed at the peak of Lookout Butte at the south edge of Cuny Table, from which miles of rough badlands were visible all the way south to White River, some fifteen miles distant.

The next afternoon, following an extended trek across Cuny Table, the Indians at last reached the Stronghold. Here they set up a semi-permanent camp.

The Brûlés at Pass Creek broke camp meanwhile and were moving westward. Depredations against friendly Indian camps along White River were a daily occurrence. The pent-up fury and excitement of the Brûlés was unleashed even more against a settlement of squaw men and mixed bloods at the mouth of Porcupine Creek. Ranches and farms were wrecked, horses were stolen, harness and wagons chopped to pieces, tables, chairs, and bedsteads broken to bits, cattle driven off to bolster the Brûlés' diminishing food supply.

The government beef ranch, headquarters of the chief agency herder, John Dwyer, was burned to the ground. Baptiste "Big Bat" Pourier, famed scout and squaw man, lost seventy-five horses and thirty-eight head of cattle. Charley Cuny, after whose father the table had been named, was completely ruined—as were dozens of others. No member of the community came out unscathed.

Hawk Head and Big Horse, reliable Indian policemen, attempted without success to turn back the raiders. Accompanied by most of the community's inhabitants, they rode in to Pine Ridge Agency to report that their own families had been captured by the Brûlé war party, which numbered nearly two hundred warriors. The leaders had told the policemen:

"Go and tell the soldiers at Pine Ridge that we are part of thirteen hundred other Brûlés, and that from now on we are going to kill every white person we meet. If the soldiers come, we are ready for them."

Near the mouth of White Clay Creek the marauders crossed White River and made camp at the edge of the Bad Lands. Scouts soon located the Ogalala outposts and presently the Brûlés moved on up to the Stronghold.

The great camp at the Stronghold now numbered thousands— undoubtedly one of the largest gatherings of American Indians since Little Big Horn. For a time it seemed that the sacred hoop of the universe might again be made whole as the great camp spread out in an ever-widening circle. In every Indian heart leaped the hope that the old lost power of the once-mighty Sioux Nation, weakened and dissipated by its fatal contact with white men, would at last be restored.

As in the past the tribes and bands camped separately, each group forming an arc in the great hoop that spanned nearly a mile across the central flat of the Stronghold. Camp criers rode everywhere, shouting directions as to where the lodges should be pitched, and much care was taken to keep the tepees well in from the plateau rim so that they would not be visible from the floor of the surrounding Bad Lands should troops approach from that quarter.

As tradition demanded, the camp circle was left open to the east and the door flaps of the lodges also faced east. Filling in both sides of the gap all along the eastern segment were the Brûlés. Next to them on the north were the Sansarcs (Itazipco). On the west were the Minneconjous, while the Ogalalas, most numerous of all, closed the circle on the south nearest the narrow neck of land which led over to Cuny Table. A few Two Kettle Sioux were camped with the Brûlés. Beyond a bare handful of families and individuals, no Hunkpapas or Blackfeet (Sihasapa) Sioux were yet present.

Old village ways were quickly revived as the Indians eagerly shed the thin veneer of civilization acquired from the whites. Wagons stood unused now that the job of hauling up the lodges was done. Horses were hobbled and turned loose into one great herd which grazed inside the camp circle. Cattle were also free to roam the flat. When the people grew hungry, a beef was shot down and butchered. No scrap of the animal's carcass went to waste.

A narrow footpath led down to a cedar brake from the Stronghold's west rim. Here, sheltered by a lone stunted cedar, was a bubbling spring which supplied water for most of the camp. As time went on an additional spring was found on the east side of the table.

The entire camp was on a wartime footing. While men fashioned and repaired weapons, some five hundred women were set to work, digging rifle pits along the approach to the Stronghold on Cuny Table in case a last-ditch stand became necessary. Scouts were sent out in every direction, some parties ranging all the way south to the Drexel Catholic Mission and the hills overlooking Pine Ridge Agency. Relays of lookouts were posted on buttes surrounding the Stronghold. So tight was the screen of scouts that it was impossible for army scouts or friendly Indians to find out what was happening in the ghost-dance camp.

Once settled on the Stronghold, the Indians soon had the ghost dance going stronger than ever. Because of his unfulfilled prediction that the end of the world would come for the white race early in December, Short Bull lost some influence among the Brûlés. Black Elk and Good Thunder, however, were still in good standing. But the prime movers of the ceremonies held on the Stronghold were three Hunkpapa brothers, married to Ogalala women. Iron Hawk, Good Crow, and Standing Elk were all medicine men and began to wield increasing power among the believers.

Kicking Bear, though still active as a medicine man, slipped into an accustomed role as fighting chief of the entire camp. The choice was both logical and timely, according to growing apprehension in the Stronghold. Although more important chiefs, such as Two Strikes, Crow Dog, and Big Road, were on hand, none had the dash and courage of Kicking Bear. Unfortunately, during the brief interim of quiet and comparative inactivity which followed the Indians' arrival at the Stronghold the white man's government decided upon two drastic courses of action.

War Against Ghosts

MILITARY operations in the Dakotas came under the jurisdiction of the commander of the Department of the Missouri, General Nelson A. Miles. The general's headquarters were in Chicago, but as the Sioux situation steadily worsened, he felt his presence was needed in Dakota and made preparations to take to the field.

In light of an official government decision to bring about the early arrest of Sitting Bull and to disarm the ghost dancers, Miles was increasingly apprehensive about recent developments which contradicted his confident prediction of November 19 that "the appearance of troops at the agencies will have a most quieting effect." Brooke's reports from Pine Ridge Agency, regarded by Miles as the main trouble spot, indicated that things were anything but quiet.

"Discontent has been growing among the tribes for months," he said in a masterpiece of understatement to a group of Chicago newspaper reporters. He admitted in the same interview, however, that the Indians had gotten beyond the control of the agents and that decisive action on the part of the military was now imperative.

"The seriousness of the situation has not been exaggerated," Miles went on. "The present conspiracy extends to more different tribes than have heretofore been hostile in the whole history of Indian warfare. . . . It is a more comprehensive plot than anything ever inspired by the Prophet or Tecumseh or even Pontiac."

General Miles attended a banquet before leaving Chicago and unexpectedly encountered Buffalo Bill Cody. The buffalo-hunter-turned-showman quickly sized up the Indian dilemma in the West as a golden opportunity for a personal triumph greater than his spectacular duel with Yellow Hand, the Cheyenne chief, in 1876. Learning that Miles intended to order Sitting Bull's arrest, Cody persuaded the general to authorize him to make the capture personally of the old Sioux chief. Buffalo Bill bringing in the wily Sitting Bull singlehanded would be an unprecedented grand *coup* and would afford Cody enormous publicity for his Wild West Show.

Accompanied by his old partner, Frank Powell, known as "White Beaver," and R. H. "Pony Bob" Haslan of Pony Express fame, Buffalo Bill arrived at Bismarck on November 27. Special conveyances were on hand to take the party down to Standing Rock Agency. Armed with the commission from Miles, Cody had almost unlimited authority. Members of the press at Bismarck, Mandan, and other points along the way were alerted to the momentous event about to occur.

But Cody had not reckoned on Agent James McLaughlin's ingenious opposition. When Buffalo Bill arrived at Standing Rock, the agent attempted to frighten him off. Cody was not in the least afraid of Sitting Bull, for during the old chief's stint with the Wild West Show in eighty-five he had gotten to know him well— well enough to realize that McLaughlin's own petty jealousy was behind the scare. Aware of Sitting Bull's weakness for sweets, Buffalo Bill bought a wagonload of candy and other presents at the local trading post. He neglected, however, to make request for a military escort from Fort Yates, an oversight construed by the officers of the garrison as a deliberate attempt to keep all the glory of Sitting Bull's arrest for himself.

Resentful of Cody's interference, the military at Fort Yates willingly cooperated in McLaughlin's plan to prevent the arrest. The agent's scheme provided for several officers, working in relays, to drink Cody under the table in the Officers' Club, while McLaughlin wired Washington to get Miles's order rescinded. In spite of the Army's cooperation, Buffalo Bill kept both his feet and his head all through a day's hard drinking, and was on the trail toward Grand River the next morning with eight newspapermen and a wagonload of gifts for Sitting Bull.

"I've got a hundred dollars' worth of stuff in that wagon for every pound old Bull weighs," Cody told the newsmen when the party stopped briefly at the cabin of squaw man William Presley Zahn.

Neither Buffalo Bill nor his gifts ever reached Sitting Bull's camp on Grand River. Near Oak Creek Indian riders, acting under McLaughlin's instructions, managed to overtake and delay Cody until the agent could notify him that the arrest order had been rescinded. Buffalo Bill reluctantly turned back.

A few days later Running Hawk, a Standing Rock policeman, rode into the camp on Grand River with a warning that the authorities were soon going to disarm all ghost dancers and take away their horses.

"A big fire is to be started here in Sitting Bull's camp," said Running Hawk.

Sitting Bull had long sensed danger. Nothing then stood in his path, had he wanted to escape, but he properly sent a letter (scribbled in halting English by Andrew Fox and delivered to Fort Yates by Bull Ghost) in which he made formal request to the agent for a pass to visit Pine Ridge in order to investigate further the ghost-dance religion. McLaughlin never bothered to answer. He had already worked out most of the details of his own plan for disposing of the old chief.

All through the ghost-dance trouble missionaries representing various denominations at Standing Rock Agency missions made frequent visits to Grand River, attempting to discourage the Indians from taking part in the dance. Despite their determination to stamp out the Indians' new religion, Sitting Bull seldom failed to welcome them to his camp.

One of the last such visits occurred in the dark days immediately following Buffalo Bill Cody's abortive mission. Spinsterish Congregationalist Mary Collins, assisted by a Yanktonnai convert named Grindstone, did her best to break up the dance. Hundreds of Hunkpapas were taking part in the ceremony and only a few broke away to join the two missionaries in a brash attempt to hold a church service in the midst of all the hubbub. As Miss Collins afterward related, "Nearer, My God, to Thee"

never sounded quite so dreadful as when sung that day by rau-
cous-voiced converts against a background of screaming, shouting ghost dancers. Seeking out Sitting Bull, Miss Collins berated
him:

"You are deceiving your people who have always trusted you.
You must go to Fort Yates and tell the officials you will have this
dance cease. Otherwise soldiers will come to kill all your people.
Your warriors will be shot and the families will go unprovided
for. You, Sitting Bull, will be responsible for this calamity. You
must send the people home."

Leaving Sitting Bull's tepee, Missionary Collins went to stare
balefully at the dance in progress. One Indian fell rigid to the
ground. Although he was apparently unconscious and in a trance,
she bent over him.

"You are not ill," she snapped. "Get up and help me send these
people home."

He rose slowly and looked sheepishly at the crowd. Seeing him
come out of a vision trance so abruptly, many dancers and onlookers seemed to lose faith in the ghost dance and turned to
go home. After that the new faith began to lose impetus among
the Sioux at Standing Rock.

Sitting Bull sensed the growing disunity of his people. Although he no longer cared whether they believed in the ghost
dance, he began riding here and there among the camps to bolster
morale. Mounted on his old gray circus horse, he chanted over
and over the old chief song he had last sung to rally his warriors
before the disastrous Sioux land cession in eighty-nine:

> " 'The Sioux Nation named me,
>   So in courage I shall live!'
>   It is reported Sitting Bull said this. . . ."

General Miles arrived in Rapid City with a minimum of fan-
fare and established headquarters in the Harney Hotel. Annoyed
that McLaughlin had thwarted his plan to take Sitting Bull
with a minimum of risk, the general bluntly indicated his disgust with civilian authorities on the reservations.

"Not until the civil agents lost control of the Indians," said

Miles, "and declared themselves powerless to preserve peace, and the Indians were in armed hostility and defiance, was a single soldier moved from his garrison to suppress the general revolt."

McLaughlin, addressing a Bismarck reporter at Standing Rock Agency, insisted that he had the ability to control his Indians and did not fall into Miles's rough categorical statement. Miles, on the other hand, openly wondered why the agent had wired President Harrison—no less!—saying that Cody's plan to visit Sitting Bull would be unduly dangerous, yet unaccountably demanded that the military be kept out of McLaughlin's affairs at Standing Rock.

In accordance with Indian Office instructions, all agents forwarded to Miles their lists of disturbing elements among the Sioux. All told, the number of ringleaders whose removal was considered desirable totaled sixty-four. Most of them were now in the Bad Lands. But topping the list was still the name of Sitting Bull—who, although McLaughlin's choice as the arch foe of Indian progress, abided by the rules and asked his agent for a pass rather than leave the reservation illegally.

For a brief time Miles's presence in Rapid City had a settling effect on whites in the Black Hills. Townsmen Tom Sweeney and Richard B. Hughes, representing the home guard in McGilly-cuddy's absence, waited on the general and persuaded him to arm the settlers and ranchers in the surrounding country. Miles complied by ordering his adjutant to requisition fifty needle guns and twenty-five hundred rounds of ammunition from nearby Fort Meade. When this shipment came in promptly on the evening train, everyone breathed a little easier.

People even began to think of things other than Indian outbreaks. A nationwide pronouncement by Postmaster General Wanamaker in Washington declared that Tolstoi's queer work, *The Kreutzer Sonata,* was downright indecent, and would be denied delivery service in the government mails. Schoolboys—and girls—were trying to get hold of a slim little volume published in eighty-three called *Poems of Passion,* widely touted as salacious literature, but of which the critics said, "Not only is this bad poetry; it could not disturb the morals of a ladybug."

Subscribers to the Rapid City *Journal* were reading juicy accounts of the death of Ed Shannon, proprietor of the Shannon Hotel in Central City, South Dakota, who was "shot and killed by Judge Gedding, despoiler of his home, who then shot and killed his wife and himself—and also a highly respected miner who was an innocent bystander."

More sedate enjoyment was offered to *Journal* readers in the serialized version of Edgar Wakeman's *Wanderings Around the British Isles.* The truly adventurous might answer ads extolling the virtues of *Heroes of the Dark Continent* by J. W. Buel—"the *only* new book on explorer Henry M. Stanley." Or taste might run to a gory recital of *The Horrors of the Johnstown Flood* of eighty-nine or a frameable engraving of the brand-new battleship, U.S.S. *Maine.*

Sooner or later, however, local talk got back to the Indian situation. Deacon Sieble shocked the entire community by saying, "If the Indians killed all the missionaries at Pine Ridge it wouldn't really be much of a loss now, would it? In fact, if it came close to satisfying the Sioux, it would be a mighty cheap settlement!"

Many citizens were beginning to think the Indian scare was just about over, in spite of the Census Bureau's unsupported claim that at least twenty people had been killed by the hostiles in November alone. Miles's headquarters issued a report from General Brooke in Pine Ridge that a punitive cavalry expedition slated to round up the hostiles in the Bad Lands had been postponed when it was heard the chiefs were talking surrender.

After weeks of tension Rapid City residents found a sort of comic relief mingled with civic pride in Judge John H. Burns's ludicrous departure from Deadwood. Attired in fringed buckskins and loudly bewailing his erstwhile inactivity, the dauntless judge left for Pine Ridge to help subdue the Sioux. As the *Journal* aptly expressed it, "This judge from Deadwood goes when the scare is about over, while our own Colonel McGillycuddy went to the front as soon as affairs became threatening. Enough said."

General Miles continued to marshal his troops with calm

precision as orders poured in from Washington. It was early yet, the general realized, to predict an end to hostilities, and more units arrived daily from far-flung outposts throughout the Northwest.

"Altogether, there are about thirty thousand Indians affected by the messiah craze," Miles allowed. "That means fully six thousand fighting men, and another six thousand that will need watching once active operations take place. Six thousand Indians can make an immense amount of trouble. Only a tenth that number were concerned in the Minnesota massacre, yet they killed more than five hundred settlers in a very brief space of time."

The general stroked his mustache importantly.

"We have about two thousand mounted men. We have plenty of infantry, but you can't catch mounted Indians with foot soldiers. These Indians are better armed now than they ever were, and their supply of horses is all that could be desired."

Then Miles went on to take another slap at the bungled mishandling of Indian affairs by corruptible civilians.

"The Sioux have been starved into fighting," he said, "rather than starve peaceably."

Troop dispositions as established by General Miles in the Dakotas were as follows: Lieutenant Colonel W. F. Drum commanded the small regular garrison at Fort Yates next to Standing Rock Agency; seven companies of the Seventh United States Infantry, under Colonel H. C. Merriam, were placed along Cheyenne River to restrain the Sioux at both Cheyenne River and Standing Rock reservations; along the south fork of Cheyenne River Lieutenant Colonel L. C. Offley took position with seven companies of the Seventeenth Infantry, while east of him, watching Big Foot's camp on the Cheyenne, was stationed Lieutenant Colonel E. V. Sumner with three troops of the Eighth Cavalry, two companies of the Third Infantry, and Lieutenant Robinson's company of Crow Indian scouts.

Two troops of the Ninth Cavalry with portions of the Eighth and Twenty-first Infantry were near Rosebud Reservation under Lieutenant Colonel R. H. Poland, and seven companies of the

First Infantry under Colonel W. B. Shafter were stationed between Rosebud and Pine Ridge agencies. Colonel E. A. Carr and six troops of the Sixth Cavalry were grouped along the Fremont, Elkhorn, and Missouri Valley Railroad (now the Chicago and Northwestern Railway) between Rapid City and Hermosa. Small regular garrisons were stationed at Forts Meade, Bennett, and Sully.

Miles held the bulk of troops, however, at Pine Ridge Agency or in position between the hostile Stronghold and nearby settlements. Northwest of Pine Ridge were scattered portions of the First, Second, and Ninth Cavalry under Colonel R. S. Tilford and Lieutenant Colonel O. I. Sanford. Farther west, at Buffalo Gap, were three troops from the Fifth and Eighth Cavalry under Captain A. G. Wells. The lion's share, of course, came under the immediate command of General Brooke at Pine Ridge Agency. Included in his jurisdiction were eight companies of the Second Infantry under Colonel A. N. Wheaton, a battalion of the Fifth Artillery under Captain G. W. Capron, and a battalion of the Ninth Cavalry under Major Guy V. Henry.

Friendly Indians seeing the Ninth for the first time were duly impressed with their first sight of colored troopers. So strange were the dusky soldiers to the Sioux, in fact, that they called them "buffalo soldiers"—both for their woolly hair and the heavy, fur-lined army greatcoats which distinguished their winter uniforms.

The most awe-inspiring sight to the Sioux, whether friendly, neutral, or hostile, was the unannounced arrival early in December of an old foe—the Seventh United States Cavalry, Custer's old command. Eight troops under Colonel James W. Forsyth marched into Pine Ridge Agency with the band from nearby Fort Robinson blaring out the old regimental favorite, "Garry Owen." Much to their present discomfort, few Indians could forget that far-off day of victory when the Little Big Horn ran crimson with white men's blood. Warriors had wiped out Long Hair Custer and his pony soldiers to the last man when troops attacked the great Indian camp. But some of Reno's and Benteen's commands had escaped to fight another day. Now, fourteen years later, many soldiers who had survived came marching into Indian country a second time. Alarm spread through the Sioux camps around the agency.

"They have come back to take revenge on us for killing Long Hair!" ran the excited whisper. "We only defended ourselves then, when we were strong and the sacred hoop was whole. Now we are starving and helpless and broken. They may kill us all!"

In many ways the Sioux outbreak in the Dakotas was a newspaperman's war. Perhaps no previous conflict in American history was so well covered by the press.[1] Six correspondents remained at Pine Ridge Agency through the entire trouble, filling a maw of sudden reader interest across the country with a welter of anecdotes and observations as well as carefully censored blow-by-blow accounts of the sporadic fighting.

A cloak of government secrecy had shrouded the reservations for such a long time that correspondents pounced on the slightest details of Indian life and lore. With eager alacrity newspapers everywhere were picking up firsthand, though often distorted, stories relating to hitherto-unknown Sioux traditions and customs. By and large, these accounts were merely highly colored and sensational reports which exaggerated Indian savagery and touted the various military commanders and Indian agents for their "expert handling" of what threatened to be "the bloodiest Indian revolt in history."

Behind them all lay an almost universal ignorance of Indian psychology, as well as Indian Office maladministration. Completely overlooking the deep religious yearning of the Sioux and other tribes, reporters constantly referred to the ghost dance as a warlike ceremony.

Some correspondents went out of their way to tell purportedly funny stories at the expense of the Sioux. "Many Indians object

[1] The press contingent at year's end at Pine Ridge alone included Buckskin Jack Kelly, the Lincoln (Nebraska) *Journal;* Crissy, Omaha *Bee;* Smith, Omaha *Herald;* Charles Seymour, Chicago *Herald;* Brackett, Chicago *Inter-Ocean;* Clark, Chicago *Tribune;* Warren K. Moorehead, Philadelphia *Press;* Charles Allen, New York *Herald;* O'Brien, Associated Press.

to being photographed," wrote Warren K. Moorehead for the Philadelphia *Press*, "as they are convinced no good can come of having their likeness in a white man's possession. They say it is 'bad medicine' and that the white man will work evil against the person whose picture he secures. Those of us who had kodaks resorted to strategy. We offered a sack of tobacco or cigarette to a blanketed man or woman, and as the Indian uncovered his or her face to light the cigarette we 'pressed the button.' "

Although the sale of alcoholic beverages or the bringing of it upon the reservations was prohibited by federal law, army officers brought in a great deal of liquid cheer which soon drew the attention of the sharp-witted Sioux. Members of the fourth estate also came liberally supplied with spirits.

One Omaha newspaper photographer named Morledge had a large flask of acid on hand with which to develop his negatives. The amber fluid had a close resemblance in color to cheap whisky sold throughout the West. A Sioux youth, George Beef Lights, came into the correspondents' headquarters at Pine Ridge Agency one day and spied the flask.

"Mniwakan!" [2] he said. "Give me whisky."

Correspondent Moorehead, sitting in a far corner of the building, was unable to reach the Indian before he had seized the flask and raised it to his lips.

"One swallow, a strangling sound, the jingling of broken glass as he dashed the bottle to the floor," wrote Moorehead in his daily dispatch, "and he ran out of the door yelling and coughing. We were convulsed with laughter, for it was very amusing to see the maddest Indian in Pine Ridge running around the yard, holding his stomach and shouting. . . . "

Many whites at Pine Ridge, members of the press and the military alike, were convinced that old Chief Red Cloud was secretly a prime mover in the outbreak. His former power as a war leader was brought up time and again, and the only war ever lost by the United States, Red Cloud's War on the Bozeman

---

[2] "Holy water"—the Sioux word for whisky.

Trail from 1866 to 1868, was reviewed by a number of correspondents. Though blind and decrepit, the old man talked freely of his early exploits and provided a lot of good copy for Eastern newspapers. Nearly every day he received newsmen in his big frame house from which the faded American flag usually fluttered.

Interviews with the old chief invariably furnished information to the effect that he was the leader of his people and always wanted them to behave. When word came to Pine Ridge that General George Crook had died, Red Cloud actually wept.

"He never lied to us," said the old chief. "His words always gave the people hope."

One visitor more perspicacious than others, however, quoted Red Cloud as saying that he thought the soldiers had come to Pine Ridge to burn his house; he could not turn some four hundred ponies out of his big corral for fear the troops might steal them. Such evidence of distrust gave added credence to the idea he was not altogether friendly. Not until correspondents began to quiz former Agent McGillycuddy were their suspicions somewhat allayed.

"Take it from me, gentlemen," McGillycuddy told the press, "old Red Cloud is still full of mischief, but has little influence on the ghost dancers. I predict that a Cheyenne River Sioux named Kicking Bear will be their top fighting leader in a last-ditch stand in the Bad Lands."

McGillycuddy's ominous prediction was well grounded, but he somewhat underestimated Red Cloud. The chief of the Ogalalas was not entirely without influence in the hostile camp. With the old man's connivance, Father Jutz of the Drexel Catholic Mission was able to penetrate the screen of hostile scouts and coax some of the chiefs among the ghost dancers to come into the agency for peace talks with General Brooke. Details of the priest's journey into the Bad Lands have not been preserved. Black Elk and others who were at the Stronghold recalled years later that a Black Robe from the Catholic mission had come to their camp

outposts and managed to persuade a number of hostile leaders
to go back with him.

On December 7 these chiefs, accompanied by many ghost
dancers, rode into Pine Ridge Agency. It was one of the last war
parades of the Sioux Nation, a show of force which caused high
excitement at the agency.

Leading the procession, a mounted warrior carried a white flag
of truce. Sub-chiefs Turning Bear, High Pine, Big Turkey, Big
Bad Horse, and Bull Dog followed, all armed with Winchesters
and decorated with war paint and feathers. Behind them rode a
group of chiefs and warriors dressed for war in fine old Sioux
costumes. A novel feature of their attire, however, were the
gaudy ghost shirts and capes. Bunches of eagle feathers were
tied into the manes and tails of their mounts, half-wild ponies
daubed with painted symbols.

Bringing up the rear was Chief Two Strike, the most prominent leader in the procession. He was seated with Father Jutz
in a dilapidated old buggy and surrounded by an honor guard
of four fierce-looking Brûlé warriors who rode along beside the
rig.

This warlike cavalry moved boldly through the agency settlement and reined up in front of General Brooke's headquarters.
They leaped to the ground, tied their ponies to trees, and entered the building for the council.

Brooke opened the powwow without delay, then went into a
tedious two-hour rigmarole of pompous statements on behalf of
the Grandfather (President Harrison) in Washington. Insisting
that the soldiers had not come to fight but to protect the settlers
and preserve the peace, the general finally suggested the Indians
come in and camp peaceably at Wounded Knee where they could
see him often and might even serve as scouts in his army.

Turning Bear rose to reply. He said it would be a bad thing
for the ghost dancers to come any nearer the agency since there
was insufficient water and grass for their horses. He could not
understand how the young men could be employed as scouts unless there was an enemy to be watched. He wondered who the

general regarded as such an enemy. Furthermore, Turning Bear explained that many of the old folks at the Stronghold no longer had horses. If they came in to camp near the agency, the Government would have to provide horses and wagons to haul in their lodges.

The council settled little but demonstrated the fact that Two Strike and other leaders were clearly anxious to bring their bands into the agency and come to terms with the Government—yet were held back by their fear of the ghost dancers, who threatened to kill them if they left the Stronghold. It was further apparent that a majority of the Indians in the hostile camp had begun to suspect they were being deceived by the prophets of the ghost-dance cult.

Brooke pressed home an immediate advantage in having the Quartermaster Department issue boxes of army hardtack and other rations to Two Strike and his cohorts. In a spirit of renewed friendliness, the peace delegation joined in a spontaneous circle dance with Sioux women from the friendly camps near the agency.

For an hour or so the dancing continued. Then several ghost dancers in the crowd decided to convince the waverers that troops had no power to harm true believers. A fanatic named Porcupine,[3] appropriately garbed in a ghost shirt made of tattered canvas, invited several warriors to fire their Winchesters at him. He stood in the center of a circle of Indians while the warriors blazed away. At the first discharge a bullet caught him in the thigh. Declaring that he was not injured in spite of his bleeding profusely, the ghost dancers would not permit the onlookers to give him any assistance. Porcupine was carried off to a lodge in the friendly camp, and it was rumored that he would soon be as good as new.

The demonstration proved disillusioning, however, and Porcupine as well as many spectators grew increasingly suspicious of the bullet-resisting power of the ghost shirts. Their friendly

[3] Not to be confused with the Cheyenne healer.

celebrating dampened by this blood letting, the peace delegation retraced their steps north to the Bad Lands.

A growing uneasiness gripped the Indians at the Stronghold. Seeds of dissension, sown during the peace talk at Pine Ridge Agency, began to bear fruit as Two Strike challenged Short Bull's tenuous hold on the Brûlés. Adding to the increasing contention between the factions was an unheralded visit to the hostile camp by a group of brave young men from the friendly bands headed by Louis Shangraux, a mixed-blood, and Chief No Neck. Closely following the peace conference, the move was well calculated by General Brooke to urge wavering chiefs to bring their bands in to the agency.

When Shangraux's party reached the camp, an unruly ghost dance was in progress, a ceremony that continued without letup for nearly thirty hours. Finally the chiefs declared a recess to hear what Shangraux and No Neck had to say.

Backed by Kicking Bear, Black Elk, and others, Short Bull answered the friendly Indians' overtures with a violent harangue.

"My followers will not give up this sacred dance!" he shouted. "None of them will move to the agency. They know better than to trust the two-tongued white men who cannot open their mouths without saying lies. Once they move to the agency they know the soldiers will take away their ponies and guns, and throw them all in the jailhouse—as they did to Crazy Horse when they killed him!"

He paused, knowing that his listeners well remembered the treacherous murder of the great Ogalala chief. Then he went on to say that the Government was not likely to let the ghost dancers go unpunished for stealing cattle from friendly Indians and plundering the mixed-blood settlement at the mouth of Porcupine Creek. With blazing eyes he faced Shangraux.

"Go back to your white friends and tell them what I say!"

But the mixed-blood was not so easily cowed. He and No Neck and their followers refused to leave the Stronghold unless the hostiles agreed to go with them.

It was now Wednesday. The ghost dance resumed with added

fury, and the Indians danced continuously through Thursday and Friday, day and night. On Saturday morning Two Strike abruptly announced that he was going to take his band into the agency. The chiefs and leaders met in heated council.

Sub-chief Crow Dog, long known for his hatred of the whites, was unpredictable. During the council, however, he unexpectedly gave support to Two Strike and agreed to go to the agency with the other Brûlés. Bull Dog, Turkey, Turning Bear, and Big Bad Horse followed suit. Short Bull met their decision with a flare of temper.

"The half-breed is at the bottom of this!" he yelled angrily. "Shangraux is a traitor! Kill him!"

Several young fanatics rushed at Shangraux with clubbed rifles. But No Neck and his Ogalalas formed a phalanx around the half-breed and Crow Dog. A pitched battle seemed imminent when the ghost dancers ran to their lodges and reappeared seconds later with cocked Winchesters. Crow Dog saved the day.

"I cannot bear to see a Sioux shed the blood of a brother Sioux," he cried.[4] Then he slowly sat down inside the circle of defenders and covered his head with his blanket.

The ghost dancers looked on in stunned apathy, suddenly aware that they had been ready to kill each other bare moments earlier. Some smiled sheepishly and backed away.

"I am going back to Pine Ridge Agency,"[5] Crow Dog said at last, taking the blanket from his head. "You may kill me if you like—to prevent my going. I am not afraid to die. But it is better to go back there now than to stay here."

On December 12 Two Strike and Crow Dog with about one hundred lodges left the ghost-dance camp. Short Bull and his cohorts yelled fierce defiance and brandished their rifles threateningly right up to the last minute. A few fanatics even lashed some of the departing Indians with their quirts. But no shots

[4] Crow Dog's stand was all the more remarkable because of his murder without compunction of Brûlé Chief Spotted Tail in 1881.

[5] Pine Ridge Agency is called Owakpamni—"agency"—or Makagi ska—"white clay"—referring to White Clay Creek which runs through the agency settlement.

were fired and no blood was shed, although subsequent army reports had it that several Sioux were killed.

With Louis Shangraux and No Neck leading the way, the main body of Brûlés left the Stronghold. Looking back from Cuny Table, they were surprised to see a large number of ghost dancers—particularly Brûlés—striking their lodges and breaking camp. Presently three hundred lodges, led by the irascible Short Bull, joined Two Strike for the long march into the agency.

Four or five miles down the trail, however, Short Bull and a few followers turned back to rejoin Kicking Bear and the three hundred or so lodges which remained at the Stronghold. Their ranks depleted, these eight hundred desperate fighting men and their families now openly defied the entire United States Army. With their last ounce of strength and determination they settled down to wait—through the winter, if need be—for the hosts of Indian ghost warriors to reinforce them.

At this point Kicking Bear took over active leadership of the ghost dancers at the Stronghold. Short Bull's temper and fatal predictions had cost him many adherents, most of whom followed Two Strike and Crow Dog into Pine Ridge.

Ranging far and wide for stray cattle, Kicking Bear and a small war party surprised an out-of-the-way beef camp in the Bad Lands between Cuny and Red Shirt Tables. Leaving several badly frightened but otherwise unharmed cowboys behind them, the Indians drove off nearly fifty head of stock. Another bunch of cowboys traded shots with the hostiles when Kicking Bear and his followers crossed Cheyenne River to raid Daly's ranch on French Creek. Thus far there were no casualties on either side.

That same day, December 12, Agent James McLaughlin was informed by Colonel Drum at Fort Yates that orders had come through by telegram from Army Headquarters in St. Paul to "secure the person of Sitting Bull." The agent had already hindered one army-approved attempt to take the old chief, and now he had no choice but to cooperate. He was able, however, to persuade Drum to let the actual arrest be made by the Indian police with troops in reserve, thus saving face for himself and the Indian Office. McLaughlin set the agency machinery into swift motion.

Sitting Bull was guilty of no crime—not even that of unauthorized absence from the reservation. McLaughlin had long complained that the chief would "commit no overt act." The sketchy information given out to the public from Standing Rock, however, alleviated any necessity for concocting an excuse. Sitting Bull's tenuous connection with the ghost dance was regarded with increasing alarm the country over. For the agent, the Sioux messiah craze provided a handy justification for the chief's seizure.

Plans called for an arrest to be made on December 20, at which time most of the Hunkpapas would be miles away from Grand River, drawing rations at Standing Rock Agency. As Sitting Bull seldom left the area immediately surrounding his camp site, he would then be alone and unprotected.

A letter from schoolteacher Jack Carignan at Grand River prompted McLaughlin to revise his schedule. It seemed that Captain Bullhead of the Indian police had gotten wind of a message sent by Kicking Bear to Sitting Bull, asking the old chief to join the ghost dancers in the Bad Lands, "as God was about to appear to them." According to Bullhead, at whose insistence Carignan was writing the agent, Sitting Bull was fitting up horses for a long ride and getting ready to go south to the Stronghold whether he got McLaughlin's permission or not. Bullhead begged the agent to order the arrest without delay for fear Sitting Bull might elude the police.

McLaughlin immediately dispatched an order instructing Bullhead to proceed with the arrest that night, Sunday, December 14. The agent addressed both Bullhead and Shave Head in the event that one or the other failed to get the message.

Other preparations were hurriedly made. Lieutenant Colonel Drum ordered Troops F and G, Eighth Cavalry, with one Gatling and one Hotchkiss gun, Captain E. G. Fechet Eighth Cavalry commanding, to move out at midnight in light marching order. The troopers were to meet the police on their way in with Sitting

Bull and prevent any interference on the part of Indians along the road. The cavalry was to start late so that no Indian runner could give the alarm before the police acted.

The agent took an added precaution. Knowing that Sitting Bull's nephew, One Bull, who now worked as an agency teamster, was fond of his uncle and would fight to the death for the old chief, McLaughlin sent him on a fool's errand all the way to Mandan to pick up a wagonload of unneeded supplies at the railhead. As One Bull confessed years later to the author, he was vaguely uneasy the day before when he left his pregnant young wife, Scarlet Whirlwind, at Sitting Bull's camp. Half Yanktonnai, half Assiniboin, the girl was nearly thirty years younger than her husband and he never liked to leave her alone for any length of time. She was now too great with child, however, to travel the rough reservation road or the rutted trail north to Mandan. One Bull reluctantly drove his team to Fort Yates, reported to Mc-Laughlin at the agency office, then started out on his long haul.

One final matter required the agent's attention. From the Officers' Club at Fort Yates McLaughlin secured enough jugs of cheap-grade whisky to fill a wagon provided with a double-size box. Confident that the Indian police would perform their arduous duty much more readily if reinforced with a little "Dutch courage," he waited until One Bull had driven off toward Mandan, then dispatched another driver with the whisky wagon south to Bullhead's place on Grand River, rendezvous for the Metal Breasts before they made the arrest attempt.

While soldiers and Indian policemen were making themselves ready for the night march on Sitting Bull's camp, the Hunkpapas held their last ghost dance on Grand River. More certain, perhaps, than ever before that the new faith must soon die, the old chief looked on calmly from the side lines.

Eagle Boy, son-in-law of one of Sitting Bull's best friends, was taking part in the ceremony. The leader was Shave Bear, a medicine man who was decked out in an elaborate ghost shirt decorated with pony tracks and rainbows and sun circles. Shave Bear offered to help the dancers see their dead friends and relatives.

Eagle Boy would be able to see his deceased grandmother if he merely touched Shave Bear's extended thumbs.

But Shave Bear's "medicine" was not working. Eagle Boy followed instructions but saw nothing. Losing faith, he went home that afternoon. Other dancers, however, were more fortunate. A few saw their dead through Shave Bear's power. All through the day they danced until late that night, when the whole camp turned in and fell asleep.

Among the visitors at Grand River that evening was McLaughlin's favorite policeman, First Sergeant Charles Shave Head. Sitting Bull accepted his presence there without question, for the Indian policemen often dropped by his camp and many of them were on friendly terms with him—or so he thought. Shave Head had never been close to the chief, partly because he had taken the life of another Sioux and was shunned by those high in tribal authority. But this night Sitting Bull was generous as usual and invited the policeman to spend the night in his cabin.

"His door was always wide open," One Bull often said of his uncle's hospitality. "He trusted everybody."

A mild protest arose from the chief's closest followers—Catch-the-Bear and Little Assiniboin (renamed Jumping Bull by Sitting Bull after his own father). Catch-the-Bear warily suggested that Shave Head stay outside the big double cabin where Sitting Bull and his elder wife, Four Times, lay down on their old buffalo-robe pallet.

"Let that man sleep in the tepee," said Catch-the-Bear.

But there was an objection. Sitting Bull himself reminded everyone that One Bull's young wife would be sleeping alone in the lodge. It would be highly improper for another man to sleep there without One Bull's knowledge or consent.

"Why don't you send that man out here?" One Bull's wife asked, stubbornly ignoring propriety, her woman's intuition sensing danger for Sitting Bull in Shave Head's presence.

"It would not be fitting," Four Times answered testily, and no more was said.

Sitting Bull's son, Crowfoot, and an adopted deaf-mute boy, known to whites as John Sitting Bull, entered the cabin and latched the door behind them. In the darkness they nearly stumbled over the prostrate form of Shave Head who had taken the floor space nearest the doorway. The youths had been busy all evening, bringing in firewood and keeping a cheery blaze going in the tepee for One Bull's pregnant wife. Now they were tired and ready for bed.

Presently all was quiet in the sleeping camp. The old chief, lying beside his aging wife, breathed the sonorous, relaxed snore of a sound sleeper.

Across the river at Bullhead's cabin the Metal Breasts gathered —Indian police who would do White Hair McLaughlin's bidding. Captain Bullhead translated the arrest order for them and read it aloud in Sioux. Long, wakeful hours followed. The police told old stories of war and fighting courage, long dimmed by fading memories. The whisky wagon was brought up from a nearby ravine, and jugs of fiery liquor were passed around until no man thought clearly any more. On impulse someone ran to fetch Gray Eagle from his house which squatted next to Bullhead's. Carried away by the bolstered courage and growing fervor of the Metal Breasts, Gray Eagle and three other men volunteered to go along with the police to arrest his brother-in-law, swelling the total force to forty-three.

White Bird and Little Soldier sat apart and drank more sparingly than the others. White Bird, who was the younger, suddenly became dubious about the night's adventure.

"Suppose those ghost shirts are bulletproof, after all?" he whispered.

Little Soldier merely patted his revolver holster in the semi-darkness. That morning McLaughlin had reassured them all. The agent had stood on a chair in the agency office and gathered them all around him as they eagerly accepted the coarse, ill-fitting blue uniforms and black slouch hats and shiny badges. Then Bullhead had handed out the guns—rifles, carbines, revolvers. Mary McLaughlin was there, too, ripping a bolt of white cloth into long strips which the Metal Breasts were to use as mufflers, so they would not mistake each other for hostiles in the darkness. There were extra rations at noon, and all the police felt warm and strong there at Fort Yates. They were ready for a fight.

Tonight, out here at Bullhead's darkened cabin, with the officers' whisky burning down their throats, it was taking time to build up their courage again. Looking across the river at Sitting Bull's sleeping camp, Little Soldier found himself wondering. He turned away quickly and asked Bullhead for another drink of whisky.

Far away, more than two hundred miles to the south, other Indians were thinking of Sitting Bull and daily expecting his arrival at the Stronghold. By day scouts ranged off to the north, watching for the approach of the Hunkpapa chief and his followers. At night signal fires were lighted to guide the party to the Stronghold. But it was a journey Sitting Bull only contemplated and never made.

Not guessing the true purpose of the fires, the friendly Ogalalas and Brûlés camped at Pine Ridge Agency could only speculate when they saw a great blaze in the Bad Lands off to the northwest. At times the light faded to a sullen glow, then flared again with new brilliance for miles along the horizon.

Old-timers, versed in fire signals of the past, said the blaze meant the hostiles were determined to fight to the death now, and would go on the warpath within one sun—a day. Any Indians who failed to join them would be forever considered enemies.

In the dark hour before daybreak the Metal Breasts gathered around a crucifix in Bullhead's cabin on Grand River. Bullhead himself muttered the Sioux words of a Christian prayer and all the policemen silently crossed themselves when he had finished.

Minutes later they moved outside and mounted their wiry little ponies. With Bullhead leading, they took the dry, rocky ford below Gray Eagle's place at a sharp trot, the ponies' iron shoes striking tiny sparks from the scattered stones. Across the river they rode, forty-three grim-faced minions of the agent, to mass for a headlong, galloping charge into the sleeping camp.

From all sides the Metal Breasts closed in on Sitting Bull's silent cabin.

Bullhead shouted a muffled command. Little Soldier rammed his rifle butt against the latched door of the cabin. Presently it opened and Shave Head stood crouching in the shadowed doorway, his duty done of opening the door to his brother policemen.

Chill morning air filled the cabin, stirring the sleeping Indians into wakefulness. A light flared as Shave Head struck a match. Bullhead, followed by half-a-dozen others, pushed past him through the doorway. A second match was struck. Several uniformed men moved in swift strides to the large double pallet on the floor. Fumbling through the bedclothes, the policemen grabbed for Sitting Bull's carbine and revolver and even his old skinning knife, for none of the Metal Breasts wanted to take chances on outright combat with the old chief.

Shave Head lighted a kerosene lamp, flooding the long room with sickly yellow light. Sitting Bull sat up on his pallet, blinking. A moment later Weasel Bear pinioned his right arm, Eagle Man his left, and lifted him to a standing position.

Bullhead placed an outstretched hand on Sitting Bull's shoulder.

"I am holding you prisoner," he said.

"We've come for you, brother," said Shave Head.

"You'll be killed here if you put up a fight," warned Sergeant Red Tomahawk, encircling the old chief's body from behind with his arms.

"All right," said Sitting Bull calmly, no trace of excitement in his voice.

No bodyguards were in the chief's cabin. Two old men had been overnight guests along with Shave Head, but they quickly ducked out the door and disappeared. Not even Crowfoot or the deaf-mute were to be seen. Aside from Sitting Bull and his captors, only Four Times apparently had the courage to remain. Half-dressed and scornful, she began scolding the policemen.

"What do you jealous Metal Breasts want with us?" she asked sneeringly.

Sitting Bull had slept naked, as was his custom, and now he stood shivering in the middle of the floor with the three policemen still hanging on to him for fear he might get away. A few old tattered garments were in the room, but the chief's good clothes were in the other cabin. As she left to fetch them for her husband, Four Times laughed derisively when Weasel Bear grabbed up a moccasin and tried to give it to Sitting Bull.

"That is my moccasin!" she cried, going out the door.

Her strident voice sounded through the camp as she roused Sitting Bull's two eldest sons.[6]

"Saddle the gray horse, boys," she shouted. "They've come for your father."

By this time people were beginning to come from their lodges, huddled in blankets and knuckling sleep from their eyes. A crowd began to gather around Sitting Bull's doorway, where a cordon of policemen stood with cocked revolvers and rifles at the ready.

Inside the cabin one of the policemen had found an old shirt and a pair of dark blue leggings made from a trade blanket. He thrust them at Sitting Bull, unmindful of the fact that the old chief could barely move, pinioned as he was by the three who held him. Without letting go of Sitting Bull's arms, Weasel Bear and Eagle Man began to force his hands and feet into shirt sleeves and leggings.

"I can dress myself," Sitting Bull protested. "You do not need to honor me this way."

The old chief had often been dressed for a special occasion by admiring followers; it was an old Sioux custom. But the Metal Breasts were merely trying to get clothes on him now, so they could take their prisoner away before the whole camp was aroused. Realizing there was no respect in the purpose of these crude policemen, Sitting Bull grew impatient.

"You could have waited until morning," he chided them, "when I'd be awake and dressed."

6 William and Henry Sitting Bull. The latter was also known as Little Soldier.

Still he did not refuse to go with the Metal Breasts. His sons had not yet brought up his gray circus horse, so he told the policemen to have the animal saddled for him. White Bird and Red Bear were sent to get the mount ready.

Sitting Bull was only half-dressed and the men who held him were pushing and dragging him toward the door. It was no way for a chief to appear before his people and the old man tried to brace himself against the door jamb to keep from being yanked outside in a state of deshabille. Eagle Man kicked his feet out from under him to force him through the doorway, and the three Metal Breasts carried him on out into the chilly dawn.

The chief was completely without fear, apparently, and seemed heartened at the sight of Catch-the-Bear, Spotted Horn Bull, Brave Thunder, and other fine old warriors of his band in the crowd around the door. As Little Soldier expressed it to the author years later:

"It was we policemen who were afraid that time!"

Without letting go of their prisoner, the policemen poked him in the back with their revolvers to urge him forward. Red Tomahawk kept his arms tight around Sitting Bull's chest and Eagle Man shouted importantly,

"Get out of the way! Stand back!"

The deaf-mute adopted son of Sitting Bull came out of the darkness suddenly, letting his excited moans mingle horribly with the shouts of the policemen. The crowd was angry at seeing their chief abused by the Metal Breasts, and it was all the police could do to force their way through the throng.

"Get around Sitting Bull!" Shave Head ordered. "Make a circle around him!"

The police did what they could to hold back the mob, but their path was blocked in every direction now as more and more people swelled the press. Hardly able to move from the cabin, some of the Metal Breasts were already counting on a fight and edged back a little to have the wall of the building behind them.

Out in the darkness women were wailing the tremolo for family warriors. Men shouted defiant insults at the policemen,[7] taunting them for acting against one of their own blood. Here and there a half-wakened child cried. A prominent old warrior, Strikes-the-Kettle, came forward to urge the Metal Breasts to release their prisoner lest they be forced to fight a losing battle against seasoned fighting men. Crawler was even more vehement.

"Kill them all!" he shouted. "Shoot down the old ones and the young ones will run!"

Henry Kills Alive, then a young man, recalled years later that a woman, Spotted Horn Bull's wife, kept up a shrill clamor at the edge of the crowd.

"These Metal Breasts are just jealous women!" she shrieked again and again.

No one ever knew exactly what prompted Sitting Bull to change his mind about going with the policemen. As a chief, he must lead his people along a course they preferred rather than one arbitrarily picked by him. He may have listened for an indication of what his tribesmen now expected of him. Perhaps his actions were inspired by a song his younger wife, Seen-by-Her-Nation, was chanting over in front of the single cabin.

> "Sitting Bull, you've always been brave.
> What are you going to do now?"

The woman was still singing above the din of the mob when White Bird led up the gray circus horse, which was fitted out with a western stock saddle and ready for the old chief to ride. The policemen began to pilot their prisoner toward his mount. Anxious to avoid further trouble, some of the volunteers tried to pacify the crowd by talking to Sitting Bull.

"Do as the agent tells you, Brother-in-law," advised Gray Eagle.

Seeing his brother-in-law among these obvious enemies infuriated the old chief. "I won't go!" he cried. "Get away from me!"

Gray Eagle grunted. "All right," he said sullenly. "I've tried to save you. Now I'm through."

He walked away toward the smaller of Sitting Bull's cabins,

[7] The Sioux language contains no curse or swear words and a man could be called nothing worse than "Woman!"

found his sister, Seen-by-Her-Nation, and ordered her to leave the camp and cross over to his own house.

"Your husband is wrong," Gray Eagle told her. "Don't stick up for him or you'll get into trouble."

She agreed and left at once.

One story of Sitting Bull's change of heart is apparently apocryphal. Certain historians say that at this point the chief's son, Crowfoot, began twitting his father, saying, "When the police or the soldiers are not here, you are brave, but when they are around you have no courage—you are afraid to fight." No Indian informant on either side had any recollection of such an incident, and none of them remembered seeing Crowfoot outside the cabin that morning alive.

Little Assiniboin told Sitting Bull that he would move in to the agency, so as to make camp there with his adopted brother. "Brother, if you die there, I will die with you," he said fervently.

He-Alone-Is-Man, a policeman, begged Sitting Bull to go quietly. "Don't be led into trouble," he pleaded. "No one will hurt you."

Even Bullhead tried to soothe the crowd. "Nobody will be harmed," he said. "We came to take Sitting Bull to the agent. White Hair wants him. White Hair has promised to build him a house near the agency, so the chief of the Hunkpapas can get things for his people whenever they need them."

Shave Head said something similar. It was obvious, however, that the smooth talk was having little effect on the crowd.

Catch-the-Bear suddenly rounded a corner of the cabin, shrouded in an old gray blanket and growling like a bear. Moving swiftly, he tossed the blanket to one side, revealing a glinting Winchester held ready to fire.

"Let him go! Let him go!" he demanded angrily.

He walked menacingly through the circle of policemen, peering into the face of each Metal Breast as he passed. The crowd remembered at once that there had long been bad blood between Catch-the-Bear and Bullhead—since the day three years ago when Bullhead had struck Catch-the-Bear a resounding blow over a sack of rations. "You have insulted me," Catch-the-Bear had said that time. "Look out. I'm going to even the score one day." [8]

Looking Elk, a policeman, tried to restrain Catch-the-Bear, who was his brother-in-law, but was shaken off. Everyone heard an ominous click as Catch-the-Bear pumped a cartridge into the chamber of his seven-shot rifle. As leader of Sitting Bull's bodyguard, a select group of hand-picked warriors,[9] he was famed for his utter fearlessness in the face of danger. He called out a harsh challenge: "Afraid-of-Bear (Bullhead), where are you? Come here!"

Bulhead answered from the cordon of policemen grouped around Sitting Bull, "I am here."

Sitting Bull must have been encouraged by Catch-the-Bear's arrival on the scene. "I am not going!" the old chief cried. "Do as you like with me, but I'm not going! Come on! Let's go!"

For all of Sitting Bull's followers it was a signal for immediate action. Catch-the-Bear whipped up his rifle and fired at Bullhead. The instantaneous flash of the Winchester caught startled expressions on the faces of the Metal Breasts.

Shot in one leg, Bullhead twisted as he fell and fired his revolver—not at Catch-the-Bear, but at Sitting Bull who was trying to jerk free of his captors. Plowing into the old chief's back on the left side, between the tenth and eleventh ribs, Bullhead's bullet inflicted a mortal wound. Sitting Bull was reeling from the impact when Red Tomahawk shot him from behind. Either shot, fired at point-blank range, would have been fatal. Sitting Bull dropped as though he had been poleaxed.

Strikes-the-Kettle immediately shot down Shave Head in a fierce spate of hand-to-hand fighting. A bloody battle raged in the morning's gray dawning as Sioux fiercely shot and clubbed and stabbed brother Sioux. The firing was rapid and continuous. One man after another went down in the dreadful holocaust.

8 This occurred at Lame Deer, Montana, in 1887, when a party of Sioux from Standing Rock Agency had visited the Crows and stopped by the Cheyenne reservation on the way home to pick up rations.

9 Not to be confused with the famous Silent Eaters, a special "dinner club" made up of members of the Hunkpapa Strong Heart warrior society and headed by Sitting Bull.

Bullhead was struck by two more bullets, one piercing his right arm, another his body. Policemen Hawk Man, Little Eagle,[10] Strong Arm (Armstrong), and Afraid-of-Soldier (Feared-by-Warriors) were shot dead. Middle was hard hit in one leg which later had to be amputated.

White Bird narrowly escaped death when a bullet spanged off his police badge. Dropping to the ground, he rolled over and over to dodge bullets until he was able to crawl around a corner of the cabin and shoot from behind projecting log ends.

All this time Sitting Bull's followers were also suffering casualties. Members of the chief's bodyguard lay dead around his crumpled body. Catch-the-Bear, Brave Thunder, Black Bird, Spotted Horn Bull, Little Assiniboin, and his son, Chase Wounded, all had fallen. Eleven Sioux had already been killed and the blood letting still was not over.

Sitting Bull's old gray circus horse, fetched to the cabin by White Bird, now did a curious thing. Hearing all the shooting, the animal fancied himself back in Buffalo Bill's Wild West Show, and sat back on his haunches in the midst of all the carnage. He even raised one hoof in salute—an old act that struck terror into the hearts of the Metal Breasts, for they believed that Sitting Bull's spirit had entered the horse's body!

The diversion gave Sitting Bull's fighting men a chance to take cover in timber along the river from which they poured in a heavy fire on the policemen around the cabin. While most of the surviving policemen were fighting for their lives, Bullhead ordered several of his men to carry him into the house and cover him with quilts. Other wounded Metal Breasts, as well as their dead, were hastily carried into the building and laid out on the already bloody floor.

Moving the bedding to accommodate Bullhead, a policeman discovered Crowfoot hiding under a mattress.

"Here's another one!" he shouted.

The boy sprang to his feet.

[10] After whom the present Grand River Hunkpapa settlement was unaccountably named.

"Uncle, don't kill me!" he begged. "I want to live! You've killed my father. Now let me go!"

It was a matter for Bullhead to decide: what to do with the cowering lad? The captain of the Metal Breasts lay on a pallet, spattered with blood and mortally wounded. There was no mercy in the man. When the policeman asked, "What shall we do with this boy?" Bullhead answered through teeth clenched tight against pain.

"Kill him!" he ordered. "They've killed me."

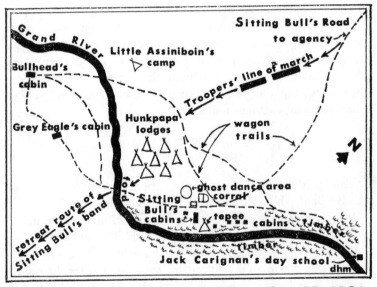

Sitting Bull's Camp on December 15, 1890

Sergeant Red Tomahawk lashed out with his pistol barrel, catching young Crowfoot on the side of his head and cleaving off his left ear. The blow sent the lad sprawling through the doorway. Outside, several Metal Breasts shot him down. He fell near his dead father and lay still.

Bullhead was not yet dead, but he had given his last command. First Sergeant Shave Head, too, was mortally wounded, his belly ripped open by Strikes-the-Kettle's bullets. Red Tomahawk took over, dispatching two messengers to summon the troops, for there was no letup in the ferocity of the Hunkpapa attack and unless help came soon, the police were done for.

By the time the soldiers arrived it was sunup. Minutes passed as Captain Fechet and his troopers lobbed in shell after shell around Sitting Bull's cabin. The Metal Breasts were caught between two fires. At last the police showed a white flag and the soldiers marched into the valley.

Sitting Bull's people hung on to the last, fighting desperately against the hated policemen whom they now considered enemies and traitors to their tribe and race. At the sight of troops, however, they retreated off to the south, three hundred and thirty-six strong, without so much as firing a shot at the soldiers. One rider,[11] clad in a red ghost shirt, daringly pirouetted his horse within close range of the combined force of troops and Indian police. He sang a defiant ghost chant:

"Father, I thought you said
We were all going to live!"

Little Soldier, as well as several troopers, fired at him, but missed. Finally he rode away after the rest of the band.

One Bull's wife, Scarlet Whirlwind, was found by her uncle, Cross Bear, a policeman, in an outbuilding used by Sitting Bull's family as a chicken coop. She had thought the snow too deep for her to run away and she did not care whether the policemen killed her or not. Cross Bear was so drunk he failed to recognize her at first. When he saw who she was, he became excited.

"Run! Get away from here!" he urged her as soldiers' bullets sang all around.

"I can't do it!" she wailed.

"Then I'll protect you," he decided.

Standing in front of her, his revolver drawn to keep other

[11] Little Soldier later identified this Hunkpapa warrior as Crow Woman, son of Red Blanket.

Metal Breasts away from her, Cross Bear shouted, "This is my niece! Don't shoot her!"

For the moment she was safe.

It was late when One Bull returned from Mandan and un-loaded his cargo at Fort Yates. He thought it strange that no police were around the agency, and even the agent's house was dark and quiet in the still of the night. Suddenly suspicious that trouble was brewing, One Bull started at once for Grand River. His alarm grew as he failed to meet any Indians on the road. Holding his team to a mile-eating trot, he planned to go direct to his uncle's camp. Between Oak Creek and Grand River, how-ever, one of his horses played out and One Bull stopped briefly at his own cabin near Carignan's day school about three miles down-river from Sitting Bull's camp.

His worst suspicions were borne out at the sight which greeted him. His cabin was a shambles. As he found out later, some of the drunken Metal Breasts had made a wide sweep of homes belonging to Sitting Bull's kinsmen. All the windows were broken. The iron stove was wrecked. Beds and pallets were torn to bits. A trunkload of prized tanned buckskins had been stolen.

The family livestock was nearly all gone—or ruthlessly killed. Several horses had disappeared from the corral. A milk cow had been cruelly butchered and no meat taken other than her kidneys —a Sioux delicacy. Nearly three hundred chickens had been slaughtered for no reason at all. As One Bull described it: "We lost everything we owned."

Rifle fire sounded from the direction of Sitting Bull's camp. Concerned at once for his wife and his uncle, One Bull drove the team toward the sound of firing. Soon he could see Indians running away off to the south. One man shouted to him, but under the whine of bullets the words were unintelligible.

Cross Bear was still standing guard over the chicken coop when One Bull rode into the fray. Several Metal Breasts leveled rifles at him and Eagle Man shouted drunkenly, "Stay where you are! Come no farther!"

Cross Bear stood weaving against the outbuilding with his revolver raised and ready to fire. One Bull waited an anxious minute or so before Eagle Man recognized him.

"This is our son-in-law, One Bull. Don't shoot him."

Eagle Man and Cross Bear were first cousins. Like most Sioux, they considered each other brothers and regarded their nephew-in-law, One Bull, as a son-in-law.

"Kill me, Son-in-law," Cross Bear told him, fumbling his revolver into its holster. "We're all drunk. We ruined each other here."

Looking around at the wreckage, One Bull could scarcely believe his eyes. "How much damage did you do?"

"We killed your uncle. Sitting Bull is dead."

"Who killed him?"

"The one who killed him is dying." Cross Bear had not yet heard that Red Tomahawk had also fired a fatal shot.

"Where is my wife? Have you killed the women, too?"

"No, she is all right. She was here a little while ago. Look in there." He waved a hand toward the chicken coop. "It was the holy water [whisky] White Hair gave us—that is what made us do these crazy things...."

Cross Bear's voice trailed off as One Bull darted into the outbuilding and held Scarlet Whirlwind tight to him for a long time before he took her home.

Once the fighting was over, the Metal Breasts and troopers began to ransack the entire camp. Sitting Bull's cabins and tepee were methodically rifled and, although no ghost shirts were found among the dead chief's belongings, two such garments were discovered in Andrew Fox's cabin nearby. These were taken by the police and later presented as souvenirs to White Hair McLaughlin. A full-length oil portrait of Sitting Bull in full regalia, signed "C. S. Weldon," was about to be destroyed by a policeman whose brother had been killed in the fighting. He had smashed the frame with his rifle butt and poked his Winchester through the canvas before a young army officer, Lieutenant Matthew

Steele, grabbed it away and later bought it from Sitting Bull's wives.

Everything of value was taken by the looters. Nothing that belonged to Sitting Bull or his followers was protected by the Metal Breasts who later turned over most of the chief's possessions to the McLaughlins. In 1893 the agent and his wife profited handsomely from these when they put them on exhibition, along with Sitting Bull's "death cabin," as part of the state of North Dakota's display at the World's Columbian Exposition and Fair at Chicago.

As the morning wore on, several relatives of dead Metal Breasts showed up. In a frenzy of grief and anger, they joined the policemen in abusing the bodies of Sitting Bull and his followers. Unspeakable desecrations were committed on the corpses. One Indian, aroused at seeing his dead kinsman, Strong Arm, found a battered neck yoke lying on the ground and used it to beat Sitting Bull's head and face into a shapeless pulp. The chief's descendants say that He-Alone-Is-Man helped to bash in the skull of Sitting Bull. They say that Red Tomahawk kicked in the features of the dead Crowfoot until the boy's face was unrecognizable. Finally, some of the troopers stepped in and put a stop to further mutilation.

Otter Robe, one of the volunteers who joined the Metal Breasts before the raid, discovered one of Sitting Bull's wives in the smaller cabin, sitting on the bed with two or three other Hunkpapa women. They all refused to get up until troopers came and yanked them outside. Under the bed Otter Robe found Sitting Bull's adopted deaf-mute son, John. He was carrying a broken-bladed jackknife which Otter Robe took away from him. One of the young man's legs bore an ugly bullet wound, but he showed no pain. Admiring his grit, Otter Robe laughingly let him go. The deaf-mute trailed his adopted relatives in their southerly retreat and finally overtook them beyond the Grand just north of Moreau River.

None of the Metal Breasts wanted their dead to be taken back to Fort Yates in the same wagon with Sitting Bull's body. But Red Tomahawk insisted that White Hair had given strict orders to bring in the chief, dead or alive. So Sitting Bull's corpse was thrown into the empty whisky wagon and the bodies of the dead policemen were piled on top of it.

White Bird and Bob-Tail-Bull were assigned to loading the bodies in the wagon. By the time the bloody job was done, both men were drenched with gore. Along with a number of other Metal Breasts, they burned their uniforms and had to take long sweat baths before they felt clean again.

Riding back to Fort Yates by way of Oak Creek, the Indian police were sober and spoke little. Their earlier elation and *esprit de corps,* nurtured so carefully by McLaughlin, seemed to have evaporated in the heat of battle against their own tribesmen.

"Well," said High Eagle, who had been a Metal Breast a long time, "we have killed our chief."

Flight

M ANY white men throughout the West rejoiced at the news of Sitting Bull's death, maintaining that his removal as an obstacle to progress had been mandatory to the further settlement of the northern plains. For years the chief's very name had been anathema to the development of vast areas in the Dakotas and Nebraska which the *honyockers* feared to homestead as long as an Indian leader of Sitting Bull's reputation still lived.

McLaughlin's smug satisfaction with the success of his project was ill-concealed. He proudly announced that "the shots that killed Sitting Bull have put a stop forever to the domination of the ancient regime among the Standing Rock Sioux."

The agent made a great show of bewailing the loss of the dead Metal Breasts, and a lot of fuss in particular was made over the dying Shave Head. McLaughlin sent a white courier eighteen miles to fetch the first sergeant's wife in order that the Shave Heads might be properly married in a Catholic ceremony before he died. The woman arrived at Shave Head's deathbed minutes late, but was consoled by the agent's promise that her husband's memory would be perpetuated by a granite shaft to be erected over his grave.

White Hair McLaughlin consistently blamed Sitting Bull for all the trouble which ended in his own death "and also the killing of much better men than he was." The dead chief was buried in quicklime like a common criminal on December 17, 1890. Not a single mourner attended his interment in an out-of-the-way corner of the Fort Yates graveyard. J. F. Waggoner, the post carpenter who built his coffin, a crude pine box, later reported that the old man's body had been terribly mutilated aside from seven bullet wounds. The chief's features had been battered beyond recognition and his jaw was around under his left ear.

Afraid of troops and policemen, no Indians ventured to bury Sitting Bull's dead followers. Reverend T. L. Riggs and his friend, Elias Gilbert, went quietly to the Grand River camp and placed the seven Indian corpses, including that of Crowfoot, in a common grave and read prayers over them, thus earning the undying gratitude of those Sioux still loyal to their chief.

By way of contrast the dead Metal Breasts were given elaborate funerals with full military honors. Old-timers who recall those gray December days say that the funeral cortege for the Indian police stretched all the way from the Fort Yates Dead House to the Roman Catholic cemetery a mile up the hill behind the agency.

On the surface the killing of Sitting Bull seemed highly propitious for McLaughlin. Approval of the agent's actions was forthcoming from nearly every official quarter, including the President of the United States. In a statement given to the New York *Herald*, Benjamin Harrison called Sitting Bull "the greatest disturbing element of his race," and hoped, now that the chief was out of the way, that the Indian difficulties in the Dakotas could be settled promptly without further bloodshed.

In a matter of days, however, the nation's press was aroused by unauthorized leaks of information from white sources in the Standing Rock country. Among his own tribesmen at least Sitting Bull had been a great man. It began to occur to inquisitive reporters that his death may have been a deliberate assassination, condoned, if not actually planned, by McLaughlin. With the death of Henry Bullhead on December 19, Sergeant Marcellus Red Tomahawk officially claimed to be the slayer of Sitting Bull. He made certain boastful revelations which indicated the arrest attempt had been only a flimsy veil for premeditated murder.

Moreover, disturbing reports were circulated that a Bismarck merchant had offered McLaughlin the sum of one thousand dollars for Sitting Bull's body. Rumors were freely bandied in the press that the corpse had been removed from the coffin before burial and taken to a dissecting room at Fort Yates. Some newspaper accounts pictured Agent McLaughlin carving up bits and pieces of the late chief's skeleton and skin, and selling them off to the highest bidders. Although such stories were unfounded, the agent suddenly found himself branded as a ghoul as well as a murderer in the public eye.

Indignant officials in the National Indian Defense Association in Washington wrote heated letters to Indian Commissioner Morgan, who launched a full-scale investigation into McLaughlin's conduct of the Sitting Bull arrest and his disposition of the chief's body. Indian Department heads speculated as to what gruesome truths lay concealed in the fact that Sitting Bull's remains had been buried in quicklime. Had this been done to hide the brutal mutilations performed on the corpse? Or was the purpose to keep relatives of the chief from enshrining his bones? No one knew. A lot of red tape had to be unraveled before McLaughlin was cleared of stigma in the minds of government officials.

Local reaction also changed abruptly. Instead of feeling relief, the *honyockers* grew increasingly apprehensive. Fearing they might fall victim to Sioux vengeance for the slaying of Sitting Bull, thousands of refugees flocked to Mandan and Bismarck for safety. Renewed alarm spread across the Dakotas. The entire Sioux Nation was daily expected to rally around the die-hard leaders of the ghost dance to avenge their revered chieftain.

General Nelson A. Miles was much annoyed. Not only was he vexed at McLaughlin's personal feuding with the Sitting Bull faction at such a critical moment; from the first he regarded the headlong flight of the chief's frightened followers as a serious contretemps that might well plunge added thousands of Indians into open rebellion. Much to the consternation of Agent McLaughlin, Miles demanded that the Government authorize the military to take over control of all the Sioux agencies. From his Rapid City headquarters the general watched developments with growing concern.

One of Sitting Bull's warriors brought word of the chief's death to the Stronghold in the Bad Lands. The ghost dancers were inflamed as news of the cruel killing passed from lodge to lodge in the great circle camp.

No one was more infuriated than Kicking Bear. Yet he heard the message in stony-eyed silence, then stalked off alone to his lodge. Short Bull, typically loquacious, began an angry harangue that lasted nearly an hour. While they listened to his tirade, however, the warriors watched Kicking Bear's silent lodge.

Presently Kicking Bear came out and strode to his hobbled pony. Fitting a worn rawhide saddle to the mount, he tied up the pony's tail and attached eagle feathers to its mane as warriors of old had done for generations. Daubs of garish paint, worked into ghost symbols, completed his noiseless preparations for battle —as forceful a signal for action as any war cry. Donning ghost shirts on the run and grabbing up their weapons, hundreds of warriors quickly joined their fighting leader.

With the Stronghold's fighting force gathered around him, Kicking Bear produced a red-stone pipe from a beaded bag. In solemn prayer he offered the pipe to heaven and earth and each of the four winds. His restless fingers felt behind his ear for the tiny medicine bundle that contained Crazy Horse's secret power. In a clear, resonant voice that could be heard throughout the Stronghold camp, he called upon the guiding spirit of Crazy Horse to help his people. Now, too, there was another spirit to be revered—that of a brave old chief of the Hunkpapas, shot down by his own tribesmen made mad by the whisky given them by a white man.

It was a time for action, a holy war against all whites. No longer could the believers be content with dancing while they waited for the coming of the Wanekia, Kicking Bear exhorted his warriors.

"It is a good day to die!" he exclaimed, echoing the ancient Sioux war yell.

And all across the Stronghold the shouts of the believers resounded. . . .

With savage ferocity, Kicking Bear and his cohorts lashed out at nearby ranches and settlements. Gus Haaser, a rider for the Flying V ranch outside of Buffalo Gap, long remembered the fierce pitched battle cowboys in his outfit had with the hostiles the day after word flashed through the Black Hills of Sitting Bull's death.

At Daly's ranch on Spring Creek fifteen settlers were holed up for hours under a withering Indian attack the same day. Three attempts were made by the redskins to fire the ranch buildings and

smoke out the defenders. A brave courier, whose name was forgotten all too soon, rode a wide, circuitous route to reach the
Sixth Cavalry bivouac near Hermosa. Commander Colonel Carr
at once sent out a detachment of one hundred troopers to the
rescue. Many shots were traded that day with the hostiles in the
first Bad Lands clash between soldiers and Indians.

A day later government supply wagons crossing Spring Creek
were attacked by about forty warriors. One trooper was badly
wounded. With seconds to spare, a troop of the Sixth Cavalry
arrived and the hostiles ran away. Following their trail to the
Stronghold, the troop, commanded by a Captain Wells, became
the first whites to scout the exact location and strength of the
ghost-dance camp. Depleted by various desertions and movements
of bands to the friendly camp at Pine Ridge, the number of hostiles was now smaller than Miles's earlier estimates. The ghost
dancers were still powerful, however, and although the white
forces now outnumbered them considerably, they were still full of
fight and well able to give soldiers and settlers a good run for
their money.

During sharp fighting at Cole's ranch on Battle Creek, the ghost
dancers suffered their first casualty. Cattleman M. D. Cole fired a
lucky shot which brought down a young warrior named Dead
Arm, a nephew-in-law of Kicking Bear. Running short of ammunition, the hostiles were forced to retreat without recovering the
youth's body. Dead Arm was buried without sentiment or ceremony on nearby Blind Man Table by the calloused cowboys.

"The ball that made him a good Indian," said Cole proudly
by way of benediction, "struck him in the left temple. He dropped
like a ton of rocks. . . ."

Ominous news came from all quarters as the rabid ghost dancers
flouted the white men and their soldiers with fanatic zeal. General
Miles now had more than half of the entire United States Army
in the field, drawn up around the Sioux reservations. With an
anxious eye on the Stronghold, he watched carefully for fresh outbreaks or signs of trouble. At Lower Brûlé Agency, southeast of
Pierre, seventeen Brûlé ghost dancers were summarily arrested

and shipped off to Fort Snelling, Minnesota, until the scare was over.

Greater tact was required with Sitting Bull's fleeing band. Army couriers out of Fort Yates were sent after the Hunkpapas and succeeded in talking a number of them into returning north to Standing Rock. About one hundred and fifty, however, pressed southwest toward Cheyenne River.

Poring over wall maps at his headquarters, Miles charted their remarkably swift progress. It was now obvious from all reports that these desperate Indians would seek asylum with equally desperate Minneconjous in the camps of Hump and Big Foot. Consolidation of such turbulent elements might well prolong the conflict. Yet the general was admittedly unable to stop their headlong flight.

Within a day of the bloody fight on Grand River, Hunkpapa runners ranging far to the south brought word of Sitting Bull's ugly death to the Minneconjous. Several days passed, however, before the tattered, freezing, panic-stricken Sitting Bull fugitives reached the mouth of Cherry Creek and sanctuary with Hump's band. Hump's son, Helper, later recalled to the author the pathetic and deplorable condition of the Hunkpapas. Half-starved, they were terribly in need of food and warm clothing. Many had frozen hands and feet; for in spite of the unusually mild days, the cold nights had been the only time these Indians had felt free to travel. They had completely lost faith in the government authorities. Their agent had turned members of their own tribe against them, and they all believed that soldiers would soon come to imprison or kill them.

General Miles now considered Hump the most formidable leader of dissatisfaction outside the Bad Lands. After the Grand River disaster, the general was little disposed to order Hump's arrest and run a certain risk of added bloodshed. Instead, he sent all the way to Texas for Captain E. P. Ewers of the Fifth Infantry, an officer of specialized experience and background. Back in the late seventies and early eighties Ewers had been in charge of Hump and his band for seven years. Of all white men, he alone had their full confidence and respect. Relieved of duty in the Southwest at Miles's behest, the captain was tranferred without delay to Fort Bennett.

Reports from the Cheyenne River, meanwhile, were increasingly ominous. Not far from Standing Butte, an old landmark used by the Indians as a lookout, a small party of whites headed by storekeeper Henry Robinson of Cheyenne City stumbled onto a belligerent band of Minneconjous.

"Hau!" Robinson called out to the Indians. *"Hau, kola!"*

But none of the Minneconjous answered his friendly greeting. These Sioux were in no mood for social intercourse with white men. One skinny bowlegged old man, Circle Lame, pulled up his ancient buffalo bow and aimed an arrow at Robinson. Straight Forehead, a much younger man, later told the author how he quickly stepped in front of the excitable old-timer and grabbed his bow away from him.

"Tokesa," he said to placate him. "After while."

Straight Forehead was sure a pitched battle would have followed had Robinson and his party failed to make themselves scarce around Standing Butte. The storekeeper was alarmed at the unfriendly manner of these Indians, and circulated reports all the way from Cheyenne City to Pierre that the Minneconjous were ready to take to the warpath.

When the news reached Miles in Rapid City, he telegraphed Captain Ewers at Fort Bennett to proceed at once to Hump's camp and use his influence on the chief. If possible, he was to induce Hump to surrender, although there was little official hope that such a coup could be brought off in light of the growing unrest along Cheyenne River.

Accompanied only by a Lieutenant Hale and two teamsters, Captain Ewers drove the sixty miles out to Cherry Creek in an old four-mule ambulance. The Minneconjous were genuinely glad to see their old friend, although his arrival was considerably upsetting to the Sitting Bull refugees. Hump was away from camp just then, searching for a stray horse. Helper, just turned sixteen, eagerly jumped on his pony and rode out to fetch his father.

Hump's band numbered about four hundred people. Most of

them were avid ghost dancers and nearly all whites for miles around were deeply afraid of these fierce Minneconjous. At the time of Ewers' visit, however, no ghost dance was in progress, and Hump's people were less excitable than usual.

Hump greeted Ewers with rare effusion. He listened patiently while the doughty captain explained that "Bear Coat" Miles, the soldier-chief, wanted Hump to bring his people in to Fort Bennett for their own safety. The chief readily agreed to do anything Ewers asked of him.

Most of the Hunkpapas followed Hump's lead and accompanied the Minneconjous in to Fort Bennett the following day. The night before the move was made, however, some thirty-eight Sitting Bull fugitives and about thirty of Hump's own warriors, including his son Helper, broke away and stole forty miles upriver to Big Foot's camp at the mouth of Deep Creek.

Once at Fort Bennett, Hump and his consolidated band caused the army no further trouble. The chief and several of his most prominent followers eventually enlisted as scouts under Captain Ewers and rendered valuable service to the military in inducing other hostiles to surrender.

The day of Sitting Bull's death a battalion of the Eighth Cavalry swooped down on Big Foot's camp from an unexpected quarter. The soldiers had moved down the Belle Fourche River from Fort Meade in the Black Hills. Catching the Indians off guard, Colonel E. V. Sumner, commander of the flying column, had put Big Foot's whole band under arrest.

Big Foot explained to Sumner that he and his band were going down to Fort Bennett and Cheyenne Agency to collect annuities guaranteed by treaty as well as to draw regular food rations.

"My people are hungry," the old chief said. "They also need axes and kettles and knives. They need winter clothing and blanket cloth and new canvas for their lodges."

Impressed by Big Foot's obvious sincerity and friendliness, Sumner accepted the old man's words as a promise that he would take his people to Fort Bennett within a few days. As an indication of good faith, the colonel withdrew his detachment upriver.

The band could take its time about leaving and would be allowed to proceed to Fort Bennett without escort.

Big Foot might have gone to the fort with his band to submit peacefully to the authorities had it not been for the arrival in his camp on December 19 of the Sitting Bull fugitives and their Minneconjou companions from Hump's camp. High excitement attended their recital of events on Grand River. Most of Big Foot's followers were enraged and ready to defy and fight the troops if they should reappear. The older people were fearful. The entire band felt keen pity and sorrow for their Hunkpapa kinsmen, and the late Sitting Bull was mourned as a near relative with the gashing of legs and hacking off of hair and other traditional signs of grief.

Word of the killing of Sitting Bull brought fever-pitch excitement to Pine Ridge Agency. Frantic alarm spread like a grass fire through the friendly Indian camps. Frightened lest soldiers or policemen attack them, one party of Sioux fled the agency on December 22, driving a large herd of ponies before them. After trading shots with a sizable force of cavalry sent out to head them off, they turned back to Pine Ridge.

That night fighting nearly broke out in Red Cloud's camp just west of the agency settlement. A mysterious blanketed figure had been making the rounds of the lodges claiming to be the Indian messiah. Police came running to make an arrest. Much to their chagrin and the astonishment of the whole camp, they found the "messiah" was actually a white man from Iowa, a harmless crank named Albert C. Hopkins, self-styled "President Pro Tem of the Pansy Society of America."

Armed only with "The Pansy Banner of Peace," which he confidently expected would guarantee him a royal welcome at the ghost-dance camp, Hopkins had planned to go to the Stronghold in the Bad Lands and preach to the ghost dancers. He claimed to be in Sioux country in the interests of peace and insisted the Indians had misinterpreted his message. Singlehanded, he would stop the Sioux war.

A few Indians protested when Hopkins was arrested. None of

the friendly chiefs professed any belief in him, however, and most of the leaders laughingly called him *"witkotko"*—a crazy fool. As Hopkins was dragged from the camp, old Red Cloud spat in his face.

"You go home," the aged chief said sternly. "You are no son of God."

Next day Hopkins was escorted south across the Nebraska line by a squad of police, and the Sioux never saw him again. His ludicrous exploits were eagerly publicized by representatives of the press, however, who saw much welcome comic relief in the white "messiah." Overnight, government authorities heard from a host of crackpots across the country.

One lady from Utica, New York, claimed to be of Iroquois blood and styled herself the "Doctor Princess Viroqua." With her sister "Wynima," she offered to "try the effect of moral suasion on the belligerent Sioux." Never taken seriously, of course, her offer was negated by the fact that neither her name nor that of her sister was pronounceable by Iroquois who knew only their own tongue, and the name "Wynima" at least was of Modoc origin.

The owner of a Wild West show in New York City, who signed himself Texas Ben, offered to help out against the hostiles. His credentials were spoiled by a dubious character reference: a written endorsement from famed outlaw Cole Younger.

A group of Minnesota *honyockers* naïvely wrote the Secretary of the Interior, offering to organize a militia company—for a consideration. Each man was to be provided with two sound horses, a good Winchester and two Colt revolvers, a three-hundred-dollar bounty, and a salary of fifty dollars a month plus rations and ammunition. For these modest appropriations the dauntless heroes would put down the Sioux outbreak. On sober second thought, the gallant Minnesotans added that they "should have in addition to this say five dollars a head." After all, they reasoned, settling "this Indian question forever" was a large order!

Big Foot was in a turmoil of indecision. The effect of the fugitives' tale of woe on the old chief was electric. News of Sitting

Bull's death at the hands of treacherous Metal Breasts employed by the agent put grave doubts in Big Foot's mind about surrendering to the capricious authorities.

On the other hand, the chief was a man of honor. He had pledged himself in effect to a certain course of action with Colonel Sumner. It went against the grain to think of violating his word—even with a member of a patently untrustworthy race.

Big Foot debated the issues with his tribesmen. Many of his people were panicky at reports that the cavalry was hovering nearby, waiting merely for an opportune moment to attack. The chief ordered his people to make ready and led them in a mass downstream exodus toward the agency.

Unknown to the Indians, General Miles had become alarmed when Sumner reported that he had permitted the Big Foot band to move to the agency without a military guard. The Eighth Cavalry was accordingly ordered to follow Big Foot, round up his band, and hold them until further notice. Big Foot and his people had reached Hump's abandoned camp at the mouth of Cherry Creek when outriding scouts advised him that cavalry was dogging his trail. The old chief rode out to meet Sumner and his troops.

Announcing that he was ready to do whatever the Army ordered, Big Foot tried to keep on friendly terms with Colonel Sumner. The detachment had just been notified, however, that some of Sitting Bull's people had been taken in by the Minneconjous. Sumner demanded to know why Big Foot had extended hospitality to the hostiles.

"They are my kinsmen," the old chief said simply. "They came to my camp hungry and footsore and almost naked. My people and I took them in and fed them and tried to make them comfortable. Even an Indian has a heart. I could not do less for my own flesh and blood."

Sumner then relented somewhat. He detailed an officer to return with Big Foot to his camp and make a head count of the band in order that food might be doled out to the hungry Indians. Three hundred and thirty-three Minneconjous and Hunkpapas were given army field rations that evening as they bedded down for the night in Hump's deserted village.

Next morning, December 22, all seemed to go smoothly as Big Foot's band moved quietly upriver, escorted back to their own village by the troops. Since the Indians made no hostile demonstrations of any sort, no attempt was made to disarm them. They all appeared friendly and amicable.

During the march, however, orders came through calling for the delivery of Big Foot and his entire band as prisoners to Fort Bennett. When the Indians reached their old log-cabin settlement on Deep Creek, Sumner told Big Foot they would all have to return down-river. The old chief protested that his women and children were cold and hungry. It would work a great hardship on all his people if they were forced out of their dwellings again in the dead of winter.

"We are in our own homes here," Big Foot said. "We are where our father, the agent, ordered us to stay. We have done nothing wrong that we should be uprooted and moved to some strange place."

The old chief looked around him at the camp. Each family had scurried into its own log cabin and had the doors barricaded against any attempt by the soldiers to dislodge them. It would be very difficult, Big Foot insisted, for him to persuade his people to leave their warm cabins.

"I have my orders," Sumner snapped. Through a white interpreter named Dunn an ultimatum was presented to the chief. Big Foot's band would be forced to obey the colonel's commands. They would be required to start for Fort Bennett the following morning. If they refused to leave their camp, troops would have to take measures to see that the orders were carried out. Indians who overheard Dunn's interpretation say that he told Big Foot that soldiers were coming in the morning to shoot them all if they refused to go.

Sumner may have been convinced that any attempt to force the Indians out of their cabins would bring on a fight. Aware that the proximity of troops might precipitate trouble and confident that Big Foot could keep his people quiet overnight, t. colonel withdrew his cavalry to their old bivouac site a few mile. upriver.

Some historians say that Big Foot promised Dunn, whom he had long befriended, that he and his band would go to Fort Bennett with the troops the next morning. Indians say that no such agreement was made by their chief. Late that evening, after Big Foot's final powwow with Sumner, the Deep Creek settlement was astir with panicky Sioux. More soldiers, belonging to a column commanded by Colonel H. C. Merriam out of Fort Bennett, were sighted down-river by several Indians. The old chief undoubtedly feared that the military was closing in for a big kill.

Prodded into action by the scattering of ghost dancers among them, the Indians hastily loaded tepee poles and canvas lodges into wagons and on pony drags. They had little in the way of provisions, but all available food was carefully packed for a desperate journey. In the dim gray hours of winter twilight the ragged members of Big Foot's band broke away from their home camp and fled south toward the ghostly fastnesses of the Bad Lands.

Scouts on lathering ponies frantically brought word of Big Foot's flight to Colonel Sumner. At first it had looked as though the Indians had intended to turn off on another trail to Fort Bennett, but it soon became apparent that the band meant to continue southward. Furious that Big Foot had slipped through his fingers, Sumner immediately sent word to General Miles, advising him of the Indians' escape. Then he established contact with Merriam's command coming up Cheyenne River. Darkness closed in before an attempt could be made to pick up Big Foot's trail. Fuming at his helplessness, Sumner put in a sleepless night. Until dawn he was on tenterhooks to begin the chase of the century.

It fell to other soldiers, however, to try to corral Big Foot and his band. When it was clear the fugitives were heading for the Bad Lands, General Miles telegraphed General Brooke at Pine

Ridge, ordering him to send out troops from the agency to make the capture.

Danger lay in Big Foot joining forces with the ghost dancers at the Stronghold, so Miles took an added precaution in alerting for immediate duty a battalion of the Seventh Cavalry then stationed at Rapid City. Divided between the general's headquarters and Pine Ridge, the regiment was regarded by most of the high army brass as the nation's top military outfit. It was no secret that officers and men of the Seventh would like nothing better than another crack at the Sioux who had defeated them so overwhelmingly at Little Big Horn.

Learning they were to march against Big Foot, who was thought to have been one of their victorious foes at Little Big Horn,[1] members of the battalion were eager for action. Heroes of the hour, Seventh Cavalry officers had a last Christmas toast with friends at Rapid City's Harney bar.

"I suppose once you find Big Foot and his band," a civilian complained, "you'll just escort them back up to Cheyenne River and Uncle Sam will have to issue them extra grub and blankets."

Colonel James W. Forsyth, grizzled commander of the Seventh, eyed him levelly. "If we get far enough from headquarters, my friend, and strike Big Foot, there'll be no strings tied to any of us."

General Miles planned to send the battalion of the Seventh along with other cavalry down Rapid Valley and across Cheyenne River into the remote northwest corner of Pine Ridge Reservation, location of the Stronghold. The troops would be augmented by another crack outfit well remembered by the general, Casey's Cheyenne Indian Scouts. Miles had sent all the way to Tongue River, Montana, for them, and their arrival by rail was hourly expected.

No one was more excited about Casey's taking part in the campaign than Frederic Remington, then covering the Sioux uprising for *Harper's Weekly*. The celebrated artist-author had arrived in

---

[1] He wasn't. Big Foot had been part of a small hunting party out combing the country north of the Little Big Horn on the day of the Custer fight, June 25, 1876.

Rapid City soon after Miles had established headquarters there, and his robust figure was a familiar sight around town.

"Lieutenant Casey could make a Sioux Indian herd sheep," Remington said admiringly, during one of his frequent visits to the *Journal* office.

Coming on the heels of a holiday, the arrival of Casey's scouts was a fitting climax to Christmas that year. While Santa Claus held sway as usual at the local Baptist church, most of the town turned out at the railroad depot to see Casey's train come in from Montana. After Remington's build-up Rapid City residents expected to see a fleet of plush Pullman palace cars bearing the elite corps of scouts. It was mildly disappointing to see an old freight engine chugging in with warm boxcars carrying wild little Cheyenne ponies, while the scouts themselves huddled shivering on flat gravel cars.

When Lieutenant Casey—the famous Big Red Nose himself with blue eyes flashing and cavalryman's mustache smartly up-curled—alighted from the caboose and saluted General Miles, the drab details of the train were forgotten in a fine bit of military pageantry well calculated to stir Dakota's whites with renewed confidence in their army. It mattered little to the citizenry that, before the day was out, brave Cheyennes would be ruthlessly pitted against their old Sioux friends and allies.

With Remington going along as an eager observer, Casey's contingent was hauled eighteen miles farther south to the army railhead at Hermosa. The Cheyenne scouts were to spearhead a flanking maneuver commanded by Colonel Carr, under whose orders the Sixth Cavalry and the detached battalion of the Seventh now operated. By skirting the Stronghold to the north and cutting a wide swath east through wild, uncharted country, it was expected that the troops might intercept Big Foot's band before it could join forces with Kicking Bear's ghost dancers.

One thing went wrong with the plan. None of the army strategists had counted on Kicking Bear striking a first savage blow at the blue-coated Cheyennes who were once his friends but now rode against him as mortal enemies. While Casey's scouts were moving stealthily down Battle Creek, the ghost dancers attacked them fiercely—with more hatred, perhaps, than was directed against the pale-faced troopers coming up behind them. Forced to battle tenaciously for every foot of ground gained, the Cheyennes were held at bay until nearly sundown. The Army, scouts and all, made camp for the night on the near northwest bank of Cheyenne River.

Across the river Kicking Bear's warriors snaked through the tangled serrated masses of the Bad Lands, latticed with golden winter sunset. Far beyond the eroded peaks squatted the flat hulk of the Stronghold, vague, mysterious, and as yet impenetrable in the dying twilight.

With the help of his faithful aging wife, Big Foot climbed up on the seat of his battered old wagon and scanned the gloomy badlands reaches for a suitable camp site. Behind him his people waited, their wagons and pony drags strung out in a long, drab procession. Few of them knew this desolate region of gaunt clay buttes and chalky alkali flats. They looked to their feeble leader, weak now with hunger and plainly ailing, to show them the un-blazed trail to safety. He stood there, tall and skeleton-thin, his eyes frost-bleared against the harsh wind, and they looked at him and wondered. Perhaps death here in these trackless wastes was better than this aimless wandering.

And yet, Big Foot, for all his increasing frailty, had a well-marked goal in mind. To the headmen and warriors he had con-fided that word had come to him from Red Cloud, his stalwart Ogalala cousin at Pine Ridge, inviting him to come south for a council. Quickly the word had spread. It was well; of all the Sioux leaders, Red Cloud alone had managed to survive and keep a semblance of strength and influence. He could not deny his Minneconjou kinsmen sanctuary and shelter from the pursuing soldiers.

Big Foot entertained no idea of doing battle with the troops that were almost sure to be dogging his trail. He half-believed the wild exhortations of the ghost-dance fanatics in his band who were led by Yellow Bird, a medicine man and avid supporter of the new faith.

"Let your heart be strong," Yellow Bird kept saying. "The bullets of the white soldiers cannot penetrate those who believe, but will fly away like birds across the prairie."

It was well, Big Foot allowed, for his warriors were poorly armed. They had a bare handful of obsolete weapons, mostly old muzzle-loaders and a few revolvers dating back to the Indian victory at Little Big Horn. Moreover, the old chief was weary and delirious with fever. Exposure and fatigue during the past two days and nights had brought on a siege of pneumonia. In making good their escape from Deep Creek, Big Foot and his people had pushed themselves far beyond the normal limits of endurance.

Most significant, perhaps, was the fact that Big Foot had long since passed his prime as a fighting chief. No longer a leader of warriors, he was now an aged advocate of peace and progress. Even his willingness to accept the ghost dance proved his ability to follow new paths. Some Indians said later that he had been coerced by his followers into leading their headlong dash for safety among Red Cloud's folk—where it was thought no soldiers would dare bother them. Although he knew the soldiers would try to apprehend his band and might even attempt to kill his people, Big Foot thought only of swift flight.

Since leaving Cheyenne River the night of the twenty-third, the band had been constantly on the move. By Christmas night Big Foot knew they must make camp, and singled out a lone butte where he had camped years earlier with a small hunting party. On the lee side of the butte his people found shelter from the chill north wind and a meager supply of brackish water. Little snow had fallen as yet and grass for the ponies was ample.

While the few scraps of available food were hungrily eaten by the half-starved women and children, Big Foot sent out relays of scouts to watch the back trail to the north. At any moment the band expected to see a column of soldiers appear on the distant horizon.

Purple dusk faded into ice-blue darkness. A pale moon rose to bathe the jagged badlands tors in eerie light. Numb with cold and fatigue, most of the people were too tired to sleep. There in the hazy moonglow many Indians claimed to have seen a frightening apparition.[2]

A figure in white buckskin or muslin garments stood motionless on a high escarpment off to the west, they said. As the phantom waved, as though beckoning them all to follow him, he faded from sight.

"It's Sitting Bull! We have seen Sitting Bull!" cried several of the Hunkpapa fugitives, rousing the camp.

The people sat up on the ground, transfixed and spine-shuddering. Few of them doubted that Sitting Bull's ghost was calling them to join the ghost dancers at the Stronghold and avenge his spirit.

Next morning a number of warriors urged Big Foot to turn west to seek the Stronghold of the ghost dancers.[3] Iron Hail, a Minneconjou warrior in his prime at the age of thirty-three, told the author years later that the reasons for a change in route seemed well founded at the time. Vast stretches of all-but-impassable badlands lay across the way south, where the wagons were sure to have rough going. White soldiers might catch up with the band at any time. Ill equipped as they were, the warriors would be no match for well-armed troops.

Moreover, food had been scarce. Although the band had passed several ranches and once even crossed a pasture filled with grazing cattle and horses, Big Foot refused to allow his people to kill livestock which did not belong to them. He had wanted no crime charged against himself or his band.

Now children throughout the camp were crying from hunger. Iron Hail's own infant child was among those suffering most from exposure and lack of food. Unable to suckle milk from their mothers' shriveled breasts, many babies were starving.

Big Foot heard the arguments in feverish silence. Beads of cold

---

[2] A similar experience among the Two Kettle Sioux on Bad River near Pierre, South Dakota, was reported that winter by Thomas Hetlund, a white rancher from that region.

[3] The Stronghold's exact location was unknown to most of the northern Sioux.

sweat showed on his forehead and upper lip. Although plainly in
agony, having contracted pneumonia, the old chief stood proudly
erect before his critics. Those who had complained the loudest
looked away, unable to meet his level gaze.

"Only with Red Cloud will we be safe, my relatives," he said
calmly.

According to Iron Hail, there was no dissension or open break
among Big Foot's fighting men. Shamefaced and silent, most of
them returned to their camps to make ready for another hard
day's traveling. A handful of malcontents—eighteen warriors and
their families, about sixty-five people in all—broke away from
the main group and started west along the badland wall to look
for the Stronghold. (Unable to locate the ghost-dance camp, they
eventually circled back to follow the trail blazed by Big Foot. On
December 30 they were discovered near Bear-in-the-Lodge Creek
south of White River by Ogalala scouts serving the Army, who
escorted them to Pine Ridge Agency without incident.)

At midday Big Foot led his followers up a precipitous winding
pass through the steep badlands escarpments.[4] Here, in a welter
of chaos and desolation, rows of barren ridges stretched as far as
the eye could see, punctuated only by spires and pinnacles and
gaunt, towering peaks of eroded clay. "Hell with the fires burned
out," Long Hair Custer had called these ghostly fastnesses during his gold-discovery expedition to the Black Hills in 1874—two
summers before he and his troops fell at Little Big Horn. After
a full afternoon's arduous climb the band crossed the rugged
summit and dropped down toward the vast White River flats
far below.

It was almost sundown when Big Foot called a halt. Lodges
were hastily set up by the women near a clump of stunted wild
plum trees, deep in the White River badlands. For the first time
since the band left Cheyenne River cook fires were permitted,
and a crier rode about giving everyone the new instructions.
Soldiers might well be following, but scouts perched on high
ridges along the back trail could give early warning of their ap-

4 This natural opening is now known as Big Foot Pass and is located in
the Badlands National Monument between Wall and Kadoka, South Dakota.

proach. Boys and young men, including Hump's son, Helper, were sent out to bring in what game they could find—badgers, prairie dogs, jack rabbits, and hawks. The catch was meager, far from enough to feed so many hungry mouths.

At last Big Foot told some of the men to slaughter a few select yearling colts in the pony herd. Only younger animals still carried flesh on their ribs; older horses, broken to harness, were yet needed for the southward trek. The Sioux cared little for horse meat, but there was nothing else available. The older women even sang the tremolo for the brave young horses when the men went out with their knives and strangling ropes. But the shrill singing could not drown out the piercing screams of dying ponies.

The sun was setting by the time it grew quiet again. An owl hooted off in the shadows. Huddled at his old woman's cook fire, Big Foot straightened at the sound of the bird's mournful cry.

"Three times the owl hooted," Big Foot said to the medicine man, Yellow Bird, who sometimes shared in the chief's evening meal.

"It means we shall have a blizzard in three days' time," Yellow Bird predicted.

"Then we must start early in the morning or we shall never reach Red Cloud's camp ahead of the snow," said Big Foot.

Pipe-on-Head, youthful grandson of the old chief, sniffed the close, fetid air of the lodge, then poked his head through the door flap to see how it looked outside. No change of wind, inside or out, indicated bad weather coming. As Pipe-on-Head solemnly confided years later to the author, only the owl's melancholy hooting had enabled Yellow Bird to foretell the storm.

Each day's travel began with a brief devotion to Wakantanka led by Big Foot himself. Sometimes Yellow Bird assisted, but usually the old chief alone would struggle to his feet and, his face sweat-glistening, would quietly express his thanks to the Great Spirit for the safety of his camp and the bounty of food enjoyed by his people the night before. He would hold his pipe aloft to the sky, then dip it earthward, finally hold it out to each of the four cardinal directions. His prayer completed, he would let his old woman and young Pipe-on-Head help him climb up to the wagon seat. Holding the reins with trembling fingers, he would lead out the ragged caravan.

The day after the owl hooted the band crossed White River near the mouth of Eagle Nest Creek where scouts found a shallow ford. Catching-Spirit-Elk, an Ogalala in his late thirties who had been visiting Big Foot's band and was returning south, recalled good camp sites along Medicine Creek, which fed into White River a few miles upriver from the ford. Before dark the ragged travelers reached the creek and made camp. Within a day, Catching-Spirit-Elk told them, they could be at Pine Ridge Agency. Big Foot confidently predicted this would be their last night of camping on the prairie.

"By tomorrow night we shall reach Red Cloud—and safety," he announced.

On Saturday, December 27, the ghost dancers abruptly left the Stronghold. For days Indians from the friendly camps had been chipping away at the hard core of resistance. Stands First, a clever Ogalala scout, had spent an entire day in the hostile camp. Although fanatics sparked by Kicking Bear and Short Bull had leveled guns at him and attempted to drown out his peaceful overtures with war cries, Stands First had persisted. Desperate, Kicking Bear sought him out in the Ogalala segment of the camp circle.

"We will listen to no more talk of peace and friendship with the treacherous whites!" Kicking Bear shouted. "No man who talks to us of peace will leave this camp alive! The white soldiers are cowards, afraid to fight us openly. You are a coward as much as they. You are a woman!"

Stands First took this sharpest of insults calmly. Standing his ground, he had the advantage—for he guessed, correctly, that Kicking Bear wanted no Sioux blood spilled here at the Stronghold.

Circumstance provided an even more clinching argument. The

ghost dancers were beginning to feel the pangs of slow starvation. Foraging parties had long since rounded up all loose livestock on the reservation. Warriors were running into increased resistance at nearby ranches where crews of cowboys and militia, armed by the state, were guarding the cattle herds day and night. Horseflesh had almost become a staple of diet, but now the pony herd was depleted. Little food remained in camp—either on the hoof or in the cook pots. Overruling the once-persuasive harangues of their leaders, the ghost dancers talked openly of surrender.

"We cannot live on words," the people argued, after listening to the fanatics.

The leaders went around lashing with their quirts those who protested, but even they realized it was hopeless to hold out any longer without warriors to rally.

The departure from the Stronghold was slow and orderly. Steady pressure came from the screen of troops and Cheyenne scouts that crossed Cheyenne River the day after Christmas. Dogging the heels of the retreating Indians, soldiers were so close to the ghost dancers that they often found cook fires still burning in camps just deserted. The troops had orders not to precipitate a fight, however, and no armed clashes occurred.

Moving south toward Pine Ridge Agency, the ghost dancers hesitated briefly at White River, crossed over to camp the night of December 27 on Grass Creek. Next day they trudged on to White Clay Creek, camping at Young-Man-Afraid-of-His-Horses' abandoned log cabin settlement [5] just upstream from the former ghost-dance encampment at No Water's. A small delegation was sent on to the Drexel Catholic Mission to ask if their white friend Father Jutz felt it safe for them to continue on to Pine Ridge Agency. All this time the ringleaders and ghost-dance prophets were compelled to string along willy-nilly with the others.

The ghost-dance troubles seemed at an end in the eyes of the authorities. While army forces gently prodded the ghost dancers

[5] This settlement was the permanent camp of the Payabya band of the Ogalalas.

along toward the agency from the west and north, General Brooke had troops out combing the northern part of the reservation for Big Foot's band. Although the capture was hourly expected, a battalion of the colored Ninth Cavalry had been sweeping the hills northeast of Pine Ridge for days and had failed to sight the Cheyenne River fugitives.

Brooke had long been holding the Seventh Cavalry in reserve. Now he ordered a battalion of Custer's old regiment to the saddle. The four troops under the command of Major S. M. Whiteside rode twenty miles northeast of the agency through a blinding dust storm to make camp near a small deserted trading post on Wounded Knee Creek.

On Sunday morning, December 28, Whiteside sent out a scouting party headed by famed old frontiersman Baptiste "Little Bat" Garnier. Little Bat took a dim view of the troopers huddled around their stoves in their warm Sibley tents, all too willing to leave the rigors of finding Big Foot's band to civilians. Looking at his strapping Ogalala scouts, the picture was perceptibly brighter. Little Bat was justifiably proud of such stalwarts as Yankton Charlie, Woman's Dress, and Highbackbone. As all three rode off with him into the frozen morning sunshine, he was confident they could flush out Big Foot without any help from the Army.

Before noon the four scouts reached Porcupine Tail Creek, ten miles east of the Wounded Knee camp, and turned upstream. Within minutes they sighted a straggling band of Indians coming down the pine-crested hills beyond Porcupine Butte, a towering landmark.

No one could mistake Big Foot's ragged fugitives. They made a sorry spectacle in their tattered blankets and buckskins, some without moccasins, many with feet and hands wrapped in bits of fur. Most of the wanderers' faces were dark from frostbite and a diet of horseflesh. Even the old bone-rack horses pulling the wagons and pony drags were too weak to keep going and made periodic stops.

There was no sign of belligerence on the part of the travel-weary caravan. Warriors in the vanguard waved, and Little Bat raised his hand in friendly greeting. Then he told Highbackbone to ride on ahead and meet them, while he and the others whirled their ponies to race back to Wounded Knee with news that Big Foot's people had at last been found.

Highbackbone was met by a fellow tribesman, Catching Spirit Elk, who was scouting the way south for the Cheyenne River band.

"Why do you come to us, Cousin?" asked Catching Spirit Elk after they exchanged greetings.

"We heard you were coming," said Highbackbone. "So we rode out to meet you. Everything will be all right."

The scout led the way down into a hollow by Porcupine Tail Creek where they could get out of the wind. It was a bright, sunny day, but the sharp, lashing wind chilled them to the bone. Highbackbone dismounted and kindled a fire and made coffee. One by one the warriors of Big Foot's band were attracted by the smoke and rode down to shake hands with Highbackbone and stare curiously at his uniform. It was soiled and threadbare, one of the old coarse blue tunics of outmoded design, but High-backbone displayed it proudly along with his yellow neckerchief and revolver and pistol belt. The warriors hunkered down all around the fire, warming their hands and drinking the blistering hot coffee until it was all gone.

By mid-afternoon Catching Spirit Elk noticed a cloud of dust rising off to the west. Presently he heard the rumble of many iron-shod hoofs on the frozen ground. He caught a flash of cavalry blue.

"Soldiers?" he asked Highbackbone.

It was puzzling to run into troops coming from the south and west. All along Big Foot and his band had expected soldiers to overtake them from the north. The scout signed yes and smiled reassuringly.

"But everything will be all right," he said. "There will be no trouble."

When Whiteside and his battalion galloped up in a swirl of dust and formed in battle order, many of the Indians got down from their wagons and began to wave empty flour sacks and other bits of white cloth at the troops. They milled about restlessly as a single Hotchkiss gun, carried on muleback, was taken down and set up threateningly in position to rake the entire caravan.

"The soldiers must only be fooling us," the Indians told each other with little conviction.

Ill of pneumonia, barely able to sit up on the seat of his wagon, Big Foot raised a white flag aloft and had his grandson drive him slowly out to meet the soldiers. As Major Whiteside came riding out of formation, Highbackbone jogged over to interpret.

"I want only peace," the old chief said. "Tell the soldier-chief I wish to parley with him."

Highbackbone relayed the request to the major.

"Nothing doing," snapped Whiteside, bristling with impatience. "Tell him I demand an unconditional surrender."

Big Foot heard the translation in stoic silence. Sickness and doubt clouded his rheumy eyes. His bony hawk face glistened with beads of perspiration.

"All right," he said at last, "I surrender."

At a brusque order from Whiteside the troops trotted forward out of battle line to form in column of fours ahead and behind the cavalcade of Indian wagons. Sending a courier to General Brooke at the agency with word that Big Foot's band had quietly surrendered to his command, the major led out the column. By pushing the Indians along at a brisk pace, he could have them encamped and bedded down before dark at the Wounded Knee campground.

Wounded Knee

WOUNDED KNEE CREEK was fast losing its old serenity. Neat rows of Sibley tents and trim picket lines of the Seventh Cavalry camp made sharp contrast with the shallow stream's gentle curving and the undulation of brown treeless hills all around. The once-peaceful valley now echoed with sounds strange and foreign—shrill bugle calls, the pawing of restless troop horses, the ominous clank of saber scabbards.

The Indians were ordered to pitch their tattered lodges on a broad flat southwest of the military encampment and against the north rim of a wide, dry ravine that crossed the flat east to west. Several abandoned Indian cabins and half-breed Louis Mousseau's tiny trading post were unoccupied by the Army or Big Foot's ragged followers.

Many of the weary travelers from Cheyenne River regarded the flat as an adequate camp site. Although it was strange country to all but a few of the northern Sioux, Catching Spirit Elk, the Ogalala, knew the place well and reassured Big Foot as to its desirability. It soon became apparent to the Indians, however, that their captors intended to give them little, if any, freedom. Here, within eighteen miles of Red Cloud and safety, Big Foot and his band were abject prisoners subject to the baffling whims of white soldiers.

Before the women finished setting up the lodges, troopers led the gun mules up a hill northwest of the flat where they unloaded two of the Hotchkiss guns and placed them in position to cover the Indian campground. At once an apprehensive whisper rustled through the band.

"Perhaps they mean to kill us!" ran the excited murmur.

"Even if the soldiers try to kill us," said Yellow Bird, moving from one family group to another, "do not be afraid. Their bullets cannot do us harm."

When there were no other signs of outright unfriendliness on the part of the troopers, the Indians gradually drifted into busy routine chores of making camp.

Later, however, just at sundown, there was another ripple of excitement among the tepees. Turned back by patrols of soldiers, the Sioux men were not allowed to take the Indian ponies to water. At last the evening watering of the pony herd was done entirely by little boys. Young Helper was considered too old and soldiers would not permit him to go down to the creek with his thirsty mount. Hump's son turned the animal over to Pipe-on-Head, who, since he was younger and smaller, was allowed to take Big Foot's tired team to water.

Returning from the creek a short while later, Pipe-on-Head looked around the family lodge in vain for his grandparents. Finally someone told him that soldiers had come to take Big Foot off to one of the soldier's tents where he would be cared for during the night. The old chief was ill with a raging fever. His old woman had had to take the reins and drive the wagon on after Big Foot's surrender to the soldiers at Porcupine Butte.

Pipe-on-Head wondered what was happening to his grandfather. Finally he worked up the courage to approach the big Sibley tents occupied by the sick old chief and several of his headmen. It was long past dark before he ventured inside to have a visit with his grandparents. After that other Indians wandered over from the tepee camp to see how their chief was getting along.

But all through the evening hours the Indians stirred with vague restlessness. Soldiers were all around now, and a rumor circulated among the tepees that more troops had been sent for and were even now on their way from Pine Ridge Agency. The people could only guess why more soldiers were coming.

Adding to the Indians' uncertainty and misery was the fact that, now the horses had been watered, no one was allowed to go after water. Seventy-six troopers of Troops A and I, Seventh Cavalry, stood dismounted sentinel duty. No Indian was permitted to pass them and those who approached with kettles and buckets to fetch water were turned back at gun point.

Presently word got out that the night guard of soldiers was headed by Captain Myles Moylan, commander of A Troop and a bitter survivor of Reno's inglorious retreat at Little Big Horn. As darkness settled over the valley Indians looked with growing discomfort at the line of warmly clad troopers, standing snug in long buffalo coats and muskrat caps. The people shivered in their lodges—partly from the increasing cold, partly from fear of the inescapable dangers that surrounded them.

Iron Hail, a sturdy warrior of thirty-three, tried to help his young wife comfort their infant child. Suckling at the mother's withered breasts, the baby whimpered from hunger. No food was at hand for adults either. In a neighboring lodge Iron Hail's aging parents, sister, and two brothers were in equally dire circumstances. Expecting to share in Red Cloud's supposed bounty by nightfall, none of Big Foot's followers had taken time to hunt for game on this last day on the trail.

Outside, an army wagon creaked into camp. A sudden chorus of shouts sounded. Iron Hail pushed aside the door flap to peer out into the fading light. A white soldier on the wagon seat saw him and roughly ordered him to come forward. Iron Hail approached the wagon uncertainly. His meager dealings with whites had taught him caution. Then a civilian scout who was driving the wagon told him in Sioux that he had been picked to issue rations to the other Indians. Major Whiteside, it seemed, did not want Big Foot's band to go hungry. Tension eased somewhat throughout the camp as boxes of army hardtack, bags of sugar, and slabs of bacon were unloaded from the wagon and dumped in a pile near Iron Hail's lodge.

One by one Iron Hail called out the names of the heads of families, but it was largely the women who thronged around him to collect rations. He recalled years later, however, his mounting uneasiness at glancing up occasionally to see soldiers on the move beyond the outlying lodges. Lugging heavy boxes of shells, the troopers were hauling a lot of ammunition up the hill where the Hotchkiss guns squatted ominously.

The women followed his watchful gaze and saw the threatening look of things. Then someone caught the flicker of cook fires around Mousseau's trading post.

"Sioux scouts," Iron Hail decided after a while.

"Surely our own relatives would not attack us," said the women, their earlier flightiness quickly abating.

"I don't know," Iron Hail answered uncertainly. It still looked precarious to him.

That night most of the soldiers of the Seventh Cavalry, bored from long inactivity at Pine Ridge, picked up their holiday celebrating where they had left off several days earlier. Big Foot's capture seemed to mark an end to the Sioux war—an added reason for jubilation now that the Seventh was away from Brooke's headquarters and out from under the general's pompous restraint. Braced by liberal draughts of whisky, troopers visited comrades in other tents and began a round of drinking that lasted well up to taps.

The officers, including Major Whiteside, were inclined to be lenient with their men. Headquarters had been advised of Big Foot's quiet surrender and by tomorrow, with the disarming of the captive band, personnel of the Seventh would be national heroes. It seemed an occasion well deserving of celebration.

"Well, it's a far cry from Little Big Horn, Captain," Major Whiteside said to grizzled Myles Moylan as the senior captain made his final report on the night guard to his battalion commander. "Spot of brandy before you go back out there?"

The Sibley, warmed by its portable stove, was comfortable, and it was tempting to sit here with this effete easterner and drink his liquor. But Moylan was on duty and something of the old soldier in him rebelled at the holiday atmosphere throughout the battalion camp. If truth were known, the senior captain had neither admiration nor patience where the green recruits and unseasoned officers grown flabby from soft desk jobs were concerned. He resented brash young field officers coming into a regiment and robbing experienced men of their seniority. All his years of faithful service added up to mighty little, he decided, when a fellow of Whiteside's stripe could take over a whole battalion, a command that by all rights should have been his own.

In a way, though, Whiteside unwittingly spoke truth. The Seventh Cavalry of 1890 was indeed a far cry from the old regiment of Custer's day. A fleeting picture of the past stabbed at his memory. He saw again that bloody afternoon at Little Big Horn. Reno's command was falling back to change front. Moylan's old A Company was at the point of pivot under devastating fire. Then, suddenly, they all saw Major Reno out in front of a headlong rout with an Indian scout's brains splattered all over him.

Yet it wasn't just Reno, Moylan thought. Nearly all of them had made a run for it. In a wild flight that sadly lacked even the dignity of an orderly retreat, half of Reno's outfit reached safety while, on all sides, painted hordes of savages came streaking through the timber, riding down officers and men as though it all were some gay, frivolous game.

Tonight, fourteen and a half years later, many of those same benighted aborigines were bedding down mere yards away. They were still dangerous adversaries—a fact conveniently overlooked by Whiteside and his desk-softened ilk. Disdainful, brusque to the point of rudeness, Myles Moylan declined the proffered brandy and left the warm tent.

Raucous laughter from the Sibley rows greeted Moylan's ears with harsh abruptness. One inebriated soldier loudly voiced the idea of calling on the ailing Big Foot, now resting under the regimental surgeon's care in one of the Sibleys. Nearly a dozen troopers came staggering to the old chief's tent and obscenely beckoned the infirm Indian leader outside for an impromptu conference. Moving swiftly to head off trouble, Captain Moylan sent the drunken troopers scattering back to their quarters, then posted a tight guard around the tent.

Off in the darkness the glow of Indian cook fires died behind the thin tepee walls and Indian voices droned off to a murmur. Yet within the camp the Sioux stirred sleeplessly at the soldiers' shouts of carousal.

Long after taps, when the troopers quieted down at last, the warriors and their families lay wakeful in their robes, listening to

the steady tread of parading sentries, the ominous click of bayo-
nets, and the sharp commands of officers echoing through the
black night whenever the guard was changed. In the troubled
minds of the Sioux these were threatening war maneuvers. And
tonight—the last night on earth for some three hundred of Big
Foot's weary followers—the Indians had no thought of making
war.

Before daybreak next morning four more troops of the Seventh
Cavalry, three Hotchkiss guns, and Lieutenant Taylor's company
of Indian scouts arrived from Pine Ridge after a forced night
march and set up temporary bivouac just north of the Sibley
tents occupied by Whiteside's battalion. General Brooke wanted
to take no chances on Big Foot slipping through the Army's grasp
again and had sent the reinforcements under the Seventh's commander, Colonel James W. Forsyth. As senior officer, Forsyth at
once took over command of the entire surrender operation.

The army plan of action was simple. Big Foot's band were to
be disarmed, preparatory to escorting them by way of Pine Ridge
Agency to the railroad across northern Nebraska. General Miles,
with War Department concurrence, had already decided that the
Indians, when captured, were to be shipped off to the east or
south until the ghost-dance scare was over.

The day broke cold, clear, and windless. A sharpness rode the
morning air that Big Foot's people recognized as a sure forerunner
of storm and snow. A bugle's harsh blare sounding reveille set
both camps astir, although the Sioux had been fitfully awake since
the pre-dawn arrival of troop reinforcements.

Mounted and in line, this fresh battalion was drawn up facing
the eastern and southern extremities of the Indian camp. The two
troops to the south were across the shallow ravine; between them
and the ravine's south rim the Ninth Cavalry's Lieutenant Taylor
and his Indian scouts were mounted and in line. Troop G was at
right angles to them across the ravine.

Moylan's night guard significantly remained dismounted and
at their assigned posts. Troop E of Whiteside's battalion stayed
mounted and took position just below the crest of the hill from

which all the Hotchkiss guns were now trained on the Indian camp. Troops B and K were dismounted and formed two sides of a hollow square around the Sibley tents occupied by Big Foot and his sub-chiefs. All in all, it was a frightening array of military might.

Presently several boxes of hardtack were issued as rations to the Indians, Iron Hail repeating his chore of the previous night in calling out the names of heads of families. Then, abruptly, a crier began walking around among the lodges, announcing in Sioux that all men should come to Big Foot's tent at once for a council.

Yellow Bird immediately began a harangue about the power-lessness of the white soldiers' bullets. Much as a matter of pre-caution, most of the Indian men donned pale ghost shirts before answering the summons to what they thought must surely be a strange meeting first thing in the morning. Left behind in the camp, the women decked themselves out in similar garments— capes and dresses. Yet none of the Indians expected trouble. A white flag above Big Foot's borrowed Sibley seemed a sure guaran-tee of safety. Gradually the men straggled over to seat themselves in a ragged semicircle facing the tent in which their sick old chief still lay.

Back among the lodges Big Foot's old woman asked Pipe-on-Head to take some willow-bark tobacco, *kinnikinick,* to his grand-father. Eager to see the council in progress, the boy delivered the tobacco promptly. Big Foot was still lying on his ragged old pallet but was anxious to have his pipe bag and smoking material. Yet, whether from sickness or some strange uneasiness, the old man seemed to think this council no place for his grandson.

"You'd better go back to your grandmother, boy," said Big Foot warningly.

Pipe-on-Head noticed no particular concern on the faces of his grandfather's followers as he jogged past them on his way back to camp. A moment later, however, he stopped dead in his tracks when a soldier with a gun in his hands shouted out something unintelligible. Then Philip F. Wells, half-breed interpreter known to the Sioux as Tokala ("Fox"), picked out twenty Indians and told them to go back to camp to get their guns. The twenty men got to their feet and strode scowling past Pipe-on-Head on their way to their lodges.

Joined by Helper and several other boys in their teens, Big Foot's grandson was standing near the council circle when the twenty men returned. All but two of them were empty-handed. Two older men carried ancient smoothbore muzzle-loaders which they laid on the ground by the interpreter.

The officers gathered around Big Foot's sick tent did not look pleased. They seemed to believe that the twenty men were holding back weapons and refusing to surrender them. Their expressions grew even more stern as Colonel Forsyth and his staff, accompanied by Father Craft from the Drexel Catholic Mission near Pine Ridge Agency, walked into the circle. The priest had come along to Wounded Knee to render such good offices as might be possible to either the regiment or the fugitives. His presence there was generally calming to the Indians. Surely no Black Robe would have any part in a treacherous undertaking.

Interpreter Wells found his present job far from his liking. As a member of Lieutenant Taylor's company of scouts, he had signed up with the Army for the duration of the ghost-dance troubles. The current strife was unduly hard on mixed-bloods, however, and Wells's familiarity with the Sioux tongue and folkways put him in the unenviable position of trying to serve both sides. He now found himself caught in the middle between two stubborn leaders—Big Foot and Colonel Forsyth.

Forsyth was determined above anything else not to repeat the mistakes made by Colonel Sumner. He was not at all disposed to be lenient with Big Foot now that he had caught up with him. Conveniently glossing over the customary courtesy granted to a surrendering foe, the colonel had the ailing chief propped up in the doorway of the Sibley tent and forced the old man to assume full responsibility in the disarming procedure.

"My people have few guns or other weapons," Big Foot insisted, gritting back the pain of fresh hemorrhage in his lungs.

With only two antiquated smoothbore guns brought in by a

group of twenty Sioux, Forsyth was unconvinced by the old chief's argument.

"You tell Big Foot he tells me his Indians have no weapons," the colonel gruffly ordered Interpreter Wells. "I am sure he is deceiving me. Tell him I know he's lying." Forsyth tried to make his face look friendlier. "Now tell Big Foot he need have no fear in giving up the weapons I know his people have, as I wish to treat him with nothing but kindness."

Forsyth's attempt at a smile in Big Foot's direction fooled nobody. But Wells translated as he was instructed. Before the interpretation was complete, however, the colonel was talking again along the same improbable tack.

"Tell him this: 'Have I not done enough for you to convince you that I intend nothing but kindness? Did I not treat you kindly, and put you in a good tent, and put a stove in it to keep you warm and comfortable? I have sent off to get provisions for your people which I expect here before long so that I can feed you well. I have even had my own doctor take care of you.' "

The old chief's fever-ridden eyes were clouded with mistrust.

"My people have no guns—only such weapons as these men have brought. I gathered up all my good guns at Cheyenne River [1] and turned them in and they were all burned up."

"You're lying!" snapped Forsyth. "In return for all my kindness to you, you lie to me!"

The colonel spoke abruptly to Major Whiteside who stood at his elbow.

"Search them. All of them. And search the camp."

At Whiteside's signal soldiers began to close in on all sides—two ranks of dismounted troopers backed up by two ranks of mounted cavalry. Indian men and boys stirred uneasily as troopers sharply brought up carbines to the ready.

As if it were all part of a preconceived plan, a squad of soldiers was ordered by Whiteside to search the camp. Since Forsyth could not spare Wells's services at council, Bat Garnier went along to interpret for the troopers and to inform the women they would

---

[1] Most Sioux refer to the Cheyenne River as Wakpa Waste—"Good River."

not be harmed. A teamster also followed the squad with a wagon. Any guns found among the Indians' personal effects were to be brought back and displayed as proof of Big Foot's supposed perfidy. Another squad of soldiers was ordered to collect weapons from the Sioux men sitting in council.

All this time the Indian women were busy dismantling lodges and packing belongings on pony drags and in wagons. A crier, anticipating an early move from Wounded Knee Creek, had announced that they were to break camp. Now the women anxiously watched the movements of the soldiers.

The search was thorough and methodical. Troopers forced the women to give up anything that might be used as weapons—axes, crowbars, knives, awls—as well as firearms. Everything was piled in the wagon. Three soldiers began untying bundles and strewing bedding and blankets around as they looked for anything made of metal that had a sharp point. Since the search had uncovered only about a dozen rifles, most of them tied together with bits of wire and rawhide and hardly usable, the soldiers seemed almost fiendishly eager to tear bundles apart and disrupt the women's careful packing.

One soldier who had blond hair and a prominent Roman nose was interested in things other than possible weapons possessed by the women. Spotting one particularly handsome young girl, he spent long minutes feeling around her waist and hips and breasts. The girl finally threw back her blanket to show that she had no concealed weapon, but the Roman-nosed soldier kept feeling her body while she stood shamefaced and terrified before him.[2]

While the search at the camp continued, Sioux men at the council were summarily ordered to give up the weapons they carried. Some were cooperative. Catching Spirit Elk, the Ogalala, readily handed over his Winchester.

"Let us give up every gun," he advised the others.

More firearms were surrendered. At this point, however, Yellow Bird got to his feet and began to go through the silent rhythmic

2 Medicine Woman survived to old age. Later married to the storekeeper at Wounded Knee, she became known throughout Pine Ridge Reservation as Mrs. Mousseau.

motions of the ghost dance. Already wearing a ghost shirt, he had his face weirdly painted with garish symbols.

At first the soldiers paid him little attention. Then he began chanting and throwing up his hands. Every so often he stooped to the earth and picked up handfuls of dry frozen dust that he threw toward the forward rank of troopers. Suddenly he turned to a group of young warriors hunkered down apart from the older men.

"Do not be afraid!" he shrilled. "Let your hearts be strong to meet what is before you. Many soldiers are around us. They have many bullets. But I have received assurance from Wakantanka, the Great Spirit, that their bullets can not penetrate us. The prairie is endless; the soldiers' bullets will not come toward you but will go over the broad prairie. If the bullets come toward you they will not penetrate you. Be not afraid!"

The young warriors earnestly answered *"Hau! Hau!"*—a solemn pronouncement of their belief in the words of Yellow Bird. Whatever happened, they would stand by him now.

Philip Wells heard much of the medicine man's tirade. Turning to Major Whiteside, he said, "That man is making mischief." He repeated all that Yellow Bird had said.

"Tell all this to Colonel Forsyth," Whiteside said, a troubled frown on his brow.

Wells found Forsyth and went through it all once more. The colonel led the way across the open semicircle. Yellow Bird was again going through the silent movements of the ghost dance, now and then hurling dust in the air.

"Tell that man to sit down and keep quiet," Forsyth snapped.

Wells complied, but the Sioux words had no effect on the medicine man. It was as though Wells had spoken some sort of gibberish to him. He kept dancing.

"Say it again." The colonel's patience was fast running out; he kept his voice low yet sharp.

This time Frog, Big Foot's brother-in-law, broke in.

"He will sit down when he gets around the circle," Frog explained to Wells.

Presently Yellow Bird danced on, moving slowly around the semicircle of seated warriors and elders. Finally he squatted down and was motionless.

"Our chief is dying," Frog said to Colonel Forsyth, speaking slowly so Wells could translate more readily. "We wish to continue our journey to Pine Ridge Agency where we shall join our cousins, the followers of Red Cloud. I speak now for my dying brother, Big Foot."

"I can take better care of Big Foot here than you could anywhere," Forsyth said tartly. "I have my own surgeon tending to him."

Before Wells had finished interpreting a sergeant hurried up to the colonel.

"There goes one of 'em with a rifle under his blanket, sir!"

"Take it away from him," Forsyth ordered.

The sergeant stepped quickly among the seated Indians, catching up with a tall young Sioux who was circling behind the group. The warrior's face flushed with anger as the sergeant snatched away his rifle. Off to one side Major Whiteside joined Colonel Forsyth.

"Tell these red devils they'll be searched one at a time," Whiteside said to Wells.

The older men submitted passively to the searchers. Like many other men in the group, Catching Spirit Elk had no other weapon to surrender but gave up his cartridge belt from which a soldier began taking bullets. Before the searching squad reached them, five or six young bucks threw off their blankets to reveal rifles which they brandished in the air. Tense moments passed as, one by one, they strode forward and laid their firearms on the growing pile. Most of the Sioux were now without weapons.

Varying tales are told—even by Indian survivors—as to how the firing started. Most reliable was the account given to the author on several occasions by Iron Hail.

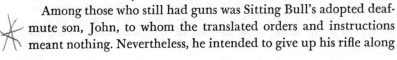

Among those who still had guns was Sitting Bull's adopted deaf-mute son, John, to whom the translated orders and instructions meant nothing. Nevertheless, he intended to give up his rifle along with the others. Unconcernedly, he ambled out toward the pile of weapons. His rifle was not pointed at anyone, and he had no thought of looking for trouble.

Acting on a signal from Major Whiteside, two soldiers started after the deaf-mute—one behind him from the east, another quartering across his path from the west. The troopers grabbed him roughly, spinning him around. Had they left him alone he would have put down his gun without the slightest resistance.

As John Sitting Bull confirmed it in sign talk with the author many years later, his rifle accidentally discharged when he was forced to grapple with the soldiers. Some Sioux say the brutal handling of the deaf-mute cost one of the troopers his life with the firing of that first shot. Be that as it may, John Sitting Bull never made such a claim. Even among the Sioux, his name as the man who first fired is not usually mentioned, his deaf-mute identity pathetically dimmed by the holocaust that abruptly followed.[3]

The shot spurred the soldiers into instant action. Almost immediately a trooper mounted on a sorrel horse came riding at a fast trot into the council circle. Leveling his carbine at the sick old chief, he pumped a bullet into Big Foot's forehead.

A terrible crash of gunfire split the morning air. Stunned and incredulous at the murder of their chieftain, the Indian men stared at the ranks of firing soldiers while the quiet little world of Wounded Knee exploded into violence. A few Sioux waved frantic hands toward the peace flag atop Big Foot's Sibley tent. The surrender had been granted more or less according to conventional terms of truce. Now, suddenly, the white flag meant nothing to these soldier-demons who fired round after round into the milling, shouting knot of Indian men.

Shocked, bewildered beyond belief, their legs numb from long sitting, the Sioux men were slow to run. One after another went

[3] According to some historians, notably James Mooney and Doane Robinson, the first shot at Wounded Knee was fired by a fanatical Minneconjou warrior named Black Fox. This is not substantiated by Indian eyewitnesses interviewed by the author. So far as is known, the above account is the first completely authenticated version.

down—many killed outright, others writhing wounded on the bloody ground. Iron Hail was one of the few still on his feet in the midst of the dead and dying.

"*Hiyupo!* Come on!" he shouted. "Let's go!"

A handful of warriors rallied around him and they made a dash for the tepee camp from which the women and children were watching them in fascinated horror. As they ran in the only direction which lay open to them, the men were suddenly caught in a downpour of death. The Hotchkiss guns on the hill began to chatter, raining lead all around the council site.

"Keep going!" Iron Hail shouted to the others.

High Hawk, a Minneconjou, was shot and fell. Iron Hail started to go back for him when a bullet knocked him flat. Unable to rescue his friend, he began to crawl back toward the camp.

The spectacle of their unarmed husbands, sons, and fathers running from the shooting soldiers struck cold terror into the onlooking women and children. All around the white flag Indian men were falling over. A few soldiers, caught in the crossfire of fellow troopers, were falling, too. The figures of the men were now so clouded by pale gun smoke that it was hardly possible to tell white man from Indian.

Among the loaded Indian wagons the women and children began to hear a strange rattling.

"Can it be hail?" an old woman asked breathlessly. "It sounds like hailstones striking our wagons."

Presently a young girl screamed in sudden pain.

"They are shooting us!" the women shouted. "Now they are shooting the helpless!"

True enough, two of the Hotchkiss guns were raking the campground as the men came running. Two troops of mounted soldiers tried to quiet their frenzied horses across the ravine, waiting for orders to charge the Indians from that sector. Under a spreading screen of smoke the women flocked toward the ravine. In its shallow defilade they might find momentary shelter from the shower of bullets that now sprayed them as well as their warriors. Men and boys were also running toward the ravine. No plan of escape was yet in their minds. Like the women they ran from sheer panic.

Indians camped for miles around could hear the distant clatter of guns at Wounded Knee. Long afterward they likened the shooting to the long, continuous tearing of a blanket. Throughout the reservation the people knew where Big Foot and his band were camped and surrounded by soldiers. They had also heard that today the old Minneconjou chief was to capitulate formally to Custer's old regiment, the Seventh Cavalry. Instinctively, they realized that all the shooting meant that everything had somehow gone wrong and that something horrendous was taking place over on Wounded Knee Creek.

"*Aaah-hey! Aaah-hey!*" the people wailed. "They are butchering over there! The soldiers are butchering them yonder!"

From camps both friendly and hostile, from ghost dancers and peaceful bands alike, young men were running for their horses and riding fast as storm wind toward the shooting over across the hills.

Black Elk was near Pine Ridge Agency that morning. Out after his horses, he heard the distant ripple of thunder as the guns fired at Wounded Knee eighteen miles away. He raced into camp with his horses. A man rode up shouting:

"The people that are coming are being fired on! Our cousins the Minneconjous are being shot down! I know it!"

Black Elk saddled a buckskin pony, then hurried into his sacred ghost shirt. Made to be worn by no one but himself, it had a spotted eagle with outstretched wings painted on the back and a daybreak star on the left shoulder. A flaming rainbow had been daubed across the garment's front from left shoulder to right hip. Red lightning streaks were marked all over the shirt. Eagle feathers were carefully tied at shoulders, elbows, and wrists. After painting his face red and putting a single spotted eagle feather upright in his hair, Black Elk felt he was ready. He was confident in the protective power of the shirt.

Spurning firearms, he carried a bow as his only weapon. He started out alone on an old trail across the hills. Presently he was followed by about twenty other young men, some wearing ghost shirts, some stripped for fighting. Loves War and Iron White Man [4] were first to catch up with him. They told him they were all going to see where the shooting was going on. With Black Elk out in front on his fast buckskin, they rode together in a tight, galloping knot of battle-eager horsemen. Trailing them at a distance was a strung-out bunch of Indian boys from the same camp, as anxious for excitement and adventure as any men of fighting age.

All this time most of Big Foot's male followers were cut off from any chance of reaching the ravine. Where only minutes earlier the Minneconjous had been sitting in council with the officers, a bloody tangle of bullet-riddled bodies now stained the ground with gore. Maddened at the sight of falling comrades shot down in the crossfire, the troopers awaited no command to open fire. The whole camp was a blazing inferno.

Many Indians, caught in the first volley, fell without a struggle. Catching Spirit Elk went down with ugly wounds in both legs. Frog huddled critically shot under a growing pile of Indian corpses. Others lay dying and helpless on the frozen ground. Of one hundred and six men and boys who had squatted in a semicircle around Big Foot's sick tent, fifty-two were already dead.

Crumpled in the doorway of the Sibley tent, Big Foot had been first of his band to die. His old woman lay inside, wounded by flying bullets pumped into the dead chief by blood-crazed troopers. A younger woman with an infant in her arms was killed as she tried to touch the flag of truce. Not knowing its mother was dead, the baby kept nursing at the woman's breast.

Yellow Bird and a few others who had guns put up a brief running fight. Breaking through the troops and heading for the camp, the medicine man dodged into a tepee. From the scant cover of the lodge he kept shooting his rifle at the soldiers until the tepee caught fire when hit by an explosive shell. With flames

[4] Later an important chief of the Ogalalas, Iron White Man died in 1936. His name, however, has been perpetuated since 1939, when it was conferred upon the author by Black Elk in a unique name-giving ceremony.

dancing all around him, Yellow Bird died gamely—riddled with the bullets to which he thought he was immune.

The soldiers were possessed with a passion for killing. Indians say the troops were drunk from the previous night's orgy. Drunk or sober, the soldiers kept up a continuous fire at any Indian who moved. It was inevitable that revenge for the defensive wiping out of Custer and half the Seventh in seventy-six should become a motive for mass slaughter.

"Remember Little Big Horn!" the soldiers yelled. "Remember Custer!"

Officers found it unnecessary to give commands. The prospect of vengeance and victory over the once-mighty Sioux was all the goad the soldiers needed. Fresh from recruiting stations in the East, never before under fire and not yet imbued with proper military discipline, the green troopers fast turned the valley of Wounded Knee into a bloody shambles.

Colonel James Forsyth stood calmly by as though watching a quiet game of charades in his own parlor. At his very elbow violence flared. A Minneconjou, dashing in on the colonel's flank, plunged a long knife into Father Craft's back, stabbing through to the lungs. Withdrawing the razor-keen blade, the Indian made a lunge toward Forsyth. Philip Wells acted quickly, tripping the colonel so that Forsyth fell away from the knife thrust. At this the angry warrior slashed the weapon across the interpreter's face. Wells's nose was left hanging by small wings back of the nostrils.

Swearing through a gush of blood, Wells swung up his rifle butt, clubbed down the Sioux, then shot him dead. Moments later he growled something about having the regimental surgeon sew his nose back in place.

Within minutes all active resistance on the part of the Indians was over. Yet the troopers kept firing. Twenty-nine soldiers were killed outright in their own deadly crossfire. About the same number were wounded—two of them mortally.

Heedless of his wound, Father Craft moved about the field, bravely administering the last rites to whites and Indians alike in spite of bullets flying all around him. At last he fell unconscious from loss of blood.

Only one soldier was actually killed at Wounded Knee by an Indian. Captain George D. Wallace, commander of K Troop and a veteran of Little Big Horn, was struck down by a warrior brandishing a stone-headed war club. His skull crushed, Wallace was found dead near the council circle with four stray bullets in his body.

Nearly all casualties suffered by the troops were unwittingly inflicted by their own comrades. Lieutenant E. A. Garlington, long-time adjutant of the Seventh Cavalry, was severely wounded. Lieutenant H. L. Hawthorne, Second Artillery, was shot in the groin and retired from action. An otherwise fatal bullet was deflected when it struck his turnip-size pocket watch.

Command of the Hotchkiss guns unaccountably fell to Corporal Paul H. Weinert, a trooper of little experience and no scruples when it came to killing noncombatants. From his hilltop Weinert lobbed two-pound high-explosive shells into the Indian camp at the rate of nearly fifty a minute—mowing down everything alive.

Under the hailstorm of bullets and shells a handful of Sioux men and boys broke through the ranks of K Troop. Led by Iron Hail, now seriously wounded, few of them ever reached the defilade of the ravine. Iron Hail got through, hoping to cross the ravine and keep going on to safety beyond. He saw at once that escape to the south was blocked by a screen of cavalry and Indian scouts, whose dim shapes loomed along the south rim through a haze of smoke and dust.

The ravine was already clogged with terrified Sioux women and children. Nearly all of them were running breathlessly to the west—away from Wounded Knee Creek. Following the only possible escape route, they were attempting to reach the sparse cover of a clump of pines at the ravine's head several hundred yards away. As troopers poured bullets into the fleeing Indians, the ravine was fast turning into a death trap.

Suddenly the dreaded explosive shells began to burst in the ravine. Weinert's Hotchkiss guns found new targets in the running fugitives. A warrior at Iron Hail's elbow was nearly blown to bits when one of the shells made a direct hit.[5]

5 The victim was a Minneconjou named Hawk Feather Shooter.

In the face of this new terror Iron Hail showed rare courage. Standing unarmed at the ravine's rim, he helped the wounded men and boys over the edge of the cut bank.

"*Hiyupo!*" he kept shouting. "Come on! It is terrible! Come on as fast as you can!"

Failing to realize that it was their own bullets which had brought down their comrades, the troopers fought on with a vengeful grievance. After the first salvos of rifle fire, the regiment deployed in every direction to drive the Sioux from cover and ride them down.

"Remember Custer!" the soldiers yelled again and again, their hoarse shouts dinning above the staccato chatter of gunfire.

In the heat of pursuit, the troops made no attempt to distinguish between men and women. Officers later claimed they shouted orders not to kill women or children, but the troopers gave the usual excuse that it was next to impossible to make out the age or sex of running Indians. Although never borne out by Indian testimony, a few soldiers insisted that some women had been armed and fighting as fiercely as the men.

Many women and children were saved by courageous Sioux scouts. Under heavy fire and at great risk, they defied death to protect the wounded and helpless from the insane wrath of the soldiers. One Ogalala scout (Feather-on-Head) even carried water to the wounded Indians. Some rescue attempts met with tragedy. Two scouts were severely injured by flying shrapnel. Mistaken by the troops for one of Big Foot's followers, Scout Highbackbone was shot dead while helping an old woman reach the shelter of the ravine.

By this time the soldiers' hunt for fugitives had become a mad free-for-all which brought mounting horror to the Sioux. Indians fell on all sides like grain before a scythe. Their broken bodies lay shattered and limp, resembling blood-splotched marionettes flung aside by some ruthless puppeteer.

Instead of following Iron Hail's lead toward the ravine, Pipe-on-Head darted through the line of troopers and started running east toward a hillside across Wounded Knee Creek. He almost stumbled over a little boy who lay trembling in the grass. Still running, Pipe-on-Head grabbed him by one hand and tried to lead him along. From the smoking ruins of the Indian camp a woman came chasing after the boys. She was Pipe-on-Head's

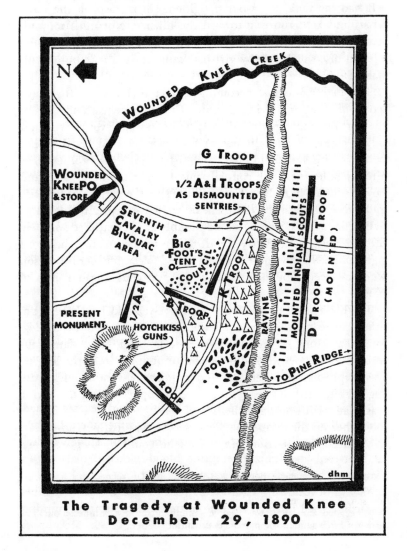

The Tragedy at Wounded Knee
December 29, 1890

mother, carrying his baby sister on her back. Grabbing both boys by the hand, she ran with them toward safety.

Bullets spat up dust all around them, screaming through the air about their heads. Suddenly a slug struck. Thinking she herself had been hit, the woman tightened her grasp on the boys' wrists and kept running toward the hillside. Not until minutes later, after they had made their way across the creek, did the woman discover her baby girl had caught a soldier's bullet and was dead.[6]

The ravine was fast becoming a river of blood, clotted with scores of dead and dying Indians. Crawling beneath the lip of the north bank, Iron Hail glanced down to see his young wife and infant child sprawled lifeless. A few paces beyond lay the dead bodies of his father, mother, and sister. Both his brothers had already fallen near the council ring. Letting the other men and boys rush past him, Iron Hail knelt beside the corpses of his wife and baby. Beneath the cut bank he waited—praying for death.

Up the ravine a woman stared dumbly at the shattered splinters of bone and gristle that were all that remained of her shell-torn right hand. Nearby another woman tried to comfort her infant son who had been shot in the mouth and was coughing out clots of blood.

Teeth clenched against pain, a twelve-year-old boy begged another lad to help him peel off the blood-drenched buckskin legging that clung to his wounded left leg. For long, dangerous minutes both boys worked under continuous fire until the legging was stripped away. Then they kept going as best they could, heading back toward the creek now since the upper end of the ravine was aflame with bursting shells.[7]

Farther up the ravine the Sioux retreat was led by Ghost Bear, a Minneconjou warrior. He did all he could to keep everyone

[6] As an old woman in her eighties, Mary Runs On related this harrowing episode to the author in 1940. Various details were subsequently confirmed by her son, James Pipe-on-Head.

[7] The good Samaritan was George Running Hawk, a Minneconjou. The name of his wounded companion is unknown.

moving on toward the clump of pines. But many of the wounded were unable to keep up with the others and began to lag behind. Mounted troopers kept riding along the south rim of the ravine, shooting down the helpless and defenseless Indians.

Suddenly a voice among the troopers called out in Sioux: "Come out of there! The fighting is over!"

As the shooting abruptly stopped, a group of unarmed little boys slowly filed out of the ravine and stood in a frightened huddle on the flat. Without warning the soldiers began shooting again, firing point-blank into the little group until all the lads lay crumbled and motionless on the ground.

The Sioux who remained alive in the ravine now numbered fewer than sixty. Only a handful reached the cover of the pine trees, and all of them now stayed well hidden or feigned death, lying motionless for hours as the day wore on.

A few other fugitives—four men and seven women—reached a low hill above the ravine where they painfully dug a trench in the frozen ground with bleeding fingers. None of them had any sort of digging tool or weapon and their survival was pure accident so far as the soldiers were concerned.

Swaggering among the dead and wounded Indians, troopers were giving the *coup de grâce* to anything that moved. Even the Indian ponies were shot down. Finding a whimpering infant at its dead mother's breast, a soldier grabbed it up squawling, threw it in the air, then shot it dead with his revolver before it hit the ground.

The massacre at Wounded Knee may well have had no survivors had not Sioux horsemen from the agency and the ghost-dance camp suddenly arrived on the ridge just west of the little valley. Led by Black Elk, about twenty of them galloped down toward the head of the ravine. All along the ravine cavalrymen were riding and shooting into it. A tiny knot of women and children huddled against the far bank. Troopers were already pointing guns at them when Black Elk's riders came to the rescue.

"Take courage! Brave up!" Black Elk shouted to the others. "These are our kinsmen. We'll try to save them."

In angry unison the rescuers shouted, "It is time to fight!"

Leading out, Black Elk let a fighting song start high in his throat.

> "A thunder-being nation am I!
> You shall live, you shall live!"

Soon the other warriors sang with him. Few in numbers, they made up for it in courage. Here were such brave fighters as Loves War, Iron White Man, and Eagle Elk, Kicking Bear's old fighting comrade. Eagle Elk had longed for battle since the death of his wife and child. Now his heart sang with the hope that he could die here on the prairie under the soldiers' guns. Grouping into a close-knitted wedge, some forty Ogalalas careered downhill toward the troopers who threatened the women and children. The soldiers fired at the attackers and then fell back, apparently convinced that more Indians lurked beyond the ridge.

"Hoka-hey! Hoka-hey!" went the old Sioux war cry, and the Minneconjou women sounded the tremolo as the warriors swept by.

The troops were actually retreating before the Ogalalas. In short order the warriors helped the women and children to safety across the ridge to the northwest.

Black Elk found a tiny baby lying all alone near the head of the ravine. Wrapping her in a bullet-torn shawl that lay nearby, he left her in a safe place and rode on. To the east the soldiers were rallying, throwing themselves prone on the ground to shoot at the rescuers.

"Wait!" Black Elk commanded his followers.

Alone, armed only with the "sacred" bow, Black Elk charged the troops. They all fired at him and bullets whistled all around him, but none found their mark. He galloped up to the soldiers' first line of defense, shouted his defiance, wheeled sharply, and came back at a dead run.

By this time more Sioux had ridden up along the ridge. Many of them were mere boys. Peering up at them, Loves War shouted to them to return to the agency since they were in danger from flying bullets. Some younger boys obeyed. But the older youths lingered on the ridge top. Soon reinforced by late arrivals from the agency camps, they began to mass for a new attack on the soldiers. The troops were now spread out in a wide, defensive position with their backs to Wounded Knee Creek. Dismounting, many troopers were frantically digging trenches in the flinty soil.

Bad as they felt about the obvious slaughter on the flat below, not all of the Ogalalas were ready to fight the soldiers. Twenty-nine-year-old Black Horn had friends among Taylor's company of scouts and wished to join them. Trying to reach the soldiers' new position, he rode a wide circle around the surrounding hills and trotted in on the troops' left flank. Although he was dressed in citizen clothes, he was carrying a Winchester for protection. A mixed-blood scout (possibly Garnier) mistook him for one of Black Elk's warriors and shouted a warning to the soldiers. As soon as Black Horn came within range the soldiers began shooting at him. He fired back in self-defense. With no chance at all of reaching his friends among the scouts, he joined Black Elk on the ridge.

Battle cries ringing on their lips, the Ogalalas swept across the valley with Black Elk well out in front. Time and again the Indians hurled themselves at the lines of dismounted cavalrymen. For all their fury, it was soon clear to the attackers that they were too few to dislodge an entire regiment of troops. Moreover, the Hotchkiss guns had been turned around so as to rake the ridge top, making it untenable for reinforcements from the ghost-dance camp. After the loss of two men the Ogalalas withdrew.

Eagle Elk did not get his wish. Although he had charged in close to the soldiers, not a bullet had so much as scratched him. Now he rode sadly away with the other warriors. Passing the handful of Minneconjou survivors he had helped rescue, he was startled to hear a woman call him by name.

"They have killed him!" she wailed. "They have killed him!"

Reining up, Eagle Elk slid off his pony and gazed dumfounded at the woman. She was older and heavier, but there was no mistaking her. She was his long-lost sweetheart, Her Eagle Robe, who had married a Hunkpapa man in Grandmother's Land and had traveled south, first with Sitting Bull's band, then with Big Foot's followers. She held a dead baby, a little boy, under her blanket, and Eagle Elk thought she had been speaking of him. She presently explained that her husband had been killed and it was his death she had been moaning about, but she refused to believe the little boy was dead and held him tight to her breast.

Saying nothing, Eagle Elk gently helped the woman mount his pony. Although many years had passed and he and Her Eagle Robe had been living almost in different worlds, she was still very much a part of him. Walking beside this woman who was both sweetheart and stranger, he led the animal across the hills toward the agency.

In spite of the futility in fighting the entrenched soldiers, the Ogalalas might have kept up some sort of holding action had it not been for signs of an approaching blizzard out of the north. With many a glance toward the threatening sky, the warriors split up into small groups as if by common consent. The troops in their trenches made no attempt to pursue them.

Black Elk stopped near the head of the ravine to pick up the tiny orphaned baby. Wrapping her snugly in the tattered shawl, he held her close to him and kept his pony at an easy gait all the way back to the agency so she would not be jostled.

His followers were thoroughly aroused. Truculent, angry at seeing their northern relatives ruthlessly butchered, they were in no mood for friendliness toward any white man. Along the way back to Pine Ridge several of them encountered a familiar lanky horseman who sat straight and tall in his saddle and displayed no trace of fear at the sight of them. McGillycuddy, their former agent, had courageously ridden out to investigate the gunfire.

"Don't you know us, Little Beard?" one Indian said mockingly.

McGillycuddy eyed him levelly. The warrior insolently edged forward until his pony stood shoulder to shoulder against McGillycuddy's mount.

"When you were our agent you promised us that if we gave you fifty of our young men to act as police, the soldiers would never come to our agency." A sneer twisted at the Indian's lips. Suddenly he threw back his blanket to reveal a fresh bullet wound from which blood still oozed. "Look at that, Little Beard! I was one of your policemen. The soldiers did this to me. What about your promise now?"

McGillycuddy never took his gaze away from the Indian's eyes.

"A promise is of no value, Thunder Cloud, when one ceases to have the power to fulfill it."

With that, McGillycuddy firmly took Thunder Cloud's pony by the bridle and rode back to the agency beside the wounded Indian.

The so-called Battle of Wounded Knee began shortly before nine o'clock the morning of December 29, 1890. By three in the afternoon it was all over. Twenty-nine troopers and one officer were killed on the Army side. Estimates vary as to the number of Indians slaughtered and their loss will never be known. Conservative guesses on the part of the military placed it as low as one hundred and forty-five killed, thirty-three wounded. But more authoritative sources indicate that the total number of Sioux men, women, and children who were killed on the field or later died from wounds and exposure was nearly three hundred!

When the troops at last began to filter out of their trenches, the approaching storm was almost upon them. Only the briefest of surveys could be made of the frightful carnage which strewed the valley. The bodies of dead women and children, obviously shot down after all resistance had ceased and every warrior was dead or wounded, were found as far as three miles from the smoldering shambles of the Sioux campground—mute evidence that Army discipline had degenerated to a point where fighting Indians had become little more than a grisly game of pursuing unarmed noncombatants.

The troops felt few pangs of conscience. Breezily cocky about their "victory" over old Big Foot, many soldiers wanted ghost shirts and dresses for souvenirs. Most of the Indian corpses were accordingly stripped and left lying naked.

One officer had promised an Indian scalp as a memento to a young lady in the East. So at least one fallen Indian was duly mutilated. The commanding officer carefully overlooked such activities, however; as Colonel Forsyth himself put it that afternoon:

"Now we have avenged Custer's death!"

His face black with caked blood, his nose held in place with strips of court plaster provided by the surgeon, Interpreter Philip Wells smiled wryly under his bandages as he felt a growing revulsion for these men who called themselves soldiers.

"Maybe so, Colonel," he admitted. "But the Seventh started the fireworks that day at Little Big Horn and had every opportunity to fight for its life.[8] These poor Indians never had a chance...."

[8] For the Indians' version of the Battle of Little Big Horn, see the author's earlier book, *Custer's Fall*.

Black Days

THE guns of Wounded Knee were heard clearly at Pine Ridge Agency. All morning scores of newspaper correspondents and curious onlookers, red men and white alike, had been riding off across the hills toward the distant thunder of gunfire. The return of an Indian messenger to the friendly Ogalala camp shortly after noon was scarcely noticed by the agency employees and civilians who remained at the settlement. Soon a runner was jogging on foot along the ridges north of the agency, carrying news of the massacre to the ghost-dance camp near Drexel Catholic Mission,[1] some four miles away. Indians say the ghost dancers learned of Big Foot's fate long before a mounted courier delivered a terse dispatch from Colonel Forsyth to General Brooke's headquarters.

In the confusion and turmoil which followed General Brooke could do little to prevent a general stampede on the part of friendly Indians who genuinely feared for their lives at the hands of the military. Hundreds of frightened Sioux lined the road north to the ghost-dance camp as lodges were struck and cook fires abandoned and wagons and pony drags hurriedly loaded.

Heading the mass exodus was Two Strike and his unruly Brûlés, corraled since December 12 at Pine Ridge. Even old Red Cloud lowered his flag to half-mast, left his big house standing empty, and fled with the others. Save for Captain Sword's fifty loyal police and a handful of friendly chiefs, few Indians remained at the agency.

With the Seventh Cavalry at Wounded Knee and the Ninth

[1] Later called the Holy Rosary Mission. The old mission buildings remain standing.

Cavalry on patrol in the Bad Lands, General Brooke was caught short-handed. The agency enclosure was not barricaded and only a small detachment of infantry was on hand to protect it. Dispatching an urgent plea for more reinforcements to General Miles in Rapid City, Brooke prepared for the worst. Reprisals were naturally to be expected. Nearly all Sioux Indians found common cause in the cruel butchery at Wounded Knee. Sentinels were hurriedly spotted around the agency and Hotchkiss guns trained on the various approaches.

Kicking Bear at once rallied his fighting force at the ghost-dance camp, now bolstered by thousands of Sioux who had previously wavered. Gone immediately was any thought of dissension among the warriors, and all sense of rivalry between Kicking Bear and Short Bull was quickly forgotten.

The strategy of Kicking Bear was simple: strike where the white man was weakest. The agency now was a vulnerable target. Time later to catch the cavalry in an ambuscade.

The ghost dancers struck at an unexpected quarter. A big band of warriors suddenly appeared on a hilltop several hundred yards north of the government boarding school, situated just west of the agency buildings. Nearly two hundred Indian boys and girls were quartered in the school, and it may have been Kicking Bear's thought to "rescue" them from the authorities.

In any case a few hotheaded young warriors began firing on the school as well as various outlying buildings. Attempts were made to set them afire. Many a Sioux elder, then attending the boarding school as a child, has long since recalled for the author how the terrified youngsters obeyed their frightened teachers and lay flat on the cold floor as bullets crashed through the windows. Hugh Top Bear, an old man of eighty-three in 1958, was then a boy of fifteen. He well remembers seeing Kicking Bear and Two Strike marshal their warriors on the hilltop for what threatened to be an all-out assault on the agency.

Meanwhile another daring ghost-dance leader, Turning Bear of the Brûlés, was pirouetting his horse down the hillside, singing a shrill ghost-dance song as he rode.

"My child, come this way,
My child, come this way!
You shall grow to be a nation!"

Although Turning Bear's own son [2] was among Two Strike's warriors and Brûlé children were then in school at Pine Ridge, many older boys, including Top Bear, wanted to join him then and there.

The ghost dancers soon met unexpected resistance, however, ironically enough from some of their own tribesmen. Everyone had apparently forgotten all about the Indian policemen still loyal to the Government. Now they came on the double to form a thin, defensive line along the schoolyard fence facing north and began blazing away at Turning Bear and other warriors who charged down the hill. Shooting to kill, they fired shot after shot, bringing down at least two ghost dancers and forcing the others back uphill.

Indians still laugh at the memory of Agent Royer letting his police take the brunt of any attack that might come while he sought safety in a nearby cellar. General Brooke, on the other hand, displayed cool courage in taking command of the defenders. Even Dr. Eastman was on the defense line. Having announced his engagement to Elaine Goodale on Christmas Day, the doctor had already provided two saddle horses for his fiancée's escape once general fighting broke out. As yet, however, both Miss Goodale and Mrs. Cook, wife of the rector, were standing by bravely on the chance they might be of some service.

As Turning Bear rode uphill, General Brooke ran out in the open.

"Stop! Stop!" he commanded the Indian police, who apparently did not understand him and kept firing.

Brooke turned desperately to Dr. Eastman. Bullets flew all around.

"Doctor, tell them they must not fire again until I order it.

[2] Owns-the-Battle, past ninety years of age, is still alive at this writing. He lives just west of Rosebud, South Dakota.

You pop at one of those fellows up there and ten of his friends rush to help him!"

Eastman immediately complied. He well understood that the defenders were in no position to repel a large attacking force of ghost dancers and that their only chance was to discourage, if possible, further fighting.

Once the police stopped firing, the scattered shots of the ghost dancers soon ceased. Kicking Bear was aware that the police force included many relatives of his own followers, and he was still determined that no Sioux should shoot down his brother Sioux. After brandishing weapons and shouting threats from the hilltop for a while, the ghost dancers gradually withdrew and moved eastward to intercept the Seventh Cavalry.

Outriding scouts from Kicking Bear's force had spotted troops approaching the agency through the gathering twilight. It was soon apparent that the Seventh had broken up into several columns for the ride back to Pine Ridge. Kicking Bear and his warriors promptly assaulted one of these columns, forcing the soldiers to give up twenty-three women and children of Big Foot's band who had been taken prisoner after the Wounded Knee massacre. The ghost dancers then fired the prairie and might well have annihilated the column had not dense smoke and approaching darkness put an end to the skirmish.

At dusk, with ghost dancers dogging their flanks and rear, the Seventh Cavalry marched into the agency, bringing their twenty-five dead and thirty-four wounded and some thirty-odd Indian women and children, most of them badly wounded. The Reverend Mr. Cook at once offered the mission chapel, later known as the Church of the Holy Cross, for use as a temporary hospital since the Army lacked sufficient Sibley tents to house the wounded Indians. Pews were torn out of the chapel and the floor covered with hay and quilts. A decorated Christmas tree was left standing.

General Brooke placed Dr. Eastman in charge of all the wounded Indians and the young physician soon had his hands full trying to take care of the poor tortured creatures single-handed. But the Army surgeons had all they could do to take care of their own wounded. Moreover, the Indians refused to allow any man in uniform to touch them. Miss Goodale, Mrs. Cook, and several of Cook's Sioux assistants served as volunteer nurses. Eastman gratefully accepted their help.

Suffering in the little chapel was terrible. Many Indians had been frightfully mangled by Hotchkiss shells and most of them were convinced they would soon die. In spite of everything the doctor and his aides could do, one after another of the pitiful women and children succumbed. Their torn bodies were quietly carried out to the churchyard to make more room for those inside.

Soon after the arrival of the troops and their wounded captives, McGillycuddy wandered over to the chapel in search of disabled friends. He had gotten back to the agency after Kicking Bear's attack and had treated Thunder Cloud's wound, then had the former policeman bedded down in his own quarters.

At the door of the chapel McGillycuddy met American Horse, one of the few remaining friendly chiefs in the settlement.

"Little Beard," said American Horse, "I want you to come in here and see my kinsman, Hunts-the-Enemy-by-Night. He is hurt bad."

McGillycuddy entered with the chief and they went to the wounded Indian's pallet. Hunts-the-Enemy-by-Night, a Minneconjou of Big Foot's band, had indeed been critically hurt. A rifle ball had gone through his cheeks, breaking out teeth on both sides and completely shattering the roof of his mouth. His left knee was also severely wounded and gangrene was fast setting in, although the mouth injury had so far proved the more troublesome.

American Horse explained to him that McGillycuddy was the Indians' friend, had been the Ogalalas' agent for seven years, and before that had been a practicing surgeon. Hunts-the-Enemy-at-Night was finally willing to let McGillycuddy examine his wounds. In giving his prognosis, McGillycuddy told him his leg would have to be amputated.

"I shall not be able to ride a horse again if I lose a leg," the warrior protested.

"If this leg isn't amputated you'll never ride a horse again anyway," McGillycuddy told him. "In three days you'll die."

Beads of sweat broke out on the warrior's face as he chewed on his lip and made a typical Indian decision.

"Then in three days I will be in the Spirit Land and I'll have both legs so I can ride after the buffalo that are there!" [3]

It was nearly dark when Black Elk rode into the deserted Ogalala camp near the agency with the little baby clutched tight against him and a warrior, Red Crow, riding beside him. Red Crow had also found a baby whose mother had been slain at Wounded Knee. The two young men looked around in vain for some woman with whom they might leave the two infants. Finding a cook pot full of dried beef in one of the abandoned lodges, they sat down inside and began to eat.

Presently soldiers who had spotted them began shooting at the tepee from the agency. One bullet struck between the two Indians and spat dust into the cook pot. But the hungry warriors kept eating until they had their fill. Then they grabbed up the babies, made a run for their horses, and rode off down White Clay Creek, following the trail of the main body of Ogalalas.

Late that night they caught up with the rest of the tribe. No tepees had been set up and people were huddled around little cook fires, ready to flee or fight should the soldiers attack them. It did not seem likely that the troops would tackle them tonight, however, for snow was already falling and a harsh wind was whipping down across the Bad Lands.

Black Elk was glad to be back among friends and relatives. As he and Red Crow rode in among the scattered families, he heard his mother singing a death song for him. She thought he had been killed when he attacked the soldiers at Wounded Knee. Now she was so happy to see him again that she wept through most of the night.

The little babies were soon turned over to women who had milk in their breasts. But hardly anyone except the smallest children slept in the stormy darkness.

Before daybreak next morning Kicking Bear led out a huge

[3] Refusing to have the leg amputated, he died two days later.

war party from the nearby ghost-dance camp. Many Ogalalas, including Black Elk, eagerly joined him for now they all wanted
revenge on the soldiers for the massacre of Big Foot and his band.
Warriors by the hundreds crossed White Clay Creek to the west
bank and rode upstream.

Striking west, the war party loped out on a high ridge overlooking the Drexel Catholic Mission. They sighted eight troops
of cavalry riding downstream—most of the Seventh under Colonel Forsyth sent out to protect the mission. This was Kicking
Bear's chance. Casting about for bait for his trap, he saw the
empty log cabins which belonged to the Ogalala Spleen band and
had his warriors set them afire. The device worked. Forsyth led
his troopers past the mission at a gallop and straight into ambush
beyond the ridge. Soon the soldiers were trapped on low ground
along the creek while sniping Sioux warriors were in great force
on all the surrounding hills.

It was the last real brush the Sioux had with the United States
Army. Kicking Bear made the most of it, using as he did the
old Indian time-tried strategy of lure and ambush.

Colonel Forsyth soon found himself in a tight spot, his troops
threatened with annihilation. He frantically sent a courier back
to the agency for reinforcements. Although he had a Hotchkiss
gun with him, the murderous weapon was of little use against
the stealthy tactics of Kicking Bear and his warriors. For here
were no disarmed Indians tricked into talking peace, no helpless
women or children, but well-armed veteran fighting men.

Black Elk was in the thick of the attack, having discarded his
bow in favor of a Winchester. For a brief time it was almost like
the old days again when the Sioux overwhelmed Crook on the
Rosebud and wiped out Custer at Little Big Horn.

"This is a day in which to do great things!" a warrior cried.

"*Hau!* It is indeed!" Black Elk called back.

Jumping off his horse, he rubbed dry earth all over his body
to show that without the help of the Powers he was nothing.
Then he grabbed up his rifle, remounted his little buckskin, and
galloped on up the high ridge.

Down along the creek the soldiers were shooting up at the

Indians. Everyone told Black Elk not to venture down there where he was certain to be killed. But he paid no attention to the warnings. He kicked the buckskin into a dead run and charged down the hillside straight at the soldiers.

The troopers showed great surprise when Black Elk rode up within a few paces of their lines and shot in their faces. All this time, however, they kept shooting at him and bullets were buzzing all around him. Unafraid, he let out a shrill war yell, then wheeled his pony and loped back up the hill. Near the top a bullet struck his belt, nearly knocking him from his mount. Hanging on to the pony's mane, he rode on to safety beyond the crest of the ridge.

The bullet cut a deep gash across the abdomen. His intestines were beginning to protrude through the gush of blood. He could stay on the little horse no longer and slumped to the ground. Presently Protector, an old man who had ridden out with the warriors, came running up the hill. Tearing a blanket into strips, he bound Black Elk's abdomen so the intestines would stay in place.

"It is a good day to die!" Black Elk cried. "Help me on my horse! Let me go and fight until I die!"

But the old man held him back.

"No, Nephew! You must not die today. Your people still need you. There will be a better day to die sometime.[4]

Finally Protector helped Black Elk on to the buckskin and led the horse down behind the ridge away from the flying bullets. By this time Black Elk was feeling the effects of the wound and was sick. He rode slowly away, confident that the soldiers would be wiped out and that the Sioux would have another great day of victory.

It seemed certain to Kicking Bear and his cohorts that a spectacular triumph was at hand. The hated Seventh Cavalry and its brutal commander were surely doomed. That the crestfallen regiment was not annihilated that day was a pure accident of chance.

[4] Black Elk lived to ripe old age and passed away in 1950.

As it happened General Brooke had no reinforcements to send to Forsyth's rescue until the providential return to Pine Ridge of the travel-weary Ninth Cavalry under Major Guy V. Henry. These black "buffalo soldiers" had ridden more than one hundred miles and had beaten off an attack by part of Kicking Bear's force on their pack train within the past thirty hours. Now they made quite a show of courage and suddenly appeared on high ground with trumpets blaring the charge. Carbines blazing, they swooped down on the Sioux besiegers. So completely unexpected was their maneuver that many Indians turned and fled. Only by lashing his warriors back with his quirt was Kicking Bear able to force a few of them into fighting a delaying action and avoiding pursuit.

Forsyth and Henry, however, decided that too many Indians were out against them and withdrew their regiments to Pine Ridge. The Sioux retired to their camp site seven miles north of the agency where their womenfolk were already packing belongings for another headlong flight into the Bad Lands.

Military outposts to the west prevented the ghost dancers from traveling far in that direction. But few Indians thought of running to any place but the Stronghold, where their women and children would be safe from the soldiers.

Presently the big campground on the Stronghold came alive again. There were more tribesmen here than ever before, including a number of Minneconjous and Hunkpapas that were refugees from Big Foot's band. Other survivors of the Wounded Knee massacre were hiding out in the nearby White River badlands.

Almost at once the Indians were faced with a food problem. Fresh meat was scarcer than ever and the hundreds of fighting men and their families looked with little enthusiasm toward the bleak days of hunger that were sure to lie ahead. Moreover, there was not the slightest solace of victory for the warriors as a bone-chilling north wind swept the Stronghold.

Back at the agency Dr. Eastman and several Indian police were ordered out in the face of lashing wind and stinging snow to look for a missing cavalryman. An officer who had been killed and seven wounded troopers of the Seventh Cavalry had been removed from the site of Kicking Bear's ambush by their comrades at arms. Upon the regiment's return to Pine Ridge, however, Private Dominic Francischetti failed to answer roll call and was presumed lost. After hours of fruitless searching, Eastman's party returned to the agency, whereupon General Brooke offered a reward for the recovery of the soldier, dead or alive.

That night and all the following day the blizzard settled like a pall of gloom over the land, carpeting the bloody field at Wounded Knee with a frozen white mantle. And off in the icy solitude of snow-covered corpses a baby suckled futilely at its mother's lifeless breast and whimpered a lonely cry against the deafening howl of the weather.

The new year of 1891 made a glum arrival at Pine Ridge Agency—as did General Nelson A. Miles. Accompanied by Lieutenant Casey's Cheyenne Scouts, a company of Crow scouts also recruited in Montana, and various other reinforcements, Miles was far from pleased with the military situation that greeted him.

On New Year's Day Kicking Bear's hungry warriors ran off a government beef herd a few miles from the agency and killed a herder, Henry Miller.[5] An estimated four thousand Indians—better than thirteen hundred fighting men—were now placed in open hostility against the United States.

One of Miles's first official acts was to relieve Colonel Forsyth from command of the Seventh Cavalry, pending an Army inquiry into the misconduct and lack of discipline displayed by the troops at Wounded Knee. The general's harshest criticism was leveled at Forsyth for deploying his regiment in such a position as to allow them to kill and wound each other. Obviously all casualties suffered by the Seventh could not have been inflicted by disarmed Indians.

General Brooke was also under a cloud for a lackluster campaign of doubt and uncertainty. Miles directed him to assume

[5] Miller was the only noncombatant killed by Indians during the entire campaign.

immediate command of all field operations and held him personally responsible.

Also on New Year's Day General Miles ordered out a party to bury the dead Indians at Wounded Knee. Nearly a hundred civilians, ten or fifteen of whom were whites, volunteered for the grim task. Several Indian members of the group, including Dr. Eastman, insisted that some of Big Foot's wounded followers might still be alive and the party was consequently provided with wagons in which to convey any survivors back to the agency. A photographer and several reporters went along, although without authorization from General Miles's headquarters.

The weather had cleared but the ground was covered with an inch or two of snow, making the journey to Wounded Knee rough and tedious. From the ridges overlooking the silent valley the bodies of the slaughtered Indians were grotesque little figures against the snow. Frozen stiff and covered with blood, they had a look as unreal as dim shapes in a nightmare.

The body of a woman blanketed with snow was found fully three miles from the site of the massacre. From that point on corpses were scattered across the flat and along the ravine, mute evidence that they had been relentlessly pursued and butchered while running for their lives.

Some members of the burial party found relatives or friends among the dead and there was much wailing and mourning. At the spot where the Indian camp had stood piles of frozen bodies lay. The corpses of eighty men sprawled in weird frozen lifelessness in the semicircle of the council ring.

The sight of such carnage was unsettling to everyone in the party. Nearly all the Indians were now singing death songs or weeping aloud. Only Dr. Eastman had the presence of mind to insist that an immediate search be made for those among the fallen who might remain alive. He set the white men to uncovering and examining every body to make sure none of them still breathed. In spite of having lain untended in bitter cold and snow for two days and two nights, a number of Big Foot's followers survived.

Among those who lived was a tiny year-old baby wrapped in a

shawl and found beside her dead mother. On the infant's head was a little cap of buckskin upon which the American flag had been carefully beaded in bright colors. Eastman brought her to the wagons with three other living babies. Of the four, she alone pulled through.

One terribly wounded Indian begged Eastman to fill his pipe for a last smoke before he died. He survived long enough, however, to be carried back to Pine Ridge and there reunite with his wife and daughters, although he succumbed a day or so later.

An old woman, blind and helpless, was found under a smoke-blackened wagon. A few other women and children were discovered in Mousseau's abandoned log store where they had managed to crawl after the departure of the soldiers. Several wagon-loads of survivors were hurriedly sent back to the agency.

It was then that a band of warriors was observed on one of the adjacent hills. Assuming they were relatives or friends of the victims, the burial party feared an attack. If the job was to be completed without interference, an escort of soldiers was needed for protection. It fell to Dr. Eastman, who owned the best horse, to go for help. He covered the eighteen miles back to Pine Ridge in short order and Casey's Cheyenne Scouts soon arrived on the scene, painted for war and ready for a clash with their old Sioux allies.

By this time a trench had been dug some fifty feet long, six feet wide, and six feet deep. Without caskets or ceremony, the bodies were thrown stiff and naked into the trench like piles of cord-wood.

Although five salaried missionaries were stationed at or near Pine Ridge Agency, not one was on hand to read prayers over the dead or comfort the bereaved. Its gruesome task completed, the burial party returned to the agency without further incident.

Desultory skirmishing resumed in the days that followed. On January 3, Kicking Bear led a strong attack against a detachment of the Sixth Cavalry patrolling Grass Creek. Repulsed, the ghost dancers were thus checked in their attempt to scrounge much-needed food from ranches bordering the reservation. Moreover, four Indians were killed—a demoralizing loss.

On January 5, Kicking Bear lashed out again, attacking an Army supply train on Wounded Knee Creek with about fifty warriors. A troop of cavalry sent out to escort the wagons into the agency found them circled to resist the Indian onslaught. Soldiers and teamsters finally drove off the Sioux, killing a number of their ponies. Later reinforced, Kicking Bear's warriors returned to the attack. A hard skirmish continued until dusk when more troops arrived in the nick of time, forcing the Indians to retreat to the Stronghold.

In the face of these reverses, a growing discontent gnawed at the ghost dancers. While Indians who were still ostensibly friendly to the Government were surreptitiously bringing food to their kinsmen in the Stronghold,[6] they also brought disquieting news. General Miles now had some one hundred forty companies of infantry and cavalry—about eight thousand soldiers—aligned against the ghost dancers. The hostiles would do well to make the best terms they could with Bear Coat Miles and move in to the agency to surrender.

Although Miles's forces now outnumbered the ghost dancers nearly seven to one, the general knew that an all-out assault on the Stronghold would cost many lives—Indians as well as whites. He decided upon the subtler strategy of starving the hungry Sioux into submission. Every day fresh reports of unrest among the hostiles reached his headquarters. And every day he tightened the chain of troops around the Stronghold, preventing the ghost dancers from moving in any direction other than south toward the agency. With the help of such friendly Ogalala chiefs as Young-Man-Afraid-of-His-Horses, American Horse, and Standing Bear (Luther's father), Miles repeatedly sent messages to the ghost dancers, reassuring them that they would be treated kindly if they surrendered.

As yet, however, few ghost-dance leaders had any real inten-

[6] Visiting Indians were not allowed to enter the Stronghold, but bags and baskets of food were brought to the plateau's precipitous edge and hauled up on ropes by the ghost dancers.

tion of giving up. Their renewed bickering was only a symptom of their terrible hunger and privation. But their stubborn resistance was causing a marked increase in apprehension among whites in the northern plains. Subsequent events added to the tumult of excitement.

The body of the Seventh Cavalry's Private Francischetti was recovered during the first week in January. The trooper's corpse had been stripped and scalp, beard, mustaches, and even the eyebrows had been taken. The arms and legs had been hacked off save for tendons which held them to the torso. The belly had been slashed open and arrows had been jammed into the naked chest. The remains were a grim reminder that the Sioux were not yet subdued.

On his way back to Rapid City, Valentine McGillycuddy had a look at the grisly cadaver displayed in a wagon near the agency sawmill. Genuinely shocked, he turned to reprimand a crowd of friendly Indians gathered around the wagon.

"I thought the Sioux had given up this barbaric practice years ago!"

"One of our people was scalped the other day at Wounded Knee," an old man answered. "For every Indian scalped there shall be a scalped white man!"

State troops were immediately called into service when a facetious resident of Chadron, Nebraska, sent out a bogus telegram on January 6 saying that his town was "surrounded by three thousand hostile Sioux" and that sixteen citizens had "already been killed by the redskins." The situation was regarded as so critical that appropriations earmarked for an annual state fair were hurriedly diverted to military purposes.

On January 7, however, genuine tragedy stalked Lieutenant Edward H. Casey, commander of the elite Cheyenne Scout corps which was General Miles's special pride. Accompanied by two Northern Cheyennes,[7] Casey was headed down White Clay Creek that morning on his way to reconnoiter the Stronghold. About eight miles north of Pine Ridge Agency he passed a small band

[7] The Cheyennes were White Moon and Rock Road, according to Willis Rowland, half-Cheyenne sergeant of Casey's Scouts.

of Sioux butchering a steer. The group were actually ghost dancers and included Helper, the errant young son of Minneconjou Chief Hump. They all appeared friendly, however, and Casey rode on. Two of the Sioux, one an Ogalala, the other a Carlisle-educated Brûlé named Plenty Horses, followed at a short distance. Presently Casey and the Cheyennes met Pete Richards, half-breed son-in-law of old Red Cloud.

"Go back," Richards warned Casey. "Red Cloud says not to come any closer. No white man is safe out there around the Stronghold.

"I'll just ride on up to that hill for a look-see," said Casey, stubbornly bent on getting at least a distant view of the Stronghold.

Richards tried hard to dissuade him. Suddenly Plenty Horses broke away from his companion and began to circle around Casey, his rifle leveled at the lieutenant, a ghost song rising shrill in his throat.

Casey's Irish temper flared at Richards and the two men were shouting at each other when a shot rang out. Casey pitched forward out of his saddle and slumped lifeless to the ground. The shot had been fired by Plenty Horses, who let out a war yell and galloped off toward the Stronghold. Casey's bolting horse was caught by four or five of Helper's Ogalala companions.

The Sioux made no move to molest the two Cheyennes, allowing them to flee to the agency. Although all of Casey's clothing, weapons, and equipment were taken by the Indians, Richards managed to recover the lieutenant's horse and helped a detachment, sent out from Pine Ridge, to bring in the body. This time no mutilations were performed on the corpse.

Riding down Rapid Valley to the Cheyenne from Rapid City,[8] McGillycuddy learned of Casey's murder before the news had been made public. Just east of the river he encountered a lone Indian who signed peace and began making friendly talk. Then the Sioux asked:

[8] Accompanied by Major John R. Brennan and W. J. McFarland of the staff of the Rapid City *Journal.*

"Father, do you know what officer was killed near the agency by an Indian?"

McGillycuddy had no idea. Had such an event occurred, he was sure he would have heard of it in Rapid City. The Indian repeated his statement.

"When did it happen?" McGillycuddy asked him.

"Two hours ago," the Sioux answered.

The agency was more than sixty miles away across country. Word could not have been carried that distance in two hours. And yet the Indian persisted.

"An officer was killed," he said again. "He was killed by an Indian. I know this. But I know nothing more."

Returning later in the day to Rapid City, McGillycuddy found that during his absence a telegram had arrived bringing official news of Casey's death. Yet somehow, in a manner known only to plains Indians, the Sioux had learned of the killing several hours before the white man's telegram had been dispatched!

A day after Casey's murder a long-overdue change in the situation came about with the peremptory dismissal of Agent Royer at Pine Ridge and similar removals of civilian agents at Rosebud and Cheyenne agencies. All Sioux agencies west of the Missouri were thus placed under the supreme command of General Miles. With the exception of Standing Rock, where McLaughlin managed to cling to his job, Army officers were put in charge, emergency beef rations were shipped in, and additional pressure brought to bear to bring about the final surrender of the ghost dancers.

Soon after the military took over complete control, old Red Cloud, heading a growing number of malcontents, sent a letter to the authorities claiming he was a prisoner of the ghost dancers and begging the soldiers to come rescue him. When no troops materialized, the old chief had his son Jack smuggle him out of the Stronghold and then was led, blind and helpless, through a howling blizzard by his courageous daughter. As he fled he was actually fired upon by his own tribesmen and was twice forced to burrow down in the snow to escape their bullets before finally reaching the safety of his big house at Pine Ridge Agency.

While the murder of Lieutenant Casey became a convenient *cause célèbre* which alleviated much of the horror of Wounded Knee still fresh in the public mind, an even more heinous crime was committed. General Miles had leniently granted a pass to a small party of friendly Ogalalas, authorizing them to hunt game in the Black Hills. Harmless old Few Tails and his aged wife, accompanied by One Feather, a peaceable young Sioux, and his wife and two children, had a successful hunt and were returning to Pine Ridge with both their wagons loaded with meat. They camped for the night on the Belle Fourche River near the mouth of Alkali Creek, a leisurely two days' trip from the agency.

Soldiers briefly visited their camp, examined their pass, and told them it was all right. Before dark another white man, a civilian named Pete Culbertson, dropped by for a little friendly palaver. The Indians were pleased that he could talk Sioux and spent a happy half-hour or so trading jokes with him about the game they had shot. Culbertson even gave One Feather's thirteen-year-old daughter a pretty string of store-bought beads.

After breakfast next morning, January 11, the Indians resumed their journey to the agency. A few hundred yards from their camp site shots rang out and Few Tails toppled from the seat of his wagon which was in the lead. The old man died instantly. Both ponies hitched to the wagon also went down. Few Tails' terrified wife jumped out and was brought to the ground by a second burst of fire. One bullet crippled the old woman's leg, another pierced her breast.

Few Tails' murderers now came out of ambush. One of the six white men was Pete Culbertson. Two others were his brothers, Andrew and Nelson, one of whom had just been released from the state penitentiary. James Juelfs, John Netland, and Alva Martin were the other three men.

Coming down the trail, One Feather saw Few Tails killed and hurriedly turned his wagon in the other direction. Before he could complete the turn, however, his wife was wounded by a bullet from Pete Culbertson's gun. Jumping from the wagon on to one of his spare ponies, One Feather shouted to his woman:

"Take the wagon! Drive on! Fast!"

The wounded woman immediately grabbed the reins and lashed the team into a dead run, while One Feather bravely turned to fight off the assailants. It was six against one, but the courageous Indian held the ruffians at bay until his wife and children got away, then raced to join them.

Eight or ten miles up the trail, however, One Feather's careening wagon was overtaken by the ruthless Culbertson gang and the shooting started all over again. While her two children lay flat in the wagon with their heads covered in blankets, the wounded woman drove on. Once again the stalwart One Feather fought off the whites until his family was out of danger. This time the Culbertsons gave up pursuit.

But now, although One Feather and his wife had never been ghost dancers or hostile sympathizers, they found themselves fired upon by *honyockers* from ranch houses along the trail. Abandoning his cumbersome wagon, he unhooked the team, mounted the children on one horse and his wife and himself on the other, and finally managed to reach Pine Ridge Agency.

Few Tails' wounded old widow lay helpless in a coma all that day and well into the night, reviving at last toward dawn of the next morning. It was freezing cold. After traveling some fifteen miles, the old woman approached a ranch house for warmth and shelter. Two white men with loaded rifles drove her away. Afraid to go near other white dwellings, hiding by day and trudging through the trackless snow by night, she eventually reached an Army outpost and, more dead than alive, gave herself up.

News of the cruel murder of Few Tails nearly disrupted General Miles's campaign for a peaceful settlement of the ghost-dance war. Even friendly chiefs upon whose cooperation Miles relied were highly angered at the unprovoked attack by whites on harmless Indian hunters. The general had insisted these chiefs surrender Casey's murderers. Young-Man-Afraid-of-His-Horse bluntly told him:

"No; I will not surrender them. But if you will bring the white

men who killed Few Tails, I will bring in the Indians who killed
the white soldier and the herder; and right out here in front of
your tepee I will have my young men shoot the Indians and you
have your soldiers shoot the white men, and then we will have
done with the whole business."

Stark hunger and despair haunted the Stronghold. The ghost
dancers were now hopelessly disillusioned and divided. Even
Kicking Bear, for all his verve, could now rally only a few stanch
warriors.

One of the last hostile forays took place near the middle of the
Moon of Frost in the Tepee—as the Sioux call January. Rumors
that soldiers were about to attack the Stronghold served to stir
some sixty warriors from their frozen lethargy. The war party
included Black Elk, now able to walk and ride a horse although
his wounded abdomen was not yet fully healed.

The warriors rode down across the White River badlands to
Grass Creek, then followed up the stream until they sighted a
corral of Army wagons set up against an expected hostile attack.
Black Elk and a few others crept up behind some hills to scout
the soldiers' defenses. Several troopers were watering harnessed
horses at the creek.

"Stay here and shoot at the soldiers," Black Elk told his companions. "I will charge down there and catch some good horses."

Mounted on his fast little buckskin, Black Elk charged while
the other warriors covered him with rifle fire. He captured seven
horses. As he wheeled to lead them away, the troopers began shooting at him. Although no bullet found its mark, two of the captured
horses were killed. Black Elk brought five animals back to the war
party.

Sharp skirmishing now broke out as more cavalry came downstream. Kicking Bear marshaled his warriors for the fight, but
there were too few Indians against all the reinforcements the
soldiers were getting.

One warrior had his horse shot from under him.[9] Black Elk

9 The warrior's name was Red Willow, an Ogalala.

quickly brought up a mount for him and saved the Indian's life. Two other Sioux were badly wounded. Black Elk was in a brave little group that rescued them from the path of the charging troops. With more casualties dropping all around, Kicking Bear led his war party back into the badlands. They reached the Stronghold long after dark.

On the evening of January 13 a serious rift developed among the hostiles. After much bickering, Little Wound, Big Road, and Two Strike led their bands to a camp site only three miles from Pine Ridge Agency and sent word to Young-Man-Afraid-of-His-Horses that they wanted peace. The leaders of the ghost-dance cult, however, remained with a great many followers in the Stronghold.

Determined to press home the advantage of the split among the hostiles, General Miles called on a handful of friendly leaders who had stayed at the agency and asked them to go to the Stronghold to make final peace with the ghost dancers. Chief Standing Bear of the Ogalalas [10] agreed to act as Miles's main emissary. Nine other leaders, including Sub-chief Fast Horse, volunteered to accompany him.

Standing Bear had a daring plan. He carried the pipe, greatly respected by all Sioux. The Indians believed that if a pipe were brought to them and they refused to accept it and smoke with the bearer, much harm might befall them. Far from sure of returning alive from this dangerous mission, Standing Bear was willing to gamble his life on the power of the pipe in dealing with the hostiles.

Seeing their relatives coming, the ghost dancers permitted the peace party to approach the Stronghold. At the neck of land leading out on to the plateau, however, a throng of armed warriors met the ten friendly chieftains and held them at gun point. Calmly ignoring their captors, the chiefs grouped themselves in a circle and sat down. Standing Bear leisurely took his pipe from his

[10] Standing Bear, because of unusually light irises, was familiarly known among his tribesmen as Totola—"Blue Eyes."

beaded tobacco bag, lighted it, and passed it solemnly around the circle.

The spectacle of the ceremony of the pipe inflamed the ghost dancers. They went wild with frantic anger. Many who were already mounted dashed up on their ponies, galloping to within inches of the seated chieftains. If the members of the peace delegation could be frightened into running for their lives, the hostiles could kill them without compunction. But Standing Bear and his fellow chiefs sat perfectly still, knowing that to flinch might well mean death.

Suddenly one of the most fanatic of the hostiles, Ten Fingers, strode through the milling horses and riders until he stood facing Standing Bear with his rifle leveled at the chief's heart.

"Why have you brought us this pipe of peace?" he demanded. "The white soldiers have killed our people without mercy. We want no peace. We want to fight the soldiers—even if we all die!"

He punctuated his words by firing a shot. The bullet struck the ground between Standing Bear's knees, spattering up dirt in the chief's face. Standing Bear sat motionless, no trace of surprise or fear on his sharp old features, his pale eyes fixed levelly on this would-be murderer. Ten Fingers' face went blank with astonishment. He turned and fled, disappearing in the crowd of ghost dancers.

Abruptly, the tension broke. Indians rushed forward, eager to smoke the pipe with such a brave man as Standing Bear. One by one the hostile leaders came forward to greet the friendly chiefs. At this point Fast Horse told the ghost dancers that the soldiers were no longer at Pine Ridge Agency. Though far from the truth, it was what the Sioux had long hoped for in their mounting desire to bring their futile war to an end. Even the leaders of the ghost-dance cult were now ready to take their famished followers to the agency.

Addressing the hostiles, Kicking Bear spoke their common mind: "My brothers, this is a hard winter. Our women and children are starving and freezing. If it were summer, I would say we should keep fighting to the end. But this we cannot do. We must make peace."

The End of a Dream

THE outbreak was over.

Some thirty-five hundred Sioux had given up. On January 15 they began streaming into Pine Ridge Agency from the nearby camp and down White Clay Creek from the Stronghold. Starving and cold, they were still a proud race of fighters defeated not by the white man's ruthless armies but by tragic circumstance and a harsh change in weather. Now they came in to the agency with their belongings loaded on creaking farm wagons and pony drags, their horse herds depleted and poor from lack of graze. The Ogalalas formed a camp near Red Cloud's old camp site just west of the agency, while the Brûlés pitched their tattered lodges along creek bottoms half a mile north of the agency buildings. By sundown almost seven hundred and fifty tepees had been set up.

From all sides troops gradually closed in on the Indians, for the authorities were taking no chances on another outbreak. Peace negotiations were hurriedly concluded, Little Wound and Little Hawk [1] speaking for the Ogalalas, Crow Dog talking for the Brûlés, and General Miles representing the Army. Young-Man-Afraid-of-His-Horses acted as mediator, while Valentine McGillycuddy was on hand to give added assurance that the Sioux would be treated with full justice.

Stipulations were simple. Weapons were to be surrendered by the Indians of their own free will. (Fearful of another Wounded Knee incident, Miles avoided the threat of force in disarming the Sioux with the result that hundreds of rifles were eventually given up voluntarily.) Supplies of beef, sugar, and coffee were to be is-

---

[1] Little Hawk was Crazy Horse's uncle.

sued at once to the Indians from the Army commissary. Finally, twenty-seven ghost-dance leaders, including Kicking Bear, Short Bull, and Mash-the-Kettle, were to be surrendered as a guaranty of good faith.

Miles's demands were readily complied with as the designated men gave themselves up as sureties for the good conduct of their people. Short Bull quickly sought to shift the blame, however, implying that all along he had been an innocent victim of fiery elements within his tribe.

"I did not want war," he told the authorities. "I only wanted to do what the Wanekia had told me to do. We went to the Bad Lands. They [the young men of the Brûlés] told me I must fight the white man. 'No! No!' I kept telling them. 'You do not hear me. I do not want to fight against the white man! The Wanekia said, "There shall be no more war!" But you do not listen!' . . . Who would have thought that dancing could make such trouble? The message I brought was peace. There was trouble, but it was not of my making!"

Short Bull's two wives were with him and they wailed and wept when their husband and his fellow prisoners were dragged away to the railroad at Rushville by a full company of soldiers. And when the ghost-dance leaders were loaded on a drafty boxcar and the train chugged off to the east, the two women gave the tremolo as though Short Bull were already dead.

Kicking Bear had submitted without a murmur. As he later told his son, he fully expected to be hanged by vengeful whites for his part in the outbreak. Yet he accepted his lot with stoic indifference. He thought fondly of Woodpecker Woman, wondering what would happen to his little family back on Cherry Creek now that Big Foot and most of his band were dead. Truly, he thought, the Wanekia and his whirlwind had failed the Sioux, leaving them nothing but the gall-bitter taste of defeat. Soon now that, too, would be over and death a welcome thing.

Most of the prisoners were sure they would never return to the Dakota prairies. When they were later summarily sentenced to two years behind bars in the guardhouse at Fort Sheridan, Illinois, none of them understood English and all got the mistaken impression that they would remain prisoners for life in the white man's jail.

The Sioux war ended officially on January 16, 1891. Although the campaign had lasted only thirty-two days, it had cost the lives of forty-eight soldiers and scouts, one white civilian, and more than three hundred Indians. In addition to the loss of the Pine Ridge beef herd and numerous sub-agency buildings, chiefly in the Little Wound community, breaking faith with the Sioux had cost the Government a staggering $1,200,000—no mean sum in that day and age.

Yet in the long run it was the Sioux who paid by far the dearest price. With those Indians who fell at Wounded Knee had died their last bright hope of a great new world. No more could they believe in a red messiah or holy shirts that would deflect bullets or a new earth that would bury their white enemies. Their final surrender to General Miles marked their inevitable turning once and for all from the "red road," path of life and purity, to the "black road," which was the path of destruction and death and the symbolic road of the white man.

Sullen in defeat, the warrior Sioux lapsed into morose apathy. A few bitter-enders, heartsick with despair and rage, ran amuck in the great camps. Rushing out with rifles, they unleashed their pent-up emotions by shooting down their own horses and dogs.

General Miles was proclaimed the "Great Peacemaker" who, after thirty years of warfare, had now brought the once-mighty Sioux to their knees. Hero of the hour, Miles ordered a grand military review in honor of his victory over the redskins. Planned as a spectacle of the armed might of the white man's government, the review was held at Pine Ridge Agency on January 22 before a captive audience of some ten thousand disgruntled Indians who were still suspicious that the soldiers might turn on them at any moment to wipe them from the face of the earth.

Surrounded by his staff, the general made an imposing figure on a fine black stallion while the troops of the frontier were paraded before him. A stifling gale of dust came up, however, threatening to disrupt the entire ceremony, and presently the trim units of cavalry, infantry, artillery, and Indian scouts could scarcely be seen for the flying sand.

Chief Standing Bear was amazed that Bear Coat Miles should get credit for something the friendly Indian leaders had done. After the review he sought out the general and eyed him coolly. He said:

"My fellow chiefs who went to the Stronghold with me to get the hostiles to surrender feel they should have recognition for remaining loyal to the white man's government all through the late trouble. They want some sort of emblem to wear to commemorate this great peace and the part they had in bringing it about."

Miles answered that he would see what he could do. Securing the names of the ten friendly chiefs who had gone to the Stronghold, he sent a list to Washington. In a short time some cheap metal buttons arrived, one for each leader to wear on his coat lapel. About the size of a quarter, the insignificant medals bore an emblazoned motto, "Peace, Good Will," a rising sun, two clasped hands, a shock of corn, and a white man's plow—each worth less than half a dollar. It was the only show of gratitude or recognition the friendly chiefs ever received!

General Miles and other military authorities were much preoccupied and embarrassed at continuing tales of horror about the Wounded Knee massacre which appeared in the national press. Accordingly, no time was lost in seeking to provide the Seventh Cavalry, in fact the entire Army, with a protective coat of whitewash.

The first step was to designate the massacre at Wounded Knee as a "battle," a convenient twist of the facts. Much was made of the fact that an Indian had fired the first shot. Since no Indian knew or would say which warrior had done so, one bloodthirsty savage after another was blamed for having precipitated the Battle of Wounded Knee. In some accounts Yellow Bird was the guilty man. In others it was an assistant medicine man, Black Fox. No one ever came up with the name of Sitting Bull's harmless deaf-mute son.

The most elaborate cover up, however, came from Congress. Twenty-nine Congressional Medals of Honor were presented to soldiers who had participated in the last Sioux campaign; *twenty-three* were awarded specifically for action at Wounded Knee!

Along in February, 1891, civil authorities caught up with the Culbertson gang. Its members would stand trial in circuit court for the murder of Few Tails. By the same token, Casey's murderer, Plenty Horses, was also to be tried in a civil court.

Plenty Horses and Leaves-His-Woman (also known as Young Skunk), the slayer of ranchman Isaac Miller, were taken under military escort to Fort Meade, South Dakota, on February 19, 1891. Valentine McGillycuddy was appointed foreman of the grand jury which convened in nearby Deadwood to determine the Indians' guilt in the killings.

Barely nineteen, Plenty Horses had spent several years at Carlisle Indian School in Pennsylvania and was considered "educated though uncivilized." As the Black Hills *Daily Times* in Deadwood expressed it, the young warrior was "by no means tender-hearted because of tender years." Actually the youth was a miserable product of Carlisle's attempt to make him over into a white man. Brought back to Rosebud Agency, he had found himself despised by his own people. In killing Casey he had sought to show his tribesmen that he was as good a fighting man as any of them.

He freely admitted his guilt. "I am an Indian," he told the grand jury. "Five years I attended Carlisle and was educated in the ways of the white man. When I returned to my people I was an outcast among them. I was no longer an Indian. I was not a white man. I was lonely. I shot the lieutenant so that I might make a place for myself among my people. Now I am one of them. I shall be hanged and the Indians will bury me as a warrior. They will be proud of me. I am satisfied."

The court adjourned to Sioux Falls as Plenty Horses' fate seemed sealed. Foreman McGillycuddy pointed out to his fellow jurors, however, that Casey had been scouting dangerously near a hostile camp and was therefore acting in effect as an enemy spy. A state of war had existed. Plenty Horses had had ample justification for killing a white officer. The judge agreed, ordering the jury to bring in a verdict of "not guilty." Acquitted, Plenty Horses returned to his tribe—a hero. Leaves-His-Woman was freed at the same time.

With far less justice demonstrated, another jury duly acquitted the members of the Culbertson gang. In those rough frontier years the mere testimony of outraged Indians was far from sufficient evidence to convict white men of murder.

Kicking Bear and his companions had languished in prison at Fort Sheridan for two months when the first breath of spring began to thaw the freezing dampness of that Illinois winter. As a harbinger of better things to come, the unhappy prisoners had a visitor, Buffalo Bill Cody, who wanted to take them all to Europe as part of his Wild West Show. Cody put up personal bond for three thousand dollars and, with General Miles's influence, secured the release of the ghost-dance leaders. They were "sentenced" to go abroad for two years, the same period they were supposed to spend in the Fort Sheridan guardhouse.

Most of the Indians welcomed a chance to travel with "Pa-huska," [2] as they called Cody. For Kicking Bear and Short Bull it was an adventure which came close to equaling their fanciful journey to the Spirit Land. En route they stopped with Buffalo Bill in Washington. High officials of the War Department made Kicking Bear look into the mouth of a cannon while his photograph was taken as pictorial proof that the savage Sioux were finally conquered. Other white men from the Smithsonian Institution grabbed Kicking Bear and put him through the harrowing ordeal of having a model made of his body, considered "representative of the finest physique in the Indian race." (Garbed in full costume, the figure is still an important part of the permanent Plains Indian exhibit in the United States National Museum in Washington, D.C.)

2 More correctly Pahin Hoska—"Long Hair."

Europeans greeted the "wild Sioux" with enthusiasm and affection, and the overseas sojourn helped heal the raw scars of defeat. But the captive show Indians longed for the vast open plains and winding rivers of home. They longed most of all for families that seemed almost like strangers in the misty past. The months abroad went on interminably. . . .

Since mid-September Wooden Lance, the young Kiowa, had searched in vain for the Wanekia. Through the bitter winter he had watched the terrible disillusionment of the Sioux, had even waited to see if their promise of the Wanekia's coming would be fulfilled. Finally he had moved on, escaping violence himself, yet still mourning the death of his favorite child. He was confident that once he found the Indian messiah the savior would enable him to talk with the spirit of his dead child. Months passed. When the Sioux became embroiled in outbreak and tragedy, he moved west from one reservation to another, visiting for weeks with each tribe, ever searching for the elusive Wanekia.

The ghost dance gradually began to be little more than a memory on the northern plains. Still Wooden Lance kept up his restless wandering. He came at last to Nevada's Mason Valley. After an almost endless pilgrimage he finally stood before the threshold of the Wanekia's own sacred dwelling. He had to wait an entire day, however, before being admitted to Wovoka's wick-iup.

When Wooden Lance entered he saw a heavy-set, lazy sort of man lying in the shadows, singing to himself, his face covered with a blanket. When the Wanekia finished his song, he uncovered his face and sleepily asked the Kiowa through an interpreter what he wanted. The reverent Wooden Lance had supposed all along that the Wanekia knew all things and had the gift of tongues. He was amazed that this stolid Paiute should be asking questions. Identifying himself, Wooden Lance spoke of his long journey and begged to see his dead child.

"That is impossible," Wovoka said listlessly. "There are no spirits here."

Cruelly disappointed, the Kiowa began to doubt that Wovoka was really the Wanekia he had come so far to see. Certainly he was not the imposing godlike creature Wooden Lance had expected to meet. Wovoka must have sensed his visitor's growing skepticism. He said:

"You need go no farther. There is only one messiah and I am he. I taught the Indians a new dance. But the Sioux twisted things and have made so much trouble that you had better go home and tell the Kiowa to drop the whole business."

Heartsick, Wooden Lance left the wickiup of the false prophet and returned to his people in Indian Territory. His unfavorable report, given at Anadarko on February 19, 1891, virtually ended the ghost dance on the southern plains. President Harrison even sent Wooden Lance a medal for squelching what the authorities hoped would be the last enthusiasm for the ritual.

A movement which had held out as much hope and promise as the ghost dance was not to die, however, without a final death-throe. Led by a medicine man, Bianki (The Eater), the Kiowa publicly revived the ceremony in September, 1894, on the Washita River. This last known ghost dance took four days and was attended by several thousand Indians from surrounding tribes. The agent's efforts to disperse the dancers met with such dogged resistance that he was obliged to give official permission—with the result that the ghost dance was no longer outlawed. But by this time the Indians of the land were so demoralized and resigned to walking the white man's road that nothing further ever came of it.

Supplanted by the Yuwipi Cult among the Sioux, the Medicine Lodge Ceremonies of the Cheyennes, and the Peyote Cult, which now embraces some 150,000 to 200,000 American and Canadian Indians, the ghost dance was forever a thing of the past.

Wovoka sadly outlived the ghost dance. Obscure, without honor or distinction even among his own tribesmen, he died unnoticed on October 4, 1932, and was buried without so much as a spirit song on the sandy shore of Walker Lake. For a brief time he had been a living symbol of the Indian's last desperate hope. News of his death caused scarcely a ripple of excitement or grief among the fanatical thousands who had once worshiped him.

Winter was tingeing the buffalo grass with pale hoarfrost that day late in November, 1892, when Kicking Bear came home. By that time the soldiers were gone from the Sioux agencies and the reservations were bleak with despair and hopelessness. Yet Kicking Bear's heart sang with gladness at the sight of his native prairies.

His wife and children met him at the new railhead at Chadron, Nebraska, and he hugged each of them close to him a long moment. Woodpecker Woman had aged much in the two and a half years since he had last seen her, but the children were taller and putting on a little flesh.

Everything was different now, he learned. His old village on Cherry Creek had been broken up and his little family and a few faithful Minneconjou followers had been living on White Clay Creek, not far from the old ghost-dance camp site at No Water's place. Back among the Ogalalas Kicking Bear was no longer an important leader of ghost dancers or even a band chief. Yet he cared little. Passing years had mellowed his restless ambition and the days when chiefs had any real importance were long gone. Only two things mattered now to Kicking Bear: his family, and his hatred for the white man.

In order to be out from under the agent's thumb, Kicking Bear moved the following summer to a remote area of chalk buttes and wild buffalo grass and low-hanging cottonwoods along Wounded Knee Creek about ten miles downstream from the site of the massacre. Other Indians followed later and the new community was called Manderson. But for a while Kicking Bear was almost alone there.

The new agent (again a civilian) was particular about school attendance as it was now the Government's policy to teach Indian children English and prohibit the use of tribal languages. Kicking Bear steadfastly opposed any attempt on the part of teachers to take his children off to school.

One day in 1899 the agent sent an Indian policeman around to

bring Kicking Bear's three sons and daughter to boarding school
at the agency. Kicking Bear met him with a leveled rifle in his
hands and refused outright to send the children away from home.
The policeman promptly reported the incident to the agent. Being
a sensible man—for a change—the agent let the matter drop.

It was Kicking Bear's last brush with the authorities. Five years
later, in 1904, he died at the age of fifty-eight.

As it had for the dream, the end came for the dreamer.

Postscript

AFTER their final surrender to General Miles in January, 1891, the Sioux never rose again. Although Kicking Bear and Short Bull and a few others talked of it occasionally, there was no serious thought of reviving the ghost dance. As one educated Indian put it years later: "After the massacre of Wounded Knee all ambition was taken out of us. We have never since been able to regain a foothold, and so we haven't progressed. . . ." [1]

Memories of that Indian winter of horror, 1890–91, were sharpened, however, when aging Buffalo Bill Cody dreamed up the idea of filming a re-enactment of Wounded Knee in 1913. He succeeded in forming a motion-picture company with the help of Essanay of Chicago and Hollywood with Cody retaining a third interest for supervising the making of the film. The old buffalo-hunter-turned-showman even succeeded in persuading General Miles and the Seventh Cavalry (which included many thirty-year men who had been recruits in 1890) to appear in it.

Short Bull, No Neck, Philip Wells, and a number of other prominent Indians and mixed-bloods who had figured in the ghost-dance conflict were still alive and attended Cody's council to set the stage. The motion picture was to be the first of a series in a historical film record of great Indian battles.

Plans called for the sham battle to take place on the very ground where Big Foot and his slaughtered band lay buried—the hilltop overlooking Wounded Knee Creek. General Miles could see nothing wrong in removing the pathetic painted sticks which marked the common Indian grave and thought it would add much realism to do the battle scene on the spot.

[1] Edison Glenn of Pine Ridge Indian Reservation as quoted by Robert Gessner in *Massacre,* published in 1931.

276

Presently a large Indian tepee village was set up along the creek. Decrepit wagons and improvised pony drags were rounded up at Denby and other nearby trading posts. The Sioux finally moved into camp and vast quantities of blank ammunition were distributed to Indians and soldiers alike, for Miles and Cody agreed that the film should have all the blood and thunder of the original action.

Many of the Indians present had actually been ghost dancers. A few were survivors of Big Foot's band and had narrowly escaped death in the massacre some twenty-three years earlier. They remained quiet and tractable, however, until word got out that the grave of the slain was about to be terribly desecrated by the movie makers.

Old-timers recall that Short Bull, then in his sixties, wandered through the village, exhorting his tribesmen and fanning their old smoldering hatred until the Sioux were ready to fight all over again. Short Bull had proposed an ingenious plot: the Indians would trade all their blank ammunition for live bullets. Shooting blanks, the Seventh Cavalry would be helpless. The tables would be turned on history!

Ben American Horse, son of the chief and brother of onetime ghost dancer Tom, was then Cody's interpreter.[2] Getting wind of Short Bull's nefarious conspiracy, he immediately warned the old showman. Short Bull and other ringleaders were promptly summoned to Cody's tent. Buffalo Bill did considerable talking that day. Long after his resonant baritone voice had become a hoarse croak, he finally convinced the Indians that they would surely be pursued, captured, and tried for murder if they attempted to turn the movie battle into a real fracas. The sham battle went before the cameras without a single casualty.

The film itself, with Buffalo Bill and General Miles featured in grandiosely distorted real-life roles, was rarely—if ever—displayed to movie-goers of the day. Soon after production ended

[2] Ben American Horse, one of the few Indians Cody called to his Denver deathbed on January 10, 1917, has been a long-time good friend and uncle (by adoption) of the author.

several prints were hurriedly confiscated by the War Department; their final disposition remains a well-kept military secret.

The ghost dance was long dead. Yet the horror of Wounded Knee lived on in the memories of Indian survivors. It had been a harsh lesson for all red men. Now they knew any hope of escape into the past was forever lost.

Indians Interviewed

Ghost Dance is based largely on personal interviews with Indians who remembered those times and took part in the actual ceremonies, dances, battles, and skirmishes as described. A small number of them were survivors of the massacre of Wounded Knee. They are as follows:

ARAPAHOES

Sherman Sage	Ethete, Wyoming
Chief Yellow Calf (George Caldwell)	" "
Sam Shotgun (Former Scout)	" "
Jack Shave Head (Former Scout)	" "
George Wallowing Bull	" "
Adam Spoonhunter	" "
Mrs. Adam Spoonhunter	" "
Tom Spoonhunter	" "
James Madison	" "
Amos Two Crows	" "
Chester Yellow Bear *	" "
Ice Man	Riverton, Wyoming

ASSINIBOINES

Red Feather	Wolf Point, Montana
Bob Tail Bear	" " "
Last Warrior	" " "
Crazy Bull	" " "
Thomas White Cloud	" " "

* Still alive in 1957.

ATSINA (GROS VENTRES)
Thin-Hair-on-Top-
    Woman   Ethete, Wyoming

BANNOCK
    Johnny Ballard *   Fort Hall, Idaho

BLACKFEET (Not involved in ghost dance, but interviewed to
        determine spread of doctrine)
    Mountain Chief   Browning, Montana
    Chewing Black Bone   "   "
    Lazy Boy   "   "
    Stabbed-by-Mistake   "   "
    Turtle   "   "

BLOODS (Not involved in ghost dance, but interviewed to de-
        termine spread of doctrine)
    White Wolf   Fort McLeod, Alberta
    Scraping White   "   "   "
    Across-the-Mountain   "   "   "

CHEYENNES
    NORTHERN
        Willis Rowland   Busby, Montana
        Frank Pine   "   "
        John Dives Backward   "   "
        Philip Rising Sun   "   "
        Wooden Leg   "   "
        Charlie Walking Bear   "   "
        Bob Tail Horse   Lame Deer, Montana
        Rufus Wallowing *   "   "   "
        Black Wolf   "   "   "

    SOUTHERN
        Yellow Eyes   El Reno, Oklahoma
        Eagle Nest   "   "

* Still alive in 1957.

COMANCHE
   Albert Attakine (Lone   Anadarko, Oklahoma
      Tepee)

KIOWA
   Chief White Horse   Anadarko, Oklahoma

KIOWA-APACHE
   Tennyson Berry   Anadarko, Oklahoma

PAWNEE
   Wolf Leggins   Cordell, Oklahoma

FLATHEAD
   Julian Antoine   Polson, Montana

HUALPAI
   Jim Mahone (Ma-hoi-na-   Seligman, Arizona
      vie) (Scout)

PAIUTE
   Johnny Shoshone   Death Valley, California

WANAPUM (Not involved in ghost dance, but interviewed to determine spread of doctrine)
   Johnny Buck (Puck-
      Hyah-Toot)   Priest Rapids, Washington
   Elijah Supelyia   "   "   "

CROWS (Not involved in ghost dance, but interviewed to determine spread of doctrine)
   Plain Bull   Prior, Montana
   Bad Man   Crow Agency, Montana
   Mountain Sheep   "   "   "

SHOSHONI

Quentin Quay (Scout)	Fort Washakie, Wyoming
Dick Washakie	" " "
Charlie Washakie	" " "
Timpana	" " "
Paree	" " "
Kidgin Edmo	" " "
Nambe Dooak	" " "
Mouse *	" " "
Willie George *	Fort Hall, Idaho

SIOUX (TETON-DAKOTA)

HUNKPAPAS

Chief Henry Oscar One Bull	Little Eagle, South Dakota
Clarence Gray Eagle *	" " " "
Philip White Bird (Policeman)	" " " "
Little Soldier (Police-man)	" " " "
Male Bear	" " " "
Louis Looking Horse	" " " "
Leo Kills Pretty Enemy	" " " "
Joseph Callous Leg	" " " "
Henry Kills Alive (Policeman)	" " " "
One Elk (Policeman)	Bull Head, South Dakota
Feather Earring	Kenel, South Dakota
Iron Hawk	Manderson, South Dakota
Fred Belt	Ogalala, South Dakota
John Sitting Bull	" " "

BLACKFEET SIOUX

Thomas White Horse	Little Eagle, South Dakota

* Still alive in 1957.

SANSARCS

Amos Clown (Old Eagle)	Thunder Butte, South Dakota
John-Did-Not-Go-Home	Red Scaffold, South Dakota
Isaac Butcher (Afraid-of-Him)	" " " "

BRÛLÉS

Dan Grass Rope	Lower Brûlé Agency, South Dakota
High Bald Eagle	St. Francis, South Dakota
Alfred Bone Shirt	" " "
Jesse White Lance *	" " "
Hollow Horn Eagle	" " "
Owns-the-Battle *	" " "
Brave Bird	" " "
Elk Thunder	Parmalee, South Dakota
Coffee	Norris, South Dakota
Johnston Little Warrior	Kyle, South Dakota
Thomas Short Bull *	Igloo, South Dakota

OGALALAS

Nicholas Black Elk, Sr.	Manderson, South Dakota
Henry Weasel (*Ogalala Hanska*) *	" " "
Howard Bad Bear *	" " "
Joe White Coyote *	" " "
Charles Kills Enemy	" " "
Henry Horse *	Wounded Knee, South Dakota
Frank Good Lance *	" " " "
Moves Camp	Wanblee, South Dakota
Daniel Blue Horse	Ogalala, South Dakota
Eagle Elk	" " "
Kills a Hundred	Buffalo Gap, South Dakota
Joseph High Eagle (Policeman)	" " " "

* Still alive in 1957.

Drags-the-Rope	Buffalo Gap, South Dakota
James Comes Again (Scout)	Hermosa, South Dakota
Andrew Knife (Knife Chief)	Pine Ridge, South Dakota
James H. Red Cloud *	" " " "
John Colhoff	" " " "
Luther Standing Bear	Los Angeles, California
Hugh Top Bear *	Kyle, South Dakota
Tom American Horse *	" " "
Black Horn	Porcupine, South Dakota
Willard White Belly *	" " "
Sam Stabber	" " "
Tom Spotted Bear (Scout) *	Denby, South Dakota
Henry Little Bear (Yellow Shield) (Scout) *	" " "
Jonas Holy Rock (Scout)	Manderson, South Dakota
Mary Fire Thunder *	" " "
Adam Lone Elk	" " "
Frank Kicking Bear *	" " "
Moses One Feather	Ogalala, South Dakota

MINNECONJOUS

Chief Joseph White Bull	Cherry Creek, South Dakota
Straight Forehead	Manderson, South Dakota

SURVIVORS OF THE WOUNDED KNEE MASSACRE

Iron Hail (Dewey Beard)	Kyle, South Dakota
Simon Helper (Wallace Hump) *	Ogalala, South Dakota
Peter Stands-for-Them	" " "
Dora High White Man *	" " "
Jackson He-Crow *	" " "
Thomas Blind Man *	" " "
Charley Blind Man *	" " "

* Still alive in 1957.

Mrs. Spotted Backbone *	" " "
Bertha Kills-Close-to-Lodge	" " "
John Little Finger	Wounded Knee, South Dakota
George Running Hawk *	" " " "
James Pipe-on-Head *	
Mrs. Big Turnip *	Manderson, South Dakota
Charles Under Baggage, Sr.	Potato Creek, South Dakota
Charley Blue Arm	Cherry Creek, South Dakota
Yellow Owl *	" " " "
Edward Owl King *	" " " "
James E. High Hawk *	Howes, South Dakota
Philip Black Moon *	" " "
Mary Runs On	Ogalala, South Dakota
Alice Straight Forehead (née Alice Moves Over) *	" " "

* Still alive in 1957.

Sources

THE TIME THE SUN DIED

—Records of the Nautical Almanac indicate the exact date, January 1, 1889, as the "time the sun died." It was a complete solar eclipse.

—Kicking Bear's tepee village on Cherry Creek has long since disappeared. The old camp site, however, is within several miles of the present community of Howes, South Dakota.

—Crazy Horse's "sacred medicine" is still in existence. It is now in the possession of Frank Kicking Bear, only surviving son of Kicking Bear. No white men and few Indians have ever seen its contents.

The use of a charm or talisman is an integral part of the old-time plains Indian culture. Smooth stones were preferred by the Sioux as battle charms. Called *tunkan*, the designation is an abbreviation of *tunkasila*, "grandfather," one of the Sioux terms for God. The *tunkan* were not only used as protective charms in battle, but were also thought to have great curative properties and were used by medicine men in healing the sick or wounded.

Various talismans were used by other tribes. The Cheyennes often made the dragonfly or butterfly a battle charm, while nearly all plains Indians considered the spider a "medicine" animal. Black prairie crickets were used to locate game. Held lightly in the hunter's palm, the direction a cricket's antennae pointed indicated where buffalo herds might be found.

—In Sioux belief the earth is considered to have two aspects, that of mother and that of grandmother. The Earth Mother is the fecund producer of all living things. The earth as grandmother is the actual ground itself, the physical substance of creation.

—The story of Crazy Horse's betrayal and death is unrivaled as an example of the white man's perfidy in dealing with Indians. As my Indian father, Black Elk, told me many times, the trouble started with Frank Grouard, the Army's interpreter at Fort Robinson, Nebraska, in the seventies. (A Sandwich Islander of Kanaka descent, Grouard was always believed by the Sioux to be a mixed-blood Indian of some alien tribe.) For reasons unknown, Grouard mistranslated Crazy Horse's offer to help the whites fight Chief Joseph's Nez Percés after their break from an Idaho reservation. Then in charge of the Department of the Missouri, General George Crook abruptly decided that the great Ogalala fighting leader was bent on taking the war trail himself. He ordered his arrest and planned to imprison Crazy Horse for life on the Dry Tortugas off Florida.

Crazy Horse had forever given up thoughts of fighting the whites again and, with reluctant resignation, had made up his mind to follow the white man's road. Spotted Tail, aging chief of the Brûlés, helped devise a ruse whereby Crazy Horse could be trapped. He arranged a council with General Bradley, commander of Fort Robinson. Crazy Horse went willingly, never suspecting that he was earmarked for treachery.

At the military post he shook hands with Army Surgeon Valentine McGillycuddy, his only friend among the whites. (So great was their mutual friendship that McGillycuddy was later remembered among the Sioux as Tasunka Witko Takola—"Friend of Crazy Horse.") McGilly-cuddy was unaware of the capture plot. Crazy Horse unwittingly followed the officer of the day to the guardhouse. Seeing cells and barred windows, the Indian was on his guard.

"This is a prison!" he shouted.

Yanking a knife from his belt, he fought his way out to the parade ground. Officer of the Day Kennington grabbed one of his wrists while his other arm was pinioned by his old Ogalala enemy, Little Big Man, now serving the whites as an Indian policeman.

"Let me go! Let me go!" cried Crazy Horse, trying to shake off the two men.

Suddenly his sharp knife found its mark and Little Big Man jerked away, blood running from a long slash across one arm.

"Stab him! Kill the son of a bitch!" Kennington yelled, trying to draw his sword and hang on to the prisoner at the same time.

A white soldier, a Ninth Infantry private, William Gentles, came running and lunged at Crazy Horse with fixed bayonet. His first attempt lodged the bayonet in the guardhouse door. Pulling the weapon free, he lunged again and again at the struggling Indian. The chief sank to the ground, writhing and groaning, blood gushing from deep wounds in his hip and abdomen.

The stabbing occurred in late afternoon on September 5, 1877. Through hours of agony in twilight and darkness, Crazy Horse lingered in a mist of pain in the post adjutant's office where Worm, his father, and Touch-the-Cloud, his closest friend, had laid him out on the floor to die.

"*Haun!*" he moaned. "I am hurt bad! My people must know it is no use to depend on me any more. This is a good day to die!"

With his old battle cry barely past his lips, Crazy Horse, greatest fighting leader of the Ogalalas, breathed his last. Black Elk, his nephew, was among the select warriors picked to stand guard over his body until it was turned over to old Worm a week or so later.

—Black Elk hinted that Crazy Horse had been buried on a scaffold near Pepper Creek, a small stream between Manderson and Holy Rosary Mission on Pine Ridge Reservation in South Dakota. He never claimed to have actually seen the grave.

Frank Kicking Bear was around eight years old when his parents took him out to pick chokecherries and pointed out what may have been Crazy Horse's grave on White Horse Creek southwest of Manderson. This was several years after the eclipse, however, and, as Frank recalls, his father had no previous knowledge of the grave's whereabouts.

—While some historians (e.g., Stanley Vestal in *New Sources of Indian History, 1850–1891*) deprecate Kicking Bear's war record and indicate his name was hardly known prior to 1890, he was actually foremost among Sioux fighting men since about 1870. Some of his exploits are mentioned in M. I. McCreight's *Flying Hawk's Tales*. (Flying Hawk was Kicking Bear's brother, about six years his junior. Another brother, Black Fox, was named after their father, a chief. Their mother, Iron Cedar Woman, was the younger of old Black Fox's two wives. She had five children; the elder wife had eight children.)

Kicking Bear and Flying Hawk took part in many raids and inter-tribal wars against Crows, Blackfeet, Flatheads, and Shoshoni, often fighting side by side, sometimes joining their kinsman Crazy Horse (their mother and Crazy Horse's mother were sisters). One time the Sioux had made a buffalo kill and were butchering when a band of Piegans (Blackfeet) attacked them. Flying Hawk ran down one attacker and fell on him, knocking him senseless. He scalped the Piegan alive, then Kicking Bear shot the scalped warrior. Three Piegans were killed in the fight. The Sioux lost only one horse. In those days both Crows and Piegans had rifles—acquired from white traders—while the Sioux fought with antiquated bows and lances and war clubs.

On another occasion the two brothers and twenty other Sioux stood off a tough bunch of Crows and a big band of Piegans in one afternoon's fighting. The Sioux might have died in battle if a big storm had not come up to end the fracas. (No plains Indian liked to fight at night or during a storm lest the friendly Powers fail to recognize their medicine markings or special battle charms which would guarantee help against their enemies.)

Kicking Bear was among the valiant warriors who rallied around Crazy Horse at the Battle of the Rosebud on June 17, 1876, when the Sioux beat back General George Crook and his column of soldiers. Black Bear, Good Weasel, Bad Heart Bull, and Kicking Bear were in the thick of the fighting as Crazy Horse held his Winchester high and shouted: "Hold on, my friends! Be strong! Remember the helpless! *This is a good day to die!*"

Eight days later Kicking Bear was at Crazy Horse's elbow during the counterattack against Reno's battalion at Little Big Horn. Kicking Bear killed at least one Arikara scout and, later, several troopers in the river when Reno's men tried to cross. One of the most significant pieces of aboriginal Indian art is Kicking Bear's painting on buckskin of the Little Big Horn Battle, now in the Southwest Museum at Los Angeles, California. His drawings show his own footprints leaving the dead Arikara's body, then crossing the river to wait for Long Hair Custer's command to come down Medicine Tail Coulee.

That fall he was with Crazy Horse and He Dog at Slim Buttes when Crook, reinforced with a thousand soldiers, won a victory over old American Horse (Iron Plume), who was mortally wounded in the battle. "It is always the friendly ones who are struck," American Horse said before he died. He had done everything possible to avoid the clash with General Crook. (American Horse was the father of Chief American Horse who figures prominently in the story of *Ghost Dance*.)

Kicking Bear's own father, Chief Black Fox, also died fighting. After he had been dead a long time, Kicking Bear and Flying Hawk went to the old man's grave. Only bones remained on the crumbling scaffold. From the back of the skull the men took a rusty old Crow arrowhead. Kicking Bear took it home and, years later, at his dying request, it was buried with him.

—Kicking Bear was on particularly safe ground in making a mystical reference to the spotted eagle. Since the spotted eagle flies highest of all winged creatures and observes everything, the Sioux traditionally regard him under certain aspects as Wakantanka, the Great Mystery. His feathers are thought to be rays of the sun. When carried or worn by an Indian, a spotted eagle feather actually becomes a manifestation of God

Himself. And in wearing a war bonnet, the Indian further identifies his spiritual self or soul with Wakantanka. Even the sight of a spotted eagle is considered an event of importance.

—*Kinnikinik* or *chanshasha* is the dried inner bark of the dogwood or red alder, mellowed with Ree twist tobacco, willow bark, or, in modern times, Bull Durham. Sometimes a small amount of Sweet Ann root is added for fragrance, and the ingredients mixed ritually.

—According to William T. Hornaday (*Extermination of the American Bison*, Smithsonian Report) the total population of the American buffalo in 1889 was a pathetic five hundred and forty-one. Thanks to federal supervision and the cooperation of the Canadian government, the species has since staged a miraculous comeback.

—In-law taboos among the Sioux applied only to opposite sexes. Some relationships involving in-laws were particularly friendly, others formal. Some of these age-old customs are maintained in Sioux households to this day.

—The Minneconjou scalp-shirt men as elected by their tribesmen in 1881 were as follows:

Hump   ⎫
Fast Bull   ⎬ reinstated
Spotted Eagle ⎭
Touch-the-Cloud
White Swan
Touch-the-Bear
White Bull (replacing his father Makes Room who retired)
Big Crow

All wore the traditional ceremonial shirts decorated with enemy scalp locks and buckskin fringe. The above list was provided by Chief White Bull himself, last of the scalp-shirt men, who died in 1947.

—George Armstrong Custer's trail into the Black Hills, blazed by his gold-seeking expedition in 1874, was later known to the Sioux as the "Thieves' Road." Two years later, in 1876, the Black Hills were forever lost to the tribes when Red Cloud signed them away on a treaty the white men never bothered to honor. Hence this appropriate name for Custer's route, which later became the main east-west artery into the area.

—Certain stringent rules were observed by most Sioux (as well as other tribes) when living in tepees. As quoted from my *Custer's Fall*, page 228: "The man of the family had the place of honor at the rear or west side of the lodge, the entrance always facing east. Youths and boys shared the space to his left. Women and girls kept to his right. . . . No one, male or female, crossed the space between the man of the family and the fireplace (in the center of the lodge)." In general, although the woman usually owned the lodge, the man came to her bed rather than she to his whenever they slept together.

—This reconstruction of family life in the Kicking Bear lodge is based largely upon the boyhood recollections of Frank Kicking Bear, only surviving member of the family.

BACKDROP

—The year 1889 was marked by a warfare of architectural styles—Romanesque, Queen Anne, Eastlake, Colonial, Victorian Gothic, and many nondescript blends, all working at cross-purposes. The unique architectural progress in Chicago as manifested by the modern conceptions of Louis Sullivan may well have been responsible for winning the Columbian Exposition of 1893 for that city. Oddly enough, however, the entire exposition had a classic-revival theme which all but retarded further development in functional design.

—Mrs. Potter Palmer is quoted by Marjorie Farnsworth in her *The Ziegfeld Follies* as saying: "You were no one, really no one, my dear, unless you had felt Sandow's muscles." When such feats began to pall, the flamboyant showman pitted Sandow against a "man-eating lion" in San Francisco, and sold tickets for staggering prices ($5 to $25). The spectators were in for much disappointment. Although Wallace, the lion, had attacked and half-eaten his keeper only a week or so before, his performance in the Ziegfeld arena was disillusioning, to say the least. Bored and coquettish, Wallace refused to fight until Sandow slapped him. When the big cat was finally goaded into charging, he ran into a terrific uppercut from the strong man's right fist. Sprawled on all fours after his disastrous leap, Wallace made a bee line for the wings, his tail between his cowardly legs. Although Sandow was undisputedly the victor, his career was virtually ended by the unequal combat.

—Even the *honyockers* were discerning when it came to stock-company productions. One Minnesota newspaper of 1889 gave a drubbing review to a performance of the Harriet Beecher Stowe classic: "Thompson's *Uncle Tom's Cabin* company appeared at the opera house last night. The dogs were poorly supported."

—One popular breakdown of eligibility for social prominence as of 1889 reads: "If you live in Boston it is 'What do you know?' If New York City is your home it is 'How much are you worth?' In Philadelphia it is 'Who was your grandfather?' Chicago society is much more fluid and undetermined, while San Francisco is noted far and wide for fast living and empty pleasures."

—The site of Red Cloud's big frame house is now indicated by a South Dakota State Highway Department marker, located at Pine Ridge Agency on U.S. Highway 18—"the direct route from Chicago to the Black Hills."

—Precious little documentation exists of the ghost dance of the early seventies as practiced by the Paiute and numerous California and Nevada tribes. One of the most authoritative sources is Cora Du Bois' *The 1870 Ghost Dance,* University of California Publications, Anthropological Records (1939). It is reprinted in Heizer and Whipple's *The California Indians.*

—The complete story of Wovoka's life is told in Paul Bailey's *Wovoka the Indian Messiah.*

—The classic source of background material on the ghost dance is the Fourteenth Annual Report of the Bureau of Ethnology, 1892–93, Part II, *The Ghost Dance Religion and the Sioux Outbreak of 1890* by James Mooney.

—Another dramatic use of a solar eclipse by an Indian shaman occurred in the summer of 1806 among the Shawnees in western Ohio. Tenskwatawa, "The Open Door," brother of Tecumseh, "The Meteor," somehow learned that an eclipse of the sun was about to take place. He announced to his tribesmen that on a given day he would prove his supernatural power by making the sun dark at midday. When twilight gloom settled over the earth and the sun went black at high noon, Tenskwatawa was at once proclaimed a true prophet. Soon his fame spread among other tribes as the Shawano Prophet. In his nationalistic effort to unite the tribes against the white men in the War of 1812, Tecumseh found his brother's influence a convenient basis for rallying all the Indians in the Northwest Territory.

—Dancing has been an integral part of many religious rituals, made strange in our modern machine age only by the remoteness of time or distance. The messiah religion of the Indians was the inspiration of a dream. Its ritual embraced the dance, the ecstasy, and the trance.

The terpsichorean art has accompanied many religions. Ancient Hebrews danced in their vineyards on the Day of Atonement. According to the Old Testament (II Samuel, 6:14) King David "danced before the

Lord with all his might." Greeks once danced to honor Apollo, Pan, Artemis, and Dionysus.

Fourteenth-century Christians in western Europe danced hand in hand and sang doggerel verses in honor of Saint John, until the clergy formed them into divisions and said prayers for them at the Church of St. Vitus at Rotestein. Well into the nineteenth century Welsh Jumpers, English Shakers and Quakers, Kentucky Revivalists, Howling Methodists, Beekmanites, Adventists, and American Wilderness Worshipers employed dance-like forms and encouraged swoons and trances. My great-grandfather, Moses McCoy, a Presbyterian, has handed down stirring tales of Holy Roller revivals in which "feigned fits and swoons were sometimes discouraged by the use of bucketsful of cold water—much to the amusement of skeptical young bucks to whom camp meetings were less religious exercises than scarce frontier recreation." (Quoted from my mother, Edna Humphreys Miller.) Still going strong, one weird cult known as the Holiness Branch of the Church of God periodically tests the faith of its followers in the remote Kentucky-Tennessee mountains by applying fire or venomous snakes to their bare flesh while they perform ecstatic dance-like gyrations.

Among Asians dancing is an organic part of religion. Metaphysical meaning can be found in each step and gesture. The tilt of a finger is loaded with religious significance. The Shinto cult of Japan employs the classical Bugaku, a prayer dance imported from China. Ceylon's devil dancers recite Buddhist verses, while high-leaping Kandyan dancers re-enact Buddhist stories as a regular part of the ritual at temple services at Amunugama. Burmese spirit dancers, Cambodian Ranayana worshipers, the Kathakali dancers of south India, the Manipuri Hindus, and the Meylevi dervishes of Islam keep alive centuries-old traditions of religious dancing.

—Belief in a messiah or savior is implicit in nearly every one of the world's great religions. The Indians who promulgated the ghost dance simply borrowed the messianic doctrine from white Christians.

The idea of Jesus' rebirth as a member of the red race grew from certain misconstrued tenets of Mormonism and other sects in which Christ's Second Coming was widely believed. A more recent instance of Jesus "appearing" as a member of another race occurred in November, 1957, when an unusually gifted black-skinned child named Elias Murambodoro was touted by many Africans in Rhodesia as Christ reincarnated. Part of Elias' divinity at least was explained by the rare fact that he had been born with a full set of teeth and early learned to preach the Gospel to his fellow natives.

—Sherman Sage told me of his own story of the Arapaho ghost dance in 1939 at Ethete, Wyoming. The preceding year Chief Yellow Calf had given me much of the data, but it was Sage himself who was the key figure in the bringing of the dance to the plains tribes. Several Shoshoni, notably Quentin Quay and Timpana, told me in 1946 of Täbinshi's quest for the Indian messiah and their tribe's practice of the new religion.

The Shoshoni found the symbolism of the ghost dance particularly acceptable. They already had a tabu against eating the flesh of birds and believed that the chickadee discovered the world. A harbinger of severe blizzards, the bird was never killed lest its death bring bad luck to the tribe.

The ghost dance among them, however, was somewhat curtailed because of old Chief Washakie's firm friendship for the late missionary-extraordinary, Reverend John Roberts of Fort Washakie. A Welshman who had ministered to the Shoshoni since 1883 and had succeeded in establishing one of the earliest Episcopal missions on the northern plains, Roberts confessed to me in 1946 that his task had been far from easy. Through his influence, Chief Black Coal of the Northern Arapahoes, a Catholic convert at nearby Ethete, held many followers in consistent opposition to the ghost dance.

JOURNEY INTO SUNSET

—As his son, Frank, later reconstructed it, Kicking Bear's route to the Wind River country of Wyoming skirted the northern portion of the Black Hills, swung south of Devil's Tower, and finally circled the southern ranges of the Big Horns. The return trip, of course, was across fairly level country all the way east to Pine Ridge Agency.

—According to Thomas Short Bull, aging son of the medicine man, at least one of Wovoka's letters to the Sioux is still in existence and in the possession of Mr. Ted Ramar, now a resident of Arizona.

—Cheez-tah-paezh or Wraps-His-Tail, fanatic medicine man of the Crows, was given a cavalry saber, painted red, by Cheyennes during their annual sun dance. Brandishing the saber (which he periodically repainted a brilliant scarlet), Wraps-His-Tail claimed that no white man's bullets or weapons could harm him. When troops were sent to Crow Agency to restore order, the Sword-bearer shrieked his war cry, then twice circled the troop formations before riding back unscathed to his whooping followers. Unaware that the soldiers were forbidden to fire without extreme provocation, the restless Crows were kept in a rising frenzy of excitement as the Sword-bearer repeatedly threw his saber into the air and caught it by the hilt as it fell. The Indians believed he could paint his face by pointing his finger at the sun, or cut down pine trees by sweeping the sword at them. All this time the soldiers held their fire and were even drenched to the skin by a sudden cloudburst—rainfall predicted by the Sword-bearer hours earlier.

Later, one of Wraps-His-Tail's most zealous disciples, Deaf Bull, precipitated a sharp pitched battle by firing on the troops. Indian policemen, riding with the soldiers, returned the fire, one bullet breaking the Sword-bearer's arm. Most of the Crows scattered fast—only one warrior named Crazy Head hanging back and catching the Sword-bearer's horse and forcing Wraps-His-Tail to face the gunfire. Two Crow policemen arrested the Sword-bearer and tested his invulnerability to flying lead by shooting him in the back of the head. With their medicine man dead, the faith of the Crows in prophets was forever shattered.

—Sells-a-Pistol-Butt is often called "Little Gun" among the Sioux.

—Short Bull's disposition was somewhat kindlier than that of Kicking Bear, hence Wovoka's partiality to him. It must not be misconstrued, however, that Short Bull was less courageous than his brother-in-law. The Brûlé had fought in the Little Big Horn Battle and many intertribal wars and had won many high honors as a fighting man and minor leader.

—The term "medicine man" as applied to Kicking Bear, Short Bull, and other Sioux leaders of the ghost dance, is a loose one. A *pejuta wicasa*— "medicine man"—was actually a healer, a doctor, one who used various herbs and other native remedies to cure sicknesses or treat injuries. These healers often were called upon to cast curative or protective spells over their patients. A *wicasa wakan*—"holy man"—on the other hand, was one who had seen a great vision or had otherwise obtained vast supernatural powers which aided him in battle or in tribal leadership. As minor chiefs, both Kicking Bear and Short Bull fell into this latter category; neither was an active healer at the time of the ghost dance. Sitting Bull, however, was both a practicing healer and a holy man of great power.

SPRING 1890

—The Sioux delegates' reports of their visit to see the Wanekia in Nevada and their "ascension into heaven" are presented here exactly as remembered and quoted by various Indians who attended the council on White Clay Creek. Aside from Cloud Horse who disagreed with his companions, the delegates corroborated each other's accounts. To avoid redundance, I have quoted only Kicking Bear, Yellow Breast, and Short Bull.

—The obvious hallucinations experienced by the Sioux delegates can be credited partly to Wovoka's clever trickery as a shaman and partly to the wishful thinking of the Sioux. A third and most valid factor was suggested to me by Thomas Short Bull, son of the Brûlé delegate. During an interview in 1957 at Igloo, South Dakota, he stated his conviction that Wovoka had given his father and the other Sioux (with the probable exception of Cloud Horse) some sort of "medicine," through which they all fell into a trance and saw visions the Paiute brought about through hypnotic suggestion. Thomas Short Bull hinted strongly this might have been peyote—cactus buds or "buttons" smuggled in from Mexico. So far as is known, this is the only Indian-substantiated connection between the ghost dance and the Peyote Cult, although it is definitely established (by J. S. Slotkin in his *The Peyote Religion*) that the Peyote religion began to be diffused rapidly among Indian tribes shortly after the ghost dance was dropped.

In 1939, at the suggestion of the late Reverend Dirk Ley, a Presbyterian missionary at Pine Ridge and a friend of my family, I attended my first Peyote meeting at Denby, South Dakota. It was led by Levi Sitting Hawk, authorized priest in the Native American Church of North America—the Peyote Cult. Having won the friendship and confidence of the Indians, I was permitted to sample the "medicine" and take part in the ritual. I became violently sick at my stomach after first eating the button, but was later told this was a customary reaction for the uninitiated. Trances and visions were subsequently induced on other occasions. I have no doubt that such visions as the Sioux delegates to Nevada described to their tribesmen could have been easily induced by eating peyote. As far as is known, however, the probability that Wovoka fed his visitors the button has never before been suggested by historians. No evidence exists that the delegates brought back peyote from Nevada, and the earliest documented Peyotism did not appear among the Teton Sioux until 1912.

—One of the earliest recollections of my adopted brother, Ben Black Elk, was the death of Good Thunder around the turn of the century. Good Thunder had two wives, one of which was the aged widow of Ben's grandfather. Ben recalls how the two old women gashed their arms and legs with knives, hacked off their braids, and wept and wailed for days in typical old-time mourning.

—The Sioux sweat lodge is always constructed so that its entrance opens to the east—the direction from which the light of wisdom comes.

—In Sioux belief, the *wagacun*—"tree that rustles," the cottonwood—represents the way of the people and symbolically connects earth with heaven. Its significance among American Indians is similar to the World Tree of the *Atharva-Veda Samhita* in Hindu scriptures. Thus the use of a dead cottonwood sapling planted in the center of the dance area and the often-expressed hope in prayer and song that the "sacred tree" shall bloom again—that is, that supernatural power will come to the believers through the symbolism of the tree.

—Tribes of the southern plains who practiced the ghost dance seemed not to have had strict tabus against wearing white man's apparel. Eyewitness accounts and a few old photographs indicate that Southern Cheyennes, Southern Arapahoes, Kiowa, and Wichitas often wore big hats and neckerchiefs and other articles of clothing acquired from whites. Only in the north, particularly among the Sioux, was the tabu in effect.

SUMMER 1890

—Luther Standing Bear's entire life story is told in his autobiography *My People the Sioux*. While his book covers much of the same material incorporated here, my account of his activities during the ghost dance era is based entirely on personal interviews with him and his younger brother, Henry.

—Sitting Bull's "war medicine," the powerful *wotawe*, was probably his most cherished possession. A yard of unbleached muslin thirty inches wide, it is dyed a deep orange-yellow and decorated with a painted green dragonfly in each corner and a red-spotted elk outlined in green in the center. He used it on a number of occasions to save his people from annihilation at the hands of enemies or to help them otherwise. Objects used in connection with the cloth were a deer tail, a bit of calamus root, and inch-wide wristlets of buffalo hide with the brown wool left intact. Wearing the wristlets, Sitting Bull usually went to a lonely hilltop to "create" rain or perform other miraculous feats. At times he would cut himself and let blood flow as a sacrifice. Occasionally a piece of red cloth might be tied to a stick to represent the blood sacrifice. His prayer vigil invariably began with a sacred song he had learned in a vision which came to him around 1872:

> I have a good friend up there.
> I have a good friend up there.
> I have an elk-friend above;
> On earth I speak for a nation.

After Sitting Bull's death, the *wotawe* came into the possession of the old chief's nephew and adopted son, One Bull. I had the privilege of seeing One Bull use the talisman to fine advantage in 1939 near Rapid City, South Dakota. A crown fire had broken out in the Black Hills National Forest near Deerfield. Seeing the distant smoke, One Bull proceeded to "create" rain which drove the fire to the ground and enabled fire fighters to stamp out the blaze. At One Bull's request I wrote a letter in English for him which we sent to the Interior Department, requesting some sort of compensation—or at least recognition—of the old Indian's service to the Government in putting out the forest fire. So far as I know, the forestry officials declined to answer, an oversight which somewhat embittered One Bull. Since his death in 1947 the *wotawe* had been in the possession of his eldest daughter, Regina One Bull Spotted Horse of Little Eagle, South Dakota.

—Secretary of the Equal Suffrage Club of Aberdeen, South Dakota, at the time of Susan B. Anthony's visit was L. Frank Baum, later the author of the Oz stories.

Many suffragettes were preoccupied with the sale and use of alcoholic beverages in what they hoped would be not only a stronghold of equal rights for the sexes but also a dry state. Answering internationally known newspaper editor William T. Stead, who contended that "a saloon is a good place to get warm," Mrs. Helen M. Gougar of Highmore snapped, "So is hell!"

—Black Elk's life story is told in John G. Niehardt's *Black Elk Speaks*.

Black Elk adopted me as his son in 1939. In 1947 I was associated with him in producing old Sioux rituals as a South Dakota tourist attraction. Many of the ceremonies had not been performed in more than fifty years. I was privileged to have many long interviews with him concerning the ghost dance, the Battle of the Little Big Horn, and other matters before his death in 1950.

—An obvious bit of trickery, Wovoka's demonstration with the shotgun pellets may well have been the first "bulletproof" garment associated with the ghost dance. Not until Black Elk's vision, however, did other Indians attempt to fashion the sacred shirts. Few such garments were in use outside of the plains.

—Eagle Elk told me of his experience in the ghost dance when I interviewed him in 1940 and 1941. For many years he was a close neighbor of Black Elk near Ogalala, South Dakota.

—The "sacred" rock owned by Mash-the-Kettle, which he could stab and fill a bucket with water, later came into the possession of Bear Lice and is now owned by his son, Nose, of White Clay, Nebraska.

FALL 1890

—Details on the Kiowa ghost dance and Wooden Lance's quest for the Indian messiah were given to me by Chief White Horse of the Kiowas, who adopted me as his son in 1943 at Anadarko, Oklahoma.

—The story of the defiance of Head Swift and Young Mule of the Northern Cheyennes was told to me by Willis Rowland, half-Cheyenne former sergeant of Casey's Scouts. I interviewed him in 1940 at Lame Deer, Montana.

—Agent Wright was reinstated at Rosebud Agency about a year after he quit his post. Apparently he suffered no loss of prestige as far as the Indian Department was concerned. Existing records do not explain his absence and the exact situation at Rosebud in the interim has long been shrouded in secrecy.

—Agency appointments at the time of the ghost dance were usually governed by political considerations rather than personal qualifications. At Pine Ridge, for example, Agent McGillycuddy, a Republican, was dismissed in 1886 when Grover Cleveland was serving his first term as President. Gallagher, a Democrat, was in turn dismissed in favor of Royer, a Republican.

—Cheyenne City never made the grade as a permanent settlement, owing largely to the ghost-dance scare.

—Some Sioux judges of the eighties and nineties, unlike those who freed Kicking Bear, doled out unbelievably harsh penalties for the most trivial offenses.

—Sitting Bull hated Agent James McLaughlin and had the utmost contempt for him. After an altercation about two runaway Hunkpapa schoolboys, the old chief told the agent to his face: "You are not the only man. You're just a hireling. You can be replaced any time."

Old-time Hunkpapas say that there had been bad blood between the two men since a time when McLaughlin had offered Sitting Bull a drink of whisky in the agency office. After that, the Indians say, the old chief never set foot in the agency office again, for Sitting Bull felt that Mc-Laughlin had been trying to make a fool of him by getting him drunk. "I don't want to go into a white man's house," Sitting Bull said. "Under a white man's roof are lies and intrigue. The air outside is pure. . . ."

—Widespread belief that ghost reinforcements would help them fight the Communists has recently gripped members of the Taoist faith in Hunan Province, China. Early in 1958, according to *Time* magazine, two Taoist leaders were condemned to death and executed for "preparing paper-made robes, swords, warships, banners, bows, and arrows in a vicious attempt to equip an army of the other world and attack the Communist Party." The modern-day counterparts of Kicking Bear were Chiang Chan-en and Li Kwei-ying (a woman).

—Kicking Bear's visit to Sitting Bull's camp was described to me by One Bull, Henry Kills Alive, Louis Looking Horse, White Bird, and several other old-time Hunkpapas in 1939 and 1940.

INDIAN SUMMER

—Sitting Bull of the Arapahoes has been undeservedly slighted in Indian history because of his name. Too many historians confused him with the Hunkpapa chief. To both Northern and Southern Arapahoes, however, he ranks among their greatest leaders. Virtually unnoticed by white men, he died of old age around 1932 at Carlton, Oklahoma. His daughter, Jennie, still lives at Clinton, Oklahoma, while a son, Stacy, now resides in Los Angeles, California.

The name Sitting Bull has occasionally cropped up among other tribes. An Ogalala named Young Sitting Bull (also known as Drum-packer) was killed by Crow Indian scouts serving the Army at Fort Keogh, Montana, on December 17, 1876. The discovery of his scaffold grave that spring gave rise to one of many false reports that the mighty Hunkpapa chief had been slain.

—Most Indians have always been innately modest. The Sioux were particularly so. Short Bull's suggestion that they go about unclothed was viewed with much displeasure, although he definitely had no immoral conduct or flagrant lasciviousness in mind when he made the suggestion.

—The Santee dialect spoken by Dr. Eastman is characterized by the frequent use of the letter "d"—as in *Dakota,* meaning "Allies," as the Sioux call themselves. (Sioux is a French corruption of a Chippewa word *Nadewessioux,* meaning "snake" or "enemy.") The Teton tribes, on the other hand, say *Lakota* in referring to themselves, while Yanktonnais and Assiniboins speak a third dialect using "n"—as in *Nakota.* There are other minor differences but the dialects are mutually understandable.

—Dr. Eastman's worthy autobiography, *From the Deep Woods to Civilization,* recounts his exemplary rise from a dreary reservation in eastern South Dakota to become one of the greatest civilized Indians America has ever known.

—Little's great-grandson, Eddie Little, is now a motion-picture actor in Hollywood and a long-time friend of the author.

WINTER 1890

—Aside from raids to capture livestock, the ghost dancers committed no depredations outside the reservations. Nearly all the frantic alarms given by the whites turned out to be exaggerations of fact or entirely false.

—Many of the details of the Ghost Dance War come from lurid accounts in the Rapid City *Journal* for the months of November and December, 1890, and January, 1891.

—As noted, agents were customarily called "Father" by their Indian charges. Officially, they were called "Major," although the title did not imply previous military service.

—Some of the data on McGillycuddy is to be found in his widow's biography of him, *McGillycuddy Agent.*

—The Sioux particularly dreaded cannon and machine guns of the Hotchkiss variety. Almost invariably the use of howitzers or Hotchkiss guns by white soldiers meant the horrible mangling and death of innocent Indian women and children. The warriors rarely feared death for themselves, but genuinely abhorred the wounding or killing of noncombatants.

—The greater part of the Bad Lands is now a National Monument.

WAR AGAINST GHOSTS

—Data on military operations in the Dakotas comes from a number of sources, particularly the Rapid City *Journal* for November, 1890. Buffalo Bill Cody's rescue attempt of Sitting Bull is widely documented, notably in *Buffalo Bill and the Wild West* by Sell and Weybright. Additional data was provided me in an interview in 1939 with Mrs. Arta Cody Boal, one of Cody's daughters, at Cody, Wyoming.

—Included among the press contingent, which operated chiefly out of the railhead at Rushville, Nebraska, was Theodore Roosevelt, doing a brief stint on the Sioux War for *Harper's Weekly*.

—Many Sioux still living well remember the ghost dancers' war parade of December 7, 1890. Quite a number of them had hoped it might help convince the soldiers they should evacuate Pine Ridge and leave the Indians completely alone. As in many other instances, bluff and bluster was a key consideration in war as the Sioux usually waged it.

—The murder of Spotted Tail by Crow Dog was one of the most celebrated assassinations in frontier history. Although a chief who had long professed friendship and admiration for the whites, he led a turbulent private life. As a youth he fell in love with Appearing Day, a chief's daughter, and killed a rival suitor, Running Bear, in order to win the maiden's hand.

As a middle-aged Lothario, Spotted Tail again fell in love—this time with the pretty young wife of crippled Medicine Bear. Taking her to his lodge, he refused to listen to Medicine Bear's friends and various Brûlé sub-chiefs, who demanded that he return the woman to her husband. Spotted Tail's actions were not only a serious breach of the Sioux moral code, but the cripple needed his wife. Although authorities differ on the motivation, it was at this time that Crow Dog vowed to slay Spotted Tail.

Armed with a rifle, Crow Dog was riding on the running gear of his wagon after delivering a load of wood at Rosebud Agency on August 5, 1881. Near the agency he saw Spotted Tail approaching on horseback. Getting down from the wagon, Crow Dog pretended to search for something in the dusty road until Spotted Tail rode up. Without a word, Crow Dog stood up and fired. Spotted Tail fell dead from his horse.

Arrested by Indian police, Crow Dog was taken to Fort Niobrara, Nebraska, and jailed in the post guardhouse. The following year, 1882, he was brought to trial for murder in Deadwood, Dakota Territory. Convicted, he was sentenced to be hanged. Since the Sioux believed their souls left their bodies through their mouths at death and hanging was thought to prevent the soul's escape, this was a harsh sentence. Crow Dog accepted his fate stoically, however, and asked only that the court permit him to visit his family on the reservation before his execution. His request was granted.

Completely honorable, Crow Dog returned voluntarily to Deadwood in time for his execution—in spite of the fact that a deputy marshal detailed to guard him lost him on the way and came trailing into Deadwood a day or so later. Meanwhile, an appeal on Crow Dog's behalf had been made to the United States Supreme Court, which ruled that the Dakota courts had no jurisdiction over crimes committed by Indians on Indian reservations. Crow Dog was set free. His code of honor assumed almost legendary proportions among Indians and white men alike.

—McLaughlin's whisky wagon for his Indian police on the eve of Sitting Bull's arrest and murder is an item heretofore overlooked by the chief's biographers and other authorities. One Bull's wife, Scarlet Whirlwind, John Sitting Bull, and Henry Sitting Bull, all of whom were present at the chief's camp, told me that the Metal Breasts were drunk by the time they came to make the arrest. White Bird and Little Soldier, both members of the Indian police force, admitted to me that McLaughlin had sent the wagonload of whisky, knowing that only under the influence of alcohol could the Hunkpapa police be induced to carry out the agent's orders.

—Sitting Bull's murder had far-reaching repercussions. According to two good friends of mine who were attending Carlisle Indian School in Pennsylvania in December, 1890, Chief Ben American Horse and the late Chief Henry Standing Bear, a dramatic fight broke out in the school's reading room when word came that Sitting Bull had been killed. John Frost, an adopted Crow and the quarter-blood son of an army surgeon who had been a friend of the school's head, Captain Richard Henry Pratt, had it in for the Sioux because his father had been killed by Sitting Bull's warriors. Reading an account of the old chief's death, he triumphed openly. Resenting the Crow's exultation, a nephew of Sitting Bull leaped upon the surgeon's son and a battle royal began. Young Frost had once made a vow to avenge his father's death and started to fulfill it then and there on the Sioux, when Captain Pratt luckily intervened. The boys were separated before either of them sustained any real injuries.

—The murder of Sitting Bull permanently split the Hunkpapa tribe. The members of McLaughlin's police force and their families were quickly ostracized by the Sitting Bull faction, as well as a number of other tribesmen who had not openly sided with the ghost dancers. Marcellus Red Tomahawk was particularly hated for having fired one of the fatal shots at Sitting Bull; and as late as 1940 his son Francis Red Tomahawk, a friend of mine, was considered an outcast by Sitting Bull's nephews, One Bull (who had taken over the chieftainship of the Hunkpapa tribe) and White Bull, both close friends of mine.

—In 1893, the larger of Sitting Bull's log cabins and Tall Bull, the dead chief's old white circus horse, were shipped to Chicago, where they were exhibited at the Columbian Exposition. No Indian is sure what happened to the horse after that, although some Hunkpapas believe that Buffalo Bill Cody, whose Wild West Show was then playing Chicago, may have taken the old horse and farmed it out on one of his various ranches in the Northwest.

—The families of Sitting Bull and Kicking Bear were closely tied many years after the ghost-dance troubles when Nancy Sitting Bull, daughter of the dead chief's eldest son, William, married Frank Kicking Bear, the prophet's only surviving son. Frank and Nancy Kicking Bear still live on their old allotment a mile or so north of the post office at Manderson, South Dakota, on Pine Ridge Indian Reservation.

—In 1953, an echo from the past reminded the Sioux Nation that their great leader was still a man of importance, even in death. For sixty-three years the old chief's remains lay rotting and undisturbed in his pauper's grave, pathetically marked by a drab wooden marker which had to be regularly replaced as tourists whittled away at it for souvenirs. Later a cairn of stones was erected by Sitting Bull's relatives, who secretly decorated it from time to time with cheap paper flowers. Later still, a cement slab and a modest marble tombstone enclosed by an iron railing marked the old chief's long-time resting place.

Sitting Bull's Hunkpapa relatives had clamored for years to have the chief's remains moved closer to his old camp on Grand River rather than let them stay in the obscure corner of the graveyard at Fort Yates, run down and deserted by the Army since 1903. But North Dakota's governors had refused to give up the body.

One April night in 1953, Clarence Gray Eagle, Sitting Bull's seventy-nine-year-old nephew and a witness to the chief's killing, led a stanch party of South Dakotans across the state line to unearth Sitting Bull's badly decomposed body and bring it back to Mobridge, South Dakota, for reburial. Taking no chances on another exhumation, Gray Eagle and his co-conspirators placed the remains in an eight-by-ten-foot steel crypt encased in concrete. As one spokesman put it, "It will take an A-bomb to move him now." Clarence Gray Eagle was laconic about his accomplishment on behalf of his tribesmen and the state of South

Dakota, which regards the new Sitting Bull grave as a fine tourist attraction: "I was tired of the white man's red tape and delays."

FLIGHT

—Thomas Short Bull, an old man of eighty-two when I interviewed him at Igloo, South Dakota, in 1957, was a lad of fourteen when his father led the Brûlé trek west to the Bad Lands. Tom did not go with them. Shortly before the outbreak, a Minneconjou named Knife visited the Short Bull family on Black Pipe Creek and adopted Tom as his son. The boy accompanied Knife north to Cheyenne River Reservation and camped with Knife's family near Cherry Creek. When the Sitting Bull fugitives fled south to take refuge with Big Foot, Knife and his followers, including young Tom, moved twenty miles west to join forces with Big Foot's band, arriving at the Deep Creek camp site only a few hours after Big Foot had departed southward to Wounded Knee—and death. "I would surely have been killed," commented Tom Short Bull, "had we arrived in time to join Big Foot."

—George Red Bear, an elderly Northern Cheyenne from Pine Ridge Reservation and one of my Indian fathers by adoption, tells me that the Cheyenne scouts were willing to fight their old Sioux friends and allies only because Casey and other Army officers had told them lies to the effect that the Sioux were mistreating Cheyennes then quartered at Pine Ridge. These Indians had not taken part in the ghost dance, and this fact helped convince their Montana relatives. Willis Rowland, once a sergeant in Casey's troop of scouts, told me much the same story years ago at Lame Deer, Montana.

WOUNDED KNEE

—Details of the tragedy of Wounded Knee have been given to me in interviews through the years with Iron Hail (Dewey Beard), James Pipe-on-Head, Peter Stands-for-Them, Simon Helper, John Sitting Bull (in sign talk), Black Elk, Howard Bad Bear, Dora High White Man, Mary Runs On, Afraid-of-Enemy, Bertha Kills-Close-to-Lodge, Charles Under Baggage, Sr., Frank Good Lance, and other Sioux Indians listed elsewhere in this book. All were actual survivors of the massacre or witnesses of the slaughter from nearby hills. The personal experiences of Black Elk, Eagle Elk, Iron Hail (Dewey Beard), Simon Helper, and

James Pipe-on-Head are given here just as they related them to me in numerous personal interviews.

—By strange coincidence, the Wounded Knee tragedy occurred on the same day that a long picturesque chapter of stagecoaching (since 1876) came to a close in Deadwood and the Black Hills of South Dakota. On December 29, 1890, the last stagecoach rolled out of Deadwood like a grand old actor taking a final curtain call. Escorted by the town's Knights of Pythias, carrying canes instead of swords, and a band plaintively playing "Fare Thee Well for I Must Leave Thee," Frank Hunter, last of the stage drivers, gathered the ribbons and cracked his whip high over the heads of six white horses for the final trip. With the arrival of the first Chicago and Northwestern train promptly at 8:45 A.M. the following morning, a bleak cold Monday, Deadwood ceased being one of the West's most flaming frontier communities and settled down to a more prosaic existence as a thriving distributing center for mines and lumbering.

—The Massacre of Wounded Knee had one redeeming feature. Lack of discipline displayed by the troops during the engagement so dismayed a young lieutenant on Brooke's staff at Pine Ridge that he later instituted a new disciplinary code that was to last in the armed services for many years. The lieutenant's name: John J. "Black Jack" Pershing.

BLACK DAYS

—The Drexel Catholic Mission, now known as the Holy Rosary Mission, has become the largest private boarding school for Indians in the United States. The old original brick buildings still show knicks and holes where stray bullets struck during the Mission fight.

—In recent months the United States Seventh Cavalry has finally made peace with the Sioux. An Associated Press dispatch dated February 18, 1958, Along the Truce Line in Korea reads: "The United States Seventh Cavalry, defeated by Sitting Bull eighty-two years ago, has made peace with the Sioux. A peace pipe made by the Seventh Cavalry soldiers was sent to Sitting Bull V, great-great-grandson of the Indian leader who wiped out the Seventh Cavalry command of General George A. Custer in the Battle of the Little Big Horn in 1876. The gift was to commemorate the birth of the young Sioux and the recent rebirth of the Seventh Cavalry under the Army's new pentomic structure. Along with the peace pipe went a letter of congratulations to the baby's parents, Vincent

(Sitting Bull IV) and Frances Cadotte of Los Angeles." (The son of One Bull's youngest daughter, Margaret One Bull Tremmel, Vincent Cadotte is one of my long-time Indian friends.)

—I knew Pete Culbertson fairly well when we both worked for Duhamels' Sioux Indian Pageant in Rapid City, South Dakota, the summer of 1940. Pete was then an old man with long hair who styled himself "Indian Pete, lifelong friend of the Sioux." This proved an exaggeration of fact when old Moses One Feather, who had survived the Culbertsons' ambush, happened to visit Indians appearing in the pageant. The old Ogalala nearly killed Indian Pete, who managed to escape briefly to another part of the country until One Feather finally went back to his home on Pine Ridge Reservation. Both One Feather and Indian Pete died a few years later of old age.

—Seventh Cavalry soldiers, transferred to Fort Meade from Pine Ridge, eventually found Few Tails' body and, after wrapping it in a soogan (a sort of comforter), buried it in a shallow grave near Alkali Creek. Coyotes soon dug up the remains. Few Tails' skull was later found by cowboy Dock Saddler and sold for $100 as a grim exhibit at the Chicago Columbian Exposition in 1893. Few Tails had apparently been shot in the mouth; several front teeth were found lodged in the back of the skull.

—Standing Bear's son, Luther, told me years ago about his father's fearless exploit in carrying the pipe to the Stronghold. Details of the incident have since been substantiated by Simon Helper, who was among the young warriors gathered at the Stronghold's neck to keep an eye on the peace delegation.

—Years after the tragedy of Wounded Knee had faded into history, a pathetic little group of Sioux survivors of the massacre and relatives of those who had been slain erected a modest granite monument above the common grave on the hilltop near Wounded Knee Post Office. Inscribed on the shaft is the following:

"This monument is erected by surviving relatives and other Ogalala and Cheyenne River Sioux Indians in memory of the Chief Big Foot Massacre, Dec. 29, 1890.

"Colonel Forsyth in command of U. S. troops.

"Big Foot was a great chief of the Sioux Indians. He often said, 'I will stand in peace till my last day comes.' He did many brave deeds for the White man and the Red man.

"Many innocent women and children who knew no wrong died here.

"The erection of this monument is largely due to the financial assist-
ance of Joseph Horn Cloud, whose father was killed here."
—A list prepared for me by Simon Helper (Wallace Hump) lists the fol-
lowing heads of families who were killed at Wounded Knee in the mas-
sacre of December 29, 1890: Chief Big Foot, William Horn Cloud, High
Hawk, Sherman Horn Cloud, Standing Bear (a Minneconjou), Scatters-
Them, Long Bull, Red Fish, White American, Swift Bear, Black Coyote,
He-Crow, Ghost Horse, Afraid-of-Bear, Little Water, Strong Fox, Living
Bear, Spotted Thunder, Shoots-the-Bear, Young Afraid-of-Bear, Yellow
Robe, Picket-Horse, Wounded Hand, Bear Cuts Body, Red Eagle, Chase-
in-Water, Pretty Hawk, Toots-its-Hole, Red Horn, He-Eagle, No Ears,
Weasel Bear, Wolfskin Necklace, Lodge Skins, Charge-at-Them, Yellow
Bird, Big Shirt, Brown Turtle, Blue American, Water-in-Horn, Scaffold
Knife, Small Side Bear, Kills Tincup, Old Horn Cloud, Courageous
Bear, Slicks-His-Hide, Grease Bone Leg, Crazy Bear, Happens, and Has-
the-Bell. (Individuals—men, women, and children—are not indicated on
Helper's list.)

THE END OF A DREAM

—Short Bull's views were later set down by Natalie Curtis in her *The
Indian Book,* published in 1907. In another interview in 1915, he em-
phasized his innocence in bringing about the outbreak. He finally died
in 1924.
—Details of Plenty Horses' trial are on record in the files of the *Black
Hills Daily Times,* Deadwood's newspaper in 1891. For excerpts from
these records, I am much indebted to Mrs. Cushman Clark of Deadwood,
South Dakota.
—The experience of Wooden Lance, the Kiowa, was related to me by
the late Chief White Horse of the Kiowas, one of my Indian fathers by
adoption. Other records of it exist, however, notably in James Mooney's
classic Part II of the Fourteenth Annual Report of the Bureau of Ethnology. Bianki's revival in 1894 was also described to me in detail by
Chief White Horse.
—Wooden Lance, highly respected among the Kiowa for his quiet dignity,
integrity, and ability, was chosen as the last principal chief of his people
soon after his return from the futile quest for an Indian messiah. He
died on August 8, 1931.

POSTSCRIPT

—The story of the making of Buffalo Bill Cody's motion picture in 1913 has been told me by Chief Ben American Horse of Kyle, South Dakota, Levi Sitting Hawk of Denby, South Dakota, and Willard White Belly of Porcupine, South Dakota, all of whom took part in the filming.

—A year or so ago, the Pine Ridge Sioux talked vaguely of reviving the ghost dance. So far as I know, nothing ever came of it.

Index

Addams, Jane, 19
Afraid-of-Hawk, 80
Afraid-of-Soldier
    (Feared-by-Warriors), 186
Alcohol, prohibitions against, 21
Allen, Charles, 167 n
Allen, James M., 145
Allen's Dance House, Manhattan,
    New York City, 21-22
American Horse, 126-127, 130-132,
    137, 249, 257
Anadarko, agency at, 88, 273
Anthony, Susan B., 72
Apiatan (Wooden Lance), 88
Arapaho Indians, 9-10, 29, 30, 31, 33,
    35, 36, 38, 44, 48, 87, 89, 101, 108,
    109
Architecture, American post-Victo-
    rian, 16
Arikara Indians, 5, 13
Asay, Ed, 149, 150
Assiniboin Indians, 87
Astor, Mrs. John Jacob, 126

Baby Doe, 17
Bad Lands, South Dakota, 152-153
Bannock Indians, 28, 29
Bartlett, George, 83
Battle of Little Big Horn *see* Little
    Big Horn, Battle of
Battle of Rosebud, 38 n
Beef issue *see* Rations, government
Ben American Horse, 277
Bennet, Judge, 141
Bettelgeau, Isaac, 93
Bianki (The Eater), 273
Big Bad Horse, 170, 173
Big Foot, 7, 9, 11-14, 16, 23, 32, 34,
    37-41, 61, 72, 77, 95, 165, 198, 200-
    244, 245, 248, 249, 251, 253, 255,
    267, 276, 277
Big Foot Pass, South Dakota, 211 n
Big Horse, 155
Big Road, 77, 138, 151, 152, 153, 158,
    264

Big Turkey, 170
Black Bird, 186
Black Elk, 5, 57-59, 76-81, 86, 137,
    138, 155, 157, 169, 172, 232, 233 n,
    239-242, 250-252, 263-264
Black Feather, 155
Black Fox, 8, 107, 230 n, 269
Black Hills *Daily Times*, 270
Black Horn, 74, 241
Black Pipe Creek, ghost dance at,
    119, 122, 136
Black Sharp Nose, 44
Blackfeet Indians, 16, 36, 40, 65, 104,
    107, 121, 133
Bland, Dr. T. A., 66
Blood Indians, 36
"Blowers," 25, 26
Blue Horse, 150
Bob-Tail-Bull, 192
"Bottle Nose Ben, the Indian Hater,"
    17
Boyle, Tim, 90
Bozeman Trail, Red Cloud's War on,
    168-169
Brave Eagle, 92, 93
Brave Thunder, 182, 186
Brennan, John R., 259 n
Broken Arm, 47, 54
Brooke, General John R., 129, 138,
    146-152, 159, 164, 166, 169-172, 205,
    215, 217, 221, 223, 245, 247-248, 253,
    254
Brûlé Indians, 16, 40, 42, 48, 62, 63,
    64, 73, 81, 85, 86, 91, 119, 120, 122,
    136-138, 140, 151, 153, 155-157, 170-
    174, 179, 197, 245-247, 259, 266,
    267
Buel, J. W., 164
Buffalo Bill *see* Cody, Buffalo Bill
"Buffalo soldiers," 166
Buffalo (American Bison) herds, 10,
    15, 31
Bull Dog, 170, 173
Bull Eagle, 95
Bull Ghost, 161

311